The Appearance of
Maye Moon

Susan Gwin

Published by Book Writing Pioneer

Cover design by Book Writing Pioneer

ISBN: Printed in the United States

KJV Genesis 1: 14-19

[14] And God said, Let there be lights in the firmament of the heaven to divide the day from the night; and let them be for signs, and for seasons, and for days, and years:

[15] And let them be for lights in the firmament of the heaven to give light upon the earth: and it was so.

[16] And God made two great lights; the greater light to rule the day, and the lesser light to rule the night: he made the stars also.

[17] And God set them in the firmament of the heaven to give light upon the earth,

[18] And to rule over the day and over the night, and to divide the light from the darkness: and God saw that it was good.

[19] And the evening and the morning were the fourth day.

A Note To The Reader
From The Author

I need to make it clear that this book is **not** a prophecy. It is a work of Christian fiction. I feel the Holy Spirit inspired me to write this book, and I have sought the Holy Spirit's guidance, and I want it to be pleasing to the Lord.

I have many physical disabilities that keep me from doing a lot of activities that I used to do, which is very frustrating at times. One evening, while attending a Wednesday evening service, my pastor preached about gifts and things that one could do in service to God around the church. I felt limited because most require the ability to stand, and I just can't stand for very long. Before going to bed, I prayed that the Lord help me to find something I could do with my limited abilities. The next morning, I woke up, and my first thought was, "What if another moon suddenly appeared in the sky? Would that be enough to make some people believe in God?" How would it be explained? What crazy theories would be created to explain the miracle? Then I thought, maybe I could write a book.

My heart is troubled by what is going on in the world. I know that God is in control, but there is so much evil everywhere you look. People's hearts have hardened to hear the word of God. Our world has become violent, greedy, lacking morals, and has gotten further and further away from God. Our churches are full of old people. What will happen when this generation passes? It is hard to know that so many people are headed to hell because they have been deceived by Satan.

Many of the scenes in the book have already happened in Biblical times. God spoke the world, the moon, and the stars into existence. Jesus healed the sick. Jesus appeared to many people after his crucifixion, but still, many people refused to believe. Jesus walked on the water in Galilee, and in this book, He walks on Maye Moon as He prepares the astronaut team for their next Mission: to heal the hearts of man around the world. Join Kathi, Jess, Pastor Scott, and the astronaut team as they lead this Miracle Mission for the Lord.

Dedication

This book is dedicated to my husband, Preston W. Gwin, who grew up in rural Humphreys County, Tennessee. He was saved in a small Pentecostal country church at a young age but believed that you lose your salvation whenever you sinned, and eventually, he drew away from the Christian way of life. God continued to work in his life, and he rededicated his life to the Lord and has been a man with more faith and trust in Jesus than anyone I have ever met. I have been amazed over the years by his wisdom, belief, and understanding of the Word of God and the difference God made in his life. When we met in 1991, he helped me to change my path and start serving the Lord. It has been a testimony of how God can change a person if only you believe. We have been blessed with a wonderful life, including our large family. Of course, there have been ups and downs, but it has been a comfort to know that we were in it together with the Lord.

Table of Contents

Blank Page Intentionally

Chapter 1

T essie and Earl dragged their colorful canvas folding chairs across the warm, sandy beach and placed them side by side. It was dusk, and there were many other older couples on the beach, like them, waiting for the moonrise. They were expecting a large full moon to rise up shortly out of the ocean. It was a cloudless night, and the bright stars began appearing and twinkling across the darkening sky. The anticipation was building. "Mom, what time did it say that the full moonrise will take place?" her husband asked. "Should be in just a few minutes. I just love the soothing deep blue color of the ocean tonight," she replied. The waves rolled in with a rhythmic, relaxing crash as it smacked the sandy land. The sounds were mesmerizing, like a soothing lullaby. Tessie and Earl waited patiently, holding hands like a couple of giddy teenagers swooning in the moonlight. They had a special love that had lasted throughout the years.

Slowly, like a bright, jolly man, the Moon peeked up out of the ocean. At first, it was just a glow, then a sliver, until finally, it reached its full glory. "Beautiful," Mom sighed. "It never gets old."

The two seniors sat quietly, still holding each other's wrinkled hands, and watched as it continued its climb upwards in the sky. Many of the other spectators began folding up their chairs and heading back to their cars, but Earl and Tessie continued to sit there a while longer, enjoying the serenity and peacefulness of the ocean. The waves were calming and hypnotizing, and they would sleep well tonight.

Tessie began humming, "What a Friend We Have in Jesus," and thought about how blessed they were to be able to retire here in Florida, where they could come to the beach as often as they wished. It was well-earned after many years of hard work. Earl told her a story of being told as a child the Moon was made of cheese. He believed it, and his sister had made fun of him. Tessie must have heard this story a hundred times, but it always made her laugh. He was just an ole' country boy from Tennessee. He squeezed her hand and said, "I love you most." "No," she answered back, "I love you most." This was their 'thing,' and they said this to one another many times throughout the day.

"Do you suppose we better pack up and head home?" Tessie asked. "I suppose so, but it is such a beautiful night. Hey, Mom, look over there. What do you think that is?" Earl questioned and stopped in his tracks.

The Appearance of Maye Moon

Tessie followed his crooked finger with her dim eyes and looked down the beach at something bluish-green and glowing coming up out of the ocean. "What is that? We already saw the moonrise." The few scattered people left on the beach were also pointing at it. Slowly, another 'Moon' rose from the horizon like a shiny great phoenix and climbed slowly up in the sky. The soft turquoise colour shined differently than the moon, but it was round and glowing like the moon. The couples' mouths gaped open wide as they continued to watch it.

The beach at night is strangely calming and mysterious. The light from the two moons has given it a luminous glow and a very eerie vibe that caused the couple to be speechless. After a few minutes of silence, Earl finally was able to whisper, "What do you think that is? Where did it come from?" Tessie just slowly shook her head in disbelief. "Pinch me, am I awake? I am sure we are awake, but I can't think of an explanation for this. There was no mention of this in the news." Earl shook his head cautiously in agreement, with amazement and disbelief written across his face.

Tessie and Earl had been together for over fifty years. After lovingly raising a brood of seven children, they decided to retire. Tessie served 30 years as a cook at the elementary school, where she treated children to the finest southern cooking in the state. Earl, a little pudgy from her fine cooking, retired from the largest newspaper in the state of Tennessee after 40 years. He worked in

3

distribution and made sure that the newspaper was delivered in tact to each customer. They both loved their jobs, but age and health got the best of them. Earl suffered a heart attack, the widowmaker, and nearly died. His surgeon put in stents at first, but a few years later, Earl needed open heart surgery. It was a rough time for Tessie, watching Earl lie in a hospital bed looking grey as a ghost. Earl pulled through, and ever since, Tessie had a tough time slowing him down. God wasn't through with him yet.

Tessie's health problems required her to take several meds each day. Her pain was non-stop from years of standing on concrete while cooking. Her arms and shoulders were in pain from lugging around heavy pots of food during the day, then going home and taking care of her large family. Tessie would not have changed anything because she loved cooking for all of the children. She would love their hugs when they entered the cafeteria. In her heart, she knew many of them did not get a nutritious meal the rest of the day. She took pride in the fact that she was known throughout the county as being a good cook—no, an excellent cook.

Together, they put in their marching papers and retired to Florida. At first, their children were not so happy about it, but after visiting them a few times, they saw how happy they were and loved the Florida coastal area too.

The Appearance of Maye Moon

The illuminated bluish-green ball trailed behind the glowing Moon by just a little bit. Earl and Tessie could tell this new Moon was a little larger than Earth's Moon. It appeared a little further away from the Earth than our Moon. It resembled a cat's eye marble Tessie had played with as a child and was quite beautiful. There had to be a logical explanation of how and why it got in the sky. Something like this doesn't just appear out of nowhere?

"Let's head home and see what the news has to say about it. Maybe FOX is reporting something about it. We can check the local news at ten. I am sure they know where it came from. We probably missed hearing about this, at first thinking it was a planned event," Earl said with a worried look. "Yeah, that is probably a good idea. Hopefully, we won't miss the coverage," Tessie answered. "Love you most," Earl said quietly. "No, love you most, Earl," she replied. "You are my girl, Tessie." There was no doubt that Tessie and Earl were in love as much as the day they married. This had to be the strangest thing they had ever seen. As they drove home, they could see the new moon out their car window and it was almost like it was following them home.

Earl and Tessie settled in their matching plaid Lazy Boys and turned on the television to their favorite national news channel, FOX, to see if there was anything mentioning this new planetary wonder up in the sky. The news channel was flashing an alert banner at the bottom of the screen, and the news people were wildly exclaiming with fear that no one was sure what this thing was. FOX was moving from location to location, showing what the new moon looked like from various places on Earth. The commentators spoke to news affiliates all over Europe, Australia, Asia, and even Antarctica. They even had coverage from the International Space Station. Expert after expert was questioned to see if they would like to speculate what it was and where it came from. The experts all concurred; they did not see this celestial object prior to its appearance in the sky. One second, it wasn't there, and the next second it was. Not one of the experts would comment on what it is or where it came from. They were truly baffled.

"I'm afraid, Earl. Look at how they are behaving. There is fear on everyone's face. I wonder if the kids are alright; all adults in their 40's and 50's. I wonder if they are watching this?" "Mom, it is too late to call them tonight. You might frighten them. Besides that, what can they do about it? What can anyone do about it? What does anyone need to do about it? I am sure there is a logical explanation. There are probably a lot of new stars in the sky every day. Maybe God thought we needed another Moon for some reason." Earl answered and tried to calm Tessie's fear. He reminded her that God is in control. They continued to watch the news channels way late into the night, but no one claimed to know what it was or where it came from. Maybe tomorrow, it will be gone as quickly as it arrived. Maybe it is just an illusion?

The Appearance of Maye Moon

As the sun rose in the sky and the two moons disappeared in the United States, news people reported that the Moon was still there on the other side of the world. Those who thought "out of sight, out of mind" were wrong. NASA began sharing theories about the size, atmosphere, temperature, distance from Earth, gravity, and anything else they could think of. What else could they say about it? They had absolutely no idea where it came from. It was way too big to be a space craft. Mars has two moons, so it is not so strange that Earth has two moons, is it?

The Moon is a natural satellite, so "Moon" is actually its name. The Romans called it Luna. In Arabic, the Moon was referred to as Merrenda. In the West, the Moon was referred to as Selene. Scientists began submitting names for this new satellite orbiting the Earth because it was already becoming confusing. One of the names submitted was Maye, named after the mother of mogul, entrepreneurial godfather, and CEO of Space X and Tesla, Elon Musk. Maye means the fifth month, which is the month that this Moon appeared. The name quickly caught on with the news media and social media, and just like that, it was named Maye Moon.

As evening approached and the sun disappeared beyond the Western horizon, people in the retirement neighborhood began sitting out in lawn chairs, waiting to see if the Maye Moon would appear again tonight. The beach was like a rock concert, with thousands of people waiting to get the first glimpse of Maye Moon.

Traffic and parking were so horrendous that Tessie and Earl decided to stay home. It was kind of exciting to be with their neighbors, who were also sitting out in colorful lawn chairs and chit-chatting away.

Tessie and Earl lived in a gated 55 and older mobile home community. Most of the people there were either snowbirds or had moved to Florida from out of state. They were all enjoying the retired lifestyle and were active enough to stay out of a nursing home.

Tessie became known for her delicious cafeteria recipes at the community pitch-ins. She found a group of ladies to play bridge with three times a week while Earl was playing poker in the other game room. She went to ceramics and quilting, too, and filled their home with her homemade crafts. Tessie had started a women's prayer group that met once a week. Earl loved to fish in the three lakes that the community had. Sometimes, they biked together or rode around in their golf cart. Most mornings, they swam in the community pool. They were retired but were not old and tired.

As they watched up in the night sky, the Moon appeared first, but not far behind it, the Maye Moon appeared. They were still in the full moon phase, and the sky was brightly lit up and shining. It really was a gorgeous sight. Tessie and Earl waved at the neighbors and joined them, looking up at the sky. It felt like there was a peacefulness and brotherhood in the community. Tessie couldn't remember when all of the neighbors watched the sky together. Most of all, she really didn't really know what they were watching. I mean, a moon just doesn't appear out of nowhere, does it?

Maye Moon became the talk of everyone, everywhere. It was a worldwide phenomenon. Selfies, trends, Twitter, Facebook, influencers, network news, podcasts, YouTube channels – Maye Moon was everywhere, internationally. The President of the United States addressed the nation and promised that our U.S. Space Force and NASA space program would get to the bottom of this phenomenon. Scientists everywhere were scrambling for answers. Rarely does a scientific occurrence happen that can't be explained. Theories began to formulate, and experts came out of the woodwork to have their 10 minutes of fame. Maye Moon was giving the media outlets something to talk about but not much to say.

Earl and Tessie were formulating their own theory. "God was the Creator of all things, so He must have placed the new moon in the sky for a special purpose. Just because the Bible does not mention this miraculous appearing does not mean that God is not responsible," Earl explained. Many of their Christian friends and family felt the same way. "Maybe it is leading to the rapture, an end-times event when the Christians on Earth will meet Jesus Christ in the sky and transport them to heaven," a church friend proposed. "I don't think that is the case," Earl said. "If it was a pre-Rapture event,

I believe it would have been included in the Bible. God is responsible for this new moon, and He will reveal its purpose in His time." "I agree, Love, in His time," Tessie replied with a smile. "Meanwhile, I am thankful we are still around to witness this glorious appearing of this beautiful new moon." "Me, too, Mom, I love you most." Earl winked. "No, I love you most," Tessie replied.

Chapter 2

Winston Warren, a special news commentator for SNN Science News Network, was preparing for his daily segment in his small, cramped, beige cubicle. The biggest news story of his career was the Maye Moon, but he just couldn't think of anything to say that had not been said. "It is not like it is every day that a moon appears in the sky unexpectedly. Some of the crazy conspiracy theories out there on social media were that the Maye Moon was a product of mass hysteria. Another theory is that it is a reflection of the Earth. It is kinda the same color as the Earth when seen from space, but how could a reflection this big appear out of nowhere? The International Space Station has confirmed it is not a shadow. Some people believe that the Russians are responsible for it. During the last few years, the Russians have been blamed for quite a few things, so why not blame them for this? No." Warren thought, "I have to wait for a scientifically plausible explanation. Surely, some scientist or physicist somewhere will figure out how this could happen. Science has all the answers, after all. We just have to be patient and wait until they have had enough time and information to develop a theory."

Science News Network's audience has grown exponentially since the Maye Moon appeared. SNN was near the bottom in ratings but has grown 44% during the last 48 hours. This is very good for Warren's career; even better if he has an answer for everyone. "At least his segment includes an interview with NASA Chief Scientist Kathi Calloway. Maybe she can shed some light on what NASA is doing to investigate the origin of Maye Moon. You look handsome on air," Winston said with confidence to himself as he looked in the mirror on his office wall.

Warren's producer counted down his on-air time, and immediately, Warren poured on the charisma and confidence he showed every evening during his show. "Good Evening. Tonight's top science story is the Maye Moon. We will have NASA Chief Scientist Kathi Calloway with us to give us her take on the Maye Moon. How did this new moon come to be in the Earth's orbit?"

Kathi joined Warren from a remote location in Cocoa Beach, Florida. She tried to match his look of confidence, but it wasn't easy considering the circumstances. "Thank you, Warren." "We at NASA have been working 24/7 to find out as much as we can about the Maye Moon. One thing we can say for sure is that this is a puzzler." Warren nodded in agreement. "The accepted scientific theory of how the universe began is with the Big Bang Theory. There was a single point of origin that exponentially grew, doubled 100 times or more in a few seconds, and inflated and created the universe, which is rapidly expanding and changing every day. Most cosmologists believe this theory." Warren again nodded

"So Kathi, can this theory be proven?" Warren asked. "Well, it is a theory, but it is widely accepted within the Scientific community, and many theoretical physicists have studied and worked together to prove this theory. The size and enormity of the universe continue to grow with time. We are discovering new planets every day. Our telescopes are becoming more advanced, like the James Webb Space Telescope, and we find out new facts about the universe all the time. It really is quite amazing."

Kathi nervously chewed on her lip and hoped that the questions did not go beyond her expertise. "Kathi, Could you explain how Maye Moon was created and appeared here in the Earth's orbit?" "We at NASA think Maye Moon is part of the Big Bang and is part of the inflation process that is going on all the time in the universe. It is part of the growth of the universe. The universe has been growing and changing for about 13.7 billion years. The Hubble Telescope has allowed us to view this star formation between colliding galaxies. The James Webb Telescope has taken us even further into space with even clearer pictures of what is happening. We are just now witnessing that growth in our own Solar

System. We always theorized that the changes from the Big Bang took place in microseconds. Maye Moon appeared so quickly that we did not even witness it appearing. Microseconds."

"Did NASA know this event was going to happen, and could they have given us a warning about it?" "No, Warren, we did not have any prior knowledge of this and found out at the same moment that the rest of the world found out. I think it gives credence to our theory that the Big Bang happened in less than a second and grew so quickly, quicker than the speed of light," Kathi explained. "So Maye Moon wasn't, and then just was?" Warren asked. "I guess you could put it that way," Kathi surmised.

"Kathi, a lot of people are posting online several theories for this great event. Is it possible that this moon was in orbit with another planet in our solar system?" Warren inquired. "No, that is not possible. Our solar system has been checked, and everything is in place, as far as we can tell. Moons are natural satellites, and there are hundreds of them. Most of them are solid, but some are formed out of gases and dust. Because of the size of the Maye Moon, I feel it would have been discovered. Another reason I do not think that it left another planet's orbit is because it would have traveled for quite some time to get here. I believe it is a new moon." Kathi explained with confidence. "What do you say to the religious community who think that God placed the Maye Moon here?" Warren asked. "Since I do not have a belief in God, I find it hard to contemplate that theory. As a scientist, I rely solely on facts and things I can test. At this point, I do not think there is any harm in believing that God created the Maye Moon if you wish," Kathi answered.

"I would like to thank you for agreeing to speak to us today, Kathi Calloway, NASA Chief Scientist. It was an interesting conversation and gave us insight into how Maye Moon was created," Warren said directly to the camera. "That was BS," Warren said in his mind. "They don't know any more than the man on the moon." He chuckled at his own wittiness.

Warren was not a religious man; in fact, he was a self-avowed Agnostic; however, after his stint with A.A., he could say he believed that there was a higher power out there in the universe somewhere. Who created the Big Bang? Warren speculated that those scientists who believed in Intelligent Design were more credible, but he really did not want to give a lot of thought to any of it. It happened billions of years ago, and we can't do anything about it anyway. He had prayed to a "higher power" when things got tough at times but did not get the "feelies" from it. It had not provided comfort nor made him feel like anyone was listening to him. Warren pictured his "higher power" as an old man sitting with a sheet wrapped around his body like a toga. He had a very long grey beard and was an aged man of wisdom who sat on a stone throne and watched as everything in the vast universe revolved around him. His "higher power" could not be bothered with the intricacies of our life here on Earth.

As expected, the media and the internet went wild over this interview, and debates between the scientific communities continued. Soon, the religious communities joined in with their theory of how this Maye Moon appearance was created. Unfortunately, Warren did not have a better explanation. Most scientists did not want to discuss the matter publicly because they did not have a good explanation.

Warren was called into his producer, Jeffrey Clark's office. "I want you to start preparing to go to Atlanta to do a show with Pastor Scott Morales. He is a televangelist and pastor of the largest mega-church in the South." "You what?" Warren gasped. "Don't you think we ought to stick to the Science boss? I could end up a laughing stock. Our show could end up a laughing stock. Why – our network could end up a laughing stock. Don't forget we are SNN, Science News Network."

"I think the only one who will end up a laughing stock is Pastor Morales. We will ask some precise questions that Morales will not be able to explain, Biblically, of course," Clark answered. "Tomorrow, he will be your main guest. Get busy preparing for the interview of the Year. Oh, and Warren, good luck."

Tessie and Earl had been channel surfing and had caught Warren's interview with Kathi Calloway. "That was a bunch of hooey, Dad," Tessie exclaimed. "The Big Bang caused this? Why, that is just crazy. Billions of years ago... blah blah blah. I should have expected that out of a Science channel."

"I know Tessie. If they fill our minds with their crazy theories enough, many people will just believe it. I remember when no one agreed with evolution being taught in school. We had a lot less trouble, and kids in school listened to their teachers. Respect. How can you respect a teacher who tells you that you came from an ape?" Earl replied. "And each day started out with prayer. Most kids today know nothing about Creation or prayer. They have managed to erase God from our schools. If the child came from a Godless home, at least they were taught to pray in school. Darwin was an evil man and has probably done more to hurt the morality in America than any man who has ever lived. He and Madeline Murray O'Hair. What an evil woman. Believe a lie and be damned. Let's pray that something happens to change the world for good. We have to get back to God!"

Chapter 3

"Okay, the plan is to interview some of your everyday common-type people and ask the question, how did Maye Moon get here?" Jess Wanamaker, a Fox reporter on the street, explained to his cameraman as they stood outside of the Fox studio in NYC. "Just keep the camera rolling, and we will edit out the duds." Jess Wanamaker was the handsome, funny addition to the Fox lineup. It was refreshing to see a conservative who was young and hip. He would also fill in on a lot of Fox shows when their normal hosts were out. Recently, he was given a Friday night timeslot for his own show. "It is a start, but Jess Wanamaker will have his own prime-time show eventually," he thought.

The first person Jess approached was a 20-something student in a running suit. "Sir, hello, I am Jess Wanamaker, Fox reporter on the street. I was wondering if you could tell us where you think the Maye Moon appeared from?" "Who knows? Maybe it is an alien spaceship, you know, like the Starship Enterprise. Maybe it came from a galaxy far, far away. "Wouldn't that be a pretty large spaceship, sir?" Jess inquired. "Yes, it would be. The Enterprise was a pretty large ship, though. You know, plenty of space for food storage for a long trip. It has to be something like that," the young man said with a serious look on his face. Suddenly, he broke out laughing. "Seriously, I don't have the faintest idea. I was just pulling your chain and trying to be funny. When you figure out where it came from, give me a call." "What a jerk." Jess thought. "Yeah, well, thanks, man," Jess replied. "I hate these types," Jess said to the camera man, "A joker in every crowd. I hope we don't run into many of these wise guys today."

The next person they stopped was a black man wearing an NYU sweatshirt. "Hello, my name is Jess Wanamaker, and I am the Fox reporter on the street. Can I ask you a question? Could you tell me where you think the Maye Moon came from?" "I believe that the Maye Moon is a gift from the universe. Since it appeared, people are focused on Maye Moon and not on COVID or the war in Ukraine. It has been so good to have something else to talk about—something positive," the man replied. "Can you explain what you mean by it is a gift from the universe?" Jess asked. "God is the universe. He is the keeper of all things in the universe. He kept Maye Moon just for a time like this. He released Maye Moon to appear on the planet Earth to send good vibes to the people of the Earth," the man answered. "Thank you for explaining your theory." "Time to move on," Jess thought. "That was a little far out for me."

Susan Gwin

The next three people that Jess stopped did not know what to think. "Let's try that woman over there," Jess said to the camera man. "Hopefully, she has a theory." "Hello, I am Jess Wanamaker from Fox News. Would you like to share with us your theory on where the Maye Moon came from?" Jess flashed a smile at her. Jess was extremely handsome and had a million-dollar smile. "Sure, I can try. I guess I can't get it wrong since no one really knows for sure. I think that Maye Moon was traveling through space like an asteroid or comet, and when it got so close to the Earth's gravitational pull, it was sucked in and stayed where it is, rotating around the Earth as a satellite," the young woman explained. "Hey, that is actually a pretty good theory," Jess replied. "Do you have any expertise in the field of Astronomy?" "No, not really. I had a freshman class at the university. I just find it very interesting." She answered. "Thanks for participating," Jess smiled. He liked her.

The next few people were duds. One had the theory that the Maye Moon was a reflection of the Earth. Another man had the theory that the Russians put it there. Some woman who was a psychologist-type thought we were all experiencing some sort of mass hysteria and that Maye Moon wasn't there at all. Another thought: The Maye Moon somehow escaped from another dimension. Approximately 12% of those interviewed thought that it was an alien space craft. Nearly the same percentage thought that it was a result of the Big Bang. Of course, many folks would not stop at all. They were in too big of a hurry to speak to anyone. Probably hadn't even noticed the Maye Moon yet.

An older, refined lady was coming by, and Jess decided to give it another shot. "Hello, Mam, I am Jess Wanamaker, Fox Reporter on the ground." "Hello Jess, I am Martha, and I watch you on Friday evenings. I really enjoy your segment. You could say that I am a fan." Martha smiled and looked eager to help. She was approximately 80 years of age and had a natural glow about her. "Thanks, Martha, I appreciate that. I was wondering, Martha, if you could share with us your theory on where the Maye Moon came from." Jess asked. "Jess, I would have to say that Maye Moon was placed here by God the Father for some special purpose. A lot of people have been down and depressed by everything that is going on in the world. COVID has taken so many loved ones from us and left a lot of people in financial ruin. Violence is rampant. The economy is getting worse every day. Young people are worried they will never have what their parents have—a home, a car, or be able to afford a family. People are worried about global warming and pollution. I believe that God has given us something to take our minds off of all these worries. God will show us the purpose of the Maye Moon in his time. It will be for good for the whole world to see." Martha again smiled at Jess. "Jess, you have an important part in sharing this message with the world." Jess was at a loss for words.

Martha smiled, turned, and walked away. "Now that gave me the heebie jeebies," Jess thought. "I have goosebumps."

Jess finally got his bearings and told the cameraman that he thought they had enough to make a segment for the Friday night show. The two men returned to their studio and began the work of preparing the segment. Jess was having trouble getting Martha's answer out of his mind. "I wonder what she meant by I would have an important part in sharing that message." Jess thought. "It was kinda spooky the way she said it. Like she knew something that God had in mind. I am sure she is a little crazy or has dementia or something." Jess began work on editing and realized that people weren't sure what to think about the Maye Moon. There were a few "out there" answers, but most were waiting for someone to tell them what to think. And then there was Martha. "Should I use Martha's footage in the segment?" he thought. "I guess so. She is a fan and a very sweet old lady."

"Jess, where do you think the Maye Moon came from?" Jess' camera man strolled by and asked him. "I would have to say I am leaning towards it came from a Black Hole... a huge Black Hole." Jess laughed. "I guess I am a member of the 'I don't know what to think' club. Scientists will debate it for years, and eventually, they will come to a well-accepted theory and put it in the textbooks, and our children's children will accept it as the truth. This is how these things go," Jess explained. "Do you have plans for lunch?"

The Appearance of Maye Moon

The two young men headed down the block and settled on a little Italian diner on the corner. Jess noticed that people seated around him were discussing the latest news, Maye Moon. Maye Moon was all the buzz. He wondered how long Maye Moon would captivate people. "It is crazy to think that people all over the world are experiencing this same thing and having these same conversations." "I know. Hey Jess, why don't you see if the producer would send us to Hawaii or some other exotic place to do the show segment?" his camera man replied. "What? New York City isn't exotic enough for you?" The waitress took their order, and the young men continued to make small talk about sports.

Chapter 4

P astor Scott Morales awoke at 6:45 a.m. to the sound of Amazing Grace playing on the alarm clock of his Tuxedo Park Atlanta mansion. It is said that Tuxedo Park is the closest thing to Beverly Hills in the Southeast. Only the best for God. Pastor Scott started his day off like most mornings: slip into his robe and slippers, visit the bathroom, comb through his hair, brush his teeth, and signal to his Guatemalan kitchen helper that he was ready for his coffee.

Mia quickly brought his Jamaican Blue Mountain coffee and asked the pastor what he would like for breakfast this morning. "I think I will have Eggs Benedict with a banana this morning. Thank you, Mia." Mrs. Barnes, Pastor Scott's Assistant, quickly entered the room. She was ready to run through his schedule for today. "Make it quick. I want to get my exercise in before my car arrives." Pastor Scott told her.

"You need to be at the church no later than 9:00 a.m. this morning. You have a 9:15 a.m. appointment with Deacon Caldwell about parking, a 9:30 a.m. appointment with the Music Director about Sunday's music, and at 10:00 a.m., you are scheduled to be interviewed by Winston Warren with Science News Network about the appearance of the Maye Moon. I have his bio here for your review. The interview is scheduled for one hour at the church. You are expected at the Baptist Women's Auxiliary luncheon from 12:00 to 1:00. Be ready to say a few words of encouragement and lead the luncheon prayer. After 1:00 p.m., your schedule is free for working on your latest book. I have coordinated these plans with your driver and put the schedule in your phone," Mrs. Barnes said. As usual, Mrs. Barnes was on top of everything.

Pastor Scott looked over some of his messages while enjoying his breakfast, then headed to his home gym for a workout. After a shower, he dressed and met with his hair stylist. A man of his stature in the community must always look his best. "Why did I agree to this interview with SNN? I guess a different audience will see me than usually sees me. Maybe I will gain some fans." Pastor Scott met his driver outside right on time, punctual as always. "Take me to the church, Carl." "Yes sir," Carl replied, but of course, he was aware of the day's schedule ahead of time. "Pastor Scott, could you pray for my cousin? She just found out she has cancer. It is pretty bad, Stage 4 Lymphoma," Carl requested. "Sure, sure, Carl." Pastor Scott wasn't really paying attention. He was busy going over the SNN bio that Mrs. Barnes had provided.

Winston Warren entered the church campus and arrived at the church a little early, so he decided to review the questions he was going to ask in his interview with Pastor Morales. The Atlantic Berea Baptist Church was described as the largest church in the Southeast. It claimed to have nearly 30,000 members, and its sanctuary was larger than a football field. Someone must have gotten gold gilded paint on sale, as it covered most of the hardware in the sanctuary, including the large pulpit and cross that hung over the baptistery. The seating for 8,500 was covered in plush purple velvet upholstery fabric with purple carpet on the floors. It looked like Barney, the dinosaur, had exploded all over the church auditorium. Crystal lighting features hung throughout the ceiling. Stained glass windows with scenes depicted from the Bible covered the east and west walls. A large balcony loomed over the sanctuary. It was mega – more than mega. Warren told his camera man to get some footage of the elaborate showroom.

"This is quite different than the tiny country church that I attended as a child," he thought. It did bring back fond memories of when life was simpler and uncomplicated. "I would have to say I am thankful that my parents made sure that I went to church and had a good upbringing. In fact, Mother and Daddy still attend that small country church. Maybe if I can get some time off, I will go one Sunday and surprise them," he reminisced.

"We better wait in the massive church foyer until we are ready for the interview," Warren told his camera man. His voice echoed throughout the sanctuary even though he was whispering. He was actually getting nervous about this interview. He felt like he was preparing to interview King Charles III or some other royalty. At last, an attractive secretary arrived and told the reporter that they would be meeting in Pastor Scott's office. A young man was leaving the office with a stack of sheet music in his hands. He was humming a song that Warren was unfamiliar with. "Pastor Scott, this is the SNN reporter, Winston Warren, here to interview you." The secretary made the introduction.

"Winston, come in, have a seat, and make yourself comfortable. We have taken the liberty of arranging an interview setting here on the left (Thank you, Mrs. Barnes). We thought that might work for what you had in mind." Pastor Scott motioned to the newly arranged interview spot. "Thank you, Pastor, that was very kind of you. Yes, I think that will work well." Warren answered. "My assistant prepared some questions you might want to ask during the interview." Pastor Scott proceeded, "We always try our best to be prepared ahead of time." "Actually, I have prepared the questions we would like to ask," Winston replied.

"As you know, we are a Science network, and we want to try to present an interview that demonstrates where religion and science intersect. At least that is a goal I have." Warren explained. "I see,"

Pastor Scott said, "Well, we can work with that as long as you do not include anything to try to tarnish the image of our church or God. We want to always be a beacon of light in this community." "I am sure you will have no problem with the questions I have prepared. I am only trying to get a theological and scriptural answer to the appearance of the Maye Moon. We speak to a lot of scientists and physicists, but this appearance should be examined from the religious perspective also," Warren explained. "Ok, well, we will do our best, but this occurrence is pretty unexplainable. Warren, Are you a religious man?" Pastor Scott asked. "Pastor, I thought I was here to ask the questions." He chuckled. "I am actually from a Christian home, but to be honest, I am now more of an Agnostic. I have drifted pretty far from my upbringing, but I do have a pretty thorough knowledge of the Bible."

Warren and Pastor Scott settled into the plush leather chairs on set. The camera man got set up, and they were ready to begin. "Good evening. We have a treat for you tonight, viewers. We will be speaking to the pastor of the mega-church, Atlantic Berea Baptist Church, Pastor Scott Morales," Warren began. "Good evening, please call me Pastor Scott like my congregation does. It is so good to be here with you at SNN." "Could you start by telling our viewers about your church and your work at Atlantic Berea Baptist?" Warren asked. "Sure, Warren. We are a traditional, fundamental Baptist church of approximately 30,000 members at last count. We have many services and groups to choose from throughout the week. Our mission is to teach the Word of God to anyone and everyone. We operate a Pre K-12 school and have a tremendous youth program. I think the best in the city. We have a homeless ministry, an addiction program, counseling, a shut-in program, a food bank, various nursing home ministries, a tragedy relief program, and we support many missionaries. We have a television broadcast and a radio program. Our next endeavor will be to open a university to train our young people about service to God. We love the Lord, and the Lord loves us. We welcome all people to come and visit us at Ted Turner Dr. NW near Centennial Olympic Park." Pastor Scott answered.

"It must be very difficult to manage the needs of 30,000 people," Warren said. "It would be if our ministry did not have the finest staff and group of volunteers in Atlanta. The Lord has been gracious to take care of the needs of His people." Pastor Scott answered.

"Pastor Scott, everyone is talking about the unexplainable phenomena known as Maye Moon. Could you share with us what the Word of God says about it?" Warren questioned. "I am sorry to disappoint you, Warren, but the Bible does not mention Maye Moon or the appearance of any new moon."

"Pastor Scott, does that mean that you are a believer in the Big Bang Theory regarding how the universe was created?" Warren inquired. "By no means, absolutely not. The Bible explains that in the beginning, God created the heavens and the Earth. God spoke the Earth and heavens into existence. On the fourth day, he created the Sun and the Moon for light and to divide the day from the night. I can't say for sure whether there was a great loud bang when he did this or not," Pastor Scott smiled when he said this. Warren smiled back. "Scientists agree that the universe is approximately 13.7 billion years old. Do you believe that God created the universe that long ago?" Warren questioned. "Not according to the Bible. I would like to see their proof for that date. As far as I know there is no solid proof for that date. In the Bible, we are provided with the genealogy starting with Adam and Eve, the first man and woman, all the way thru to Jesus Christ. Those records support the Creation theory that the Earth and universe are approximately 6000-6500 years old." Pastor Scott replied.

"Does the Bible have all of the answers? Where was God before he created the heaven and the Earth?" Warren asked sincerely. Pastor Scott explained, "There are a lot of things that we are not meant to know here on Earth. All things will be explained to those who reach heaven. We do know that God always was and always will be. He is omnipotent. I look forward to understanding all of the mysteries. I have a lot of questions myself. I usually try to accept by faith that God's way is the only way."

The Appearance of Maye Moon

"Pastor Scott, do you think that God created Maye Moon?" Warren asked. "I have no doubt that God did." Pastor Scott answered. "Why do you think that it was God who created Maye Moon?" Warren asked. "I do not think that anyone on Earth has the power to do it, so it must have been God." Pastor Scott said positively. "Why? What would be the purpose?" Warren questioned. "I believe that God will let us know in His time and in His way. Until then, we should just enjoy its beauty each and every day."

"One final question, Pastor Scott, can God, religion, and Science co-exist?" Warren asked. "I don't know why not. They always have." Pastor Scott smiled and was happy with his answers. "That should convert some new readers to buy my latest book," He thought as he returned to his chauffeured limo.

Winston Warren was glad that the interview was over. Actually, there were a lot of things that were discussed that he wanted to think about. "It would be nice to have that kind of faith that God exists and that He created the Maye Moon for some important reason that would help mankind. I really don't have time for the whole church thing," Warren thought. "How can you live without it?" a still, small voice in his mind answered. Warren got goosebumps.

Tessie and Earl attended their small church on Sunday morning and heard many of the same points that Pastor Scott had made. Several visitors came to church this week hoping to hear about the Maye Moon. Their pastor was a humble preacher who served the Lord every day with very little to show for it. He was known for giving to others and supporting missionaries all over the world. His old used car could use a new set of tires, but that is just money that could help spread God's Word to a lost and dying world. His greatest pleasure was leading a lost soul to Christ. His wife was just as dedicated to the ministry. They had four children to take care of on their small salary, but God always provided.

Tessie and Earl were 100 % sure that God was responsible for placing the Maye Moon in the sky. Some day, they will understand the reason behind it. Maye Moon showed up three weeks ago, and there has been a renewed spirit of love and hopefulness that the world needed after the COVID virus.

Sunday morning, Pastor Scott was met with a surprise at his church. A group of approximately 50 protestors and a television crew were waiting at the entrance. The protestors were carrying various signs supporting Science. They began to shout obscenities and untruths at the members who were trying to enter the church. Church security was trying to peacefully get them to leave, but they were not budging. Many members were returning to their cars so they would not be caught on camera. Pastor Scott decided that his only recourse was to call the police to clear them out. "This will definitely make national news," He thought. "That's not in our best interest." He was being labeled as the Pastor of the Moonies, not to be confused with the Family Federation for World Peace and Unification Church, started by Reverend Sun Myung Moon in 1954. Many people refer to the Moonies as a dangerous cult. "We definitely do not need this kind of publicity. I must call in some favors and try to squash this story right away," Pastor Scott thought.

Monday morning, Pastor Scott called in three of his trusted members and met with them in his office. Although they had some good connections the damage was already done. Videos had already been posted on the internet and had gone viral. He would have to run a PR campaign reminding the community of the goodwill the church had done and was doing. The term "Moonies" had caught on and anyone who believed God was responsible for the Maye Moon was then referred to as a "Moonie." "At least it is not just our church labeled as "Moonies," Pastor Scott thought. "We must make this work in our favor. Maybe this will die out quickly."

Chapter 5

T oday, in a Fox News special report, Space X announced that they will be working on a larger manned rocket capable of landing on Maye Moon and have it ready by the end of the year. Four astronauts will be aboard and will be conducting a variety of tests and collecting samples from the new moon. The publicist from Space X, Arlene Turner, released the information exclusively to America's News Headquarters, who put it in their top spot. "We are anxious to verify and find out more information about Maye Moon. You will witness a lot of testing and practice launches leading up to the Miracle Mission launch taking place at Cape Canaveral in Florida," Arlene explained. "We are very excited to embark on this new adventure on the Space Coast."

"What does Elon Musk think about the new moon being named after his mother?" the reporter asked. "Elon and Maye Musk both feel very honoured to have the new moon named after her," Arlene answered. "Is Elon scrapping his Mars mission?" the reporter asked. "No way, that has always been the ultimate goal of Space X, but it will take place when the time is right. Right now, the time is right for Maye Moon," Turner answered.

Soon after their announcement, the Chinese, the Koreans, and the Russians also announced they planned to do their own flights to Maye Moon. It will be a modern-day space race. Lorraine Maxwell, Chief Operating Officer of Space X, said in a brief media conference, "We are confident that Space X will win the Space Race once again. After all, Space X had already been planning for a space launch to Mars before Maye Moon appeared. The company will just transition the plan to visit Maye Moon first. Our founder, Elon Musk, makes things happen. He has been very successful in operating many corporations, and this should be no different."

Later in the day, the President of the United States, President George McIntosh, announced in a televised news conference that the U.S. was prepared to put as many resources as Space X needed towards accomplishing this mission. "Space X has done so much good for the world, and we want to support them in any way we can. I feel it is important that we show the world that we are still the leader in the space exploration field. The U.S., through NASA, was the pioneer of the aeronautics field. We feel that the Maye Moon should become a territory of the United States so that we can be sure that if it has resources that can benefit mankind, they will be fairly distributed. We understand that this is a far-reaching goal in the future, but we must think and plan ahead."

"What? What was he thinking saying that?" John Stafford, McIntosh's White House Chief of Staff, thought. Stafford interrupted the news conference and said, "There will be no more questions." He quickly escorted President McIntosh out of the conference to an area where reporters were not permitted.

President McIntosh's comments were like a bomb exploding, and leaders from nearly every country were angered and making their own claims of how to divide up Maye Moon fairly. Each country had its own agenda on how they could capitalize from Maye Moon. What had provided some peacefulness in the beginning, was setting up a climate of hostility between country leaders. At this point, no one really was sure what resources were on the surface of Maye Moon yet.

President McIntosh's cabinet Secretary of Energy asked for a meeting with him to discuss some newly discovered findings. "Thank you for meeting with me, Mr. President. I come bearing good news." "I can definitely use some good news, Madam Secretary," the President replied. "Our department has been working energetically to expand our solar power grid throughout the United States. We have found that this month, solar production is up 8%. Maye Moon seems to be the cause for the increase. Because the Maye Moon is larger than the moon, it has more than doubled the size of the Sun reflection at night. Solar panels are now producing more energy at night. This is another step closer to our goal of cleaner, cheaper, sustainable energy and less dependency on fossil fuels," the Secretary of Energy explained.

"Amazing! This is such good news. Are you sure of your findings?" the President nearly shouted. "Yes, home energy bills are indicating that this is really happening." the Madam Secretary answered. "We must share these findings with the public as soon as possible. Please have your team work with my Press Secretary to discuss how to make the announcement. I am so pleased," the President exclaimed. "Let's also look at a plan for another tax incentive to encourage more homes to add solar panels. Thank you for sharing that news with me today. I needed it."

"Madam Secretary, I suppose we should share this information with NASA and the Space Force. All things related to Maye Moon should be shared. I also think we should have a Maye Moon Summit and invite guests from the United Nations. We need to start influencing Ambassadors from other countries to support us in our goal of making Maye Moon a U.S. territory. This might be a hard task to accomplish, but we need to start making strides towards that goal. I will work on forming a committee to work on this Summit, and I definitely want you to be a part of it." The President stated. "As you wish, Sir," she answered, but in her mind, she was questioning the sanity of the President. "He wants to make Maye Moon a territory of the United States? That is absurd," she thought.

At the daily press briefing, Press Secretary Anna Alexander announced that solar energy outputs had increased by 8%, thus lowering energy costs for many homes in America supporting solar energy. "The President has asked Congress to extend the 26% tax abatement to homeowners who choose to invest in solar power for their homes."

"Could you address the animosity created by President McIntosh's comments about the U.S. making the Maye Moon a territory of the United States? a bold news reporter asked. Anna replied, "I wouldn't call it animosity. I would call it a surprise. The President will be announcing a summit in the near future to address any concerns that any leader may have about his announcement. I am sure after such an agenda has explained all the benefits, there will be many countries on board with this idea."

"Does the President actually believe that he has the power to make a satellite sovereign territory of the U.S.?" another daring reporter questioned. "These are questions that cannot be asked at this time. Once the U.S. wins the space race to Maye Moon, we will be able to define that relationship. Thank you all for coming." Anna quickly exited the room. "What was the President thinking when he made that comment?" she thought to herself. "He certainly makes this job hard at times."

Chapter 6

J ess and his camera man headed out to get some new Maye Moon footage for his show. His question of the day was, "Do you believe God or the Big Bang was responsible for the Maye Moon?" They decided to stand in front of St. Patrick's Cathedral on 5th Avenue. It was only a 3-minute walk from the Rockefeller Center and was a tourist "must-see" site in Manhattan. The architecture was just inspiring. Jess attended services there each week.

Jess approached the first person he saw, a man who was in his 70s, wearing a hat and using a cane. "Hello, Sir, I am Jess Wanamaker, and I am the Fox News reporter on the street. Could I ask you a question?" "Sure, Jess," the older man answered. "Do you believe it was God or the Big Bang who was responsible for the Maye Moon?" Jess asked. "Definitely God, Jess, definitely God," he stated positively. "You sound pretty sure of that," Jess stated. "I have lived a long time, and I have witnessed the way God works in mysterious ways many times. I went to school when teachers did not have to worry about talking about God. In fact, I went to school at

St. Patrick's. I love this place," the man replied with a look of genuine love. "I appreciate you speaking with us today. Hope you have a wonderful day," Jess replied with his million-dollar smile.

The next person Jess approached was a young mother with a baby in a baby carriage. "Hi, I am Jess Wanamaker, Fox News reporter on the street. Beautiful child, is it a boy or a girl?" "This is Matthew, and he is four months old. He is my first. My name is Penny," she answered with a smile. "Penny, Could I ask you a question? Do you believe it was God or the Big Bang that was responsible for Maye Moon?" "I believe it was God. I believe in creation," she answered. "My son will be raised in church, and I thank God every day for him. I was a different person five years ago. I had gone astray and was doing drugs, partying, and living on the streets. God cleaned up my life, and I thank Him for it every day. Without Him, there would be no Sun or Moon. Maye Moon was a gift," she smiled again. "Thank you, Penny, for speaking with us, and I hope that you and Matthew have a beautiful day."

"You too, Jess. Just let God take control of everything," and there was that smile again.

The camera man followed Jess on to the next person, a man in a business suit. "Hello sir, I am Jess Wanamaker, Fox News reporter on the street. I am wondering if you would mind answering a question I have. Jess inquired. "Sure, if it doesn't take too long. I am on my way to a meeting at the Rockefeller Center," he answered. "No, this doesn't take long at all. Do you believe it was God or the Big Bang who was responsible for the Maye Moon?" Jess asked. "Actually, I have thought about this. I am not a very religious man, but I do believe that God has created this moon. It is hard to believe that something like that can appear in less than a second that does not have a creator. Who God is exactly is something I am not sure about. I am thinking about it a lot and plan to explore different views of God to get a better understanding," the business man replied. "I bet that surprises you," he smiled. "It surprised my mother. Thanks for asking."

Jess approached a young man with a back pack. "Hi, I am Jess Wanamaker, Fox News reporter on the ground. Could I ask you a question?" "Fox News, the propaganda channel? Sure, go ahead and ask," the young man sneered. "Do you believe it was God or the Big Bang who was responsible for the Maye Moon?" Jess asked. "Well, since I do not believe in God, I guess my choice would have to be the Big Bang. Science is based on the proven. You cannot prove that there is a God." "Who created Science?" Jess asked. "Science just is. Like Mathematics, it just is," the young man smirked. "Gotta run."

Jess saw an older woman coming his way. It was Martha, a grand old dame that he had interviewed before. "Hi Martha, how are you doing?" Jess asked. "Hi Jess, I am doing well. I saw you over here and just had to stop and say hello to my favorite Fox News reporter. I see you are still conducting interviews," Martha replied. "May I participate again?" "I would love for you to take part. My question today is, Do you believe it was God or the Big Bang who created the Maye Moon?" Jess asked. "That is a very good question. God is the creator of all things, big or small. I believe God sent us the Maye Moon for a very special purpose. Maye Moon's purpose will be revealed very soon. I know that, Jess. You are going to have a special part in that," Martha looked deeply into the camera when she said that. "Martha, you are such a sweetheart, but I am a lowly reporter on the street just trying to get to the bottom of this," Jess smiled that million-dollar smile. "Jess, you will see. Yes, you will see," she replied as she walked away.

"I think that is enough for today, man. Let's head back to the studio." Jess told the camera man. The hair on his arm was standing at attention again.

After getting back to the studio, Jess heard that President McIntosh was planning to make Maye Moon a territory of the U.S. "I think I should shelf this episode for a week and hit the street with the question of whether the U.S. should make Maye Moon a territory. That should be an interesting one for sure," Jess told his producer. "I think you are right, Jess. Move forward with that idea," he responded.

The Appearance of Maye Moon

Jess and his cameraman loaded up and went back out to interview more regular everyday Joe's to find out what was on the people's minds. "Let's head over to the Statue of Liberty to conduct our surveys. Isn't it a little ironic that the country of liberty is already discussing taking control of the Maye Moon?" Jess mused.

It took the new van a little while to arrive at the Statue of Liberty, but as always, there were a lot of tourists milling about, there for the picking. Just seeing the statue up close always warmed Jess' heart. The Lady is bigger and grander than you think when you see her in person. Jess' Italian grandparents arrived at Ellis Island in the early 1900s, and he could only imagine what it was like back then. And now, the U.S. is planning a mission to a moon that didn't even exist back then. Unreal.

Jess approached the first person, a lady in her mid-50s, and said, "Hi, I am Jess Wanamaker, Fox News reporter on the street, and I was wondering if I could ask you a question?" "Jess, Jess Wanamaker, is that really you? I watch you all of the time. I am a huge fan. My name is Maggie, and I would love for you to ask me a question," she swooned. "President McIntosh is planning to make Maye Moon a U.S. territory. What do you think about that?" "I hadn't heard about this. This is awful. Why would he think he should do this? How could we control a moon? I am totally against this. Why, he could put us in a war over this. We need to focus on the country we have," she answered. "I appreciate your opinion,

43

Maggie. I hope you enjoy your time here in New York City. Where are you from, Maggie?" Jess asked. "I am here from Dayton, Ohio. Thank you, Jess."

The next person was an older gentleman wearing a Veteran's hat in his mid-70s. "Hello, sir. Thank you for your service. I am Jess Wanamaker, a Fox News reporter on the street, and I would like to ask you a question. Do you mind?" "No, young man, ask me a question," he said. "President McIntosh is planning to make Maye Moon a U.S. territory. What do you think about this plan?" Jess asked.

"I fought in Nam to keep this country free from communism. I think we must be proactive to keep the communists and socialists from trying to take over Maye Moon and to keep them from claiming any resources that might be there. I agree with President McIntosh taking a proactive role in doing this. Americans have footed the bill for most of the space program, so why shouldn't we control Maye Moon? We are the fairest country and most giving to other countries in the world," He said with conviction. "Sir, those are all good points. Thank you for participating, and again thank you for your service to our country." Jess held out his hand to shake hands with the gentleman. "Good day, Sir," the old man replied.

Jess tried to speak to a teenage girl about the question, but she was oblivious to what was going on. "I wish the schools made students more aware of the current issues," Jess thought. By the end of the day, Jess found that more people seemed to support the President than did not. That kinda surprised Jess, but it is really hard to predict what people will think in this day and age. "It is a crazy world out there," Jess thought.

Chapter 7

T essie awoke to a hot body next to her. Poor Earl's body was sweating and hot to the touch, but his teeth were chattering, and he was freezing. "Tessie, can you get me another blanket? I'm cold." He managed to say. "Earl, I am going to get the thermometer too." Tessie hurried to get another thick blanket to make Earl feel more comfortable. She went to the medicine cabinet, got her trusty thermometer, and quickly returned to their bedroom. "Earl, when did you start feeling bad?" she asked. "I'm not sure. Sometime during the night." Earl answered. "I ache all over."

Tessie removed the plastic tube and popped the thermometer into Earl's mouth. "Hold it still a couple of minutes, Earl." After a short time, Tessie removed the thermometer and found that Earl's temperature was 103 degrees. Earl seemed to be having some trouble breathing. "We are not taking any chances. I am calling an ambulance to take you to the hospital." "Now, Tessie, I will be alright. I don't want to go to the hospital," Earl whispered. "This is one time when I wear the pants in this family, I insist," Tessie replied. Earl knew better than to argue with her about it. Besides, he just did not feel well enough to argue about it.

Tessie dialed 911 and told the operator that she needed an ambulance for her husband. As she held back her tears, she tried to answer the operator's questions. She felt helpless and confused but managed to get through the call. She went to the front door and waited for them to arrive. Neighbors were already milling about, having coffee, walking their dogs, starting their days.

Finally, after approximately 15 minutes, the ambulance arrived, and two paramedics came in with a medical bag. "Good morning, mam. What seems to be the trouble?" one young man asked. "It's my husband. He is very sick and running a high fever," Tessie replied. "Which way is he? You should wait here while we check him out. I think you need to sit down and try to relax," He directed. The two paramedics headed down the narrow hallway to Earl and Tessie's bedroom. After a couple of minutes, they returned to get a stretcher to remove Earl from the bed and transport him to the hospital.

Neighbors were gathering around like a flock of birds, whispering, waiting to see what would transpire. An ambulance is a frequent event in a 55+ community. The paramedics assured Tessie that they would take good care of Earl. "Can I ride along?" Tessie asked. "No, ma'am. We have not allowed that since COVID. The best thing for you to do is to stay put. We do not want you to get sick also." Tessie nodded. She blew Earl a kiss goodbye. "I love you most, Earl," she said with tears in her eyes. She squeezed his hand. "No, Mom, I love you most," he managed to reply. "Don't worry about me, Tessie. If something happens, I will be with Jesus, waiting for you to join me some day." "I know, Earl, but I am not ready to lose you, so you fight to get better. Jesus doesn't mind waiting. I will be praying for you." The paramedics got in the ambulance with Earl, and the ambulance started down the street to the community exit.

The neighbors started approaching Tessie with concern and questions. She was teary and shaky and did not feel like talking right then. "Sorry, but I must make some phone calls to my children," Tessie told them. "We will be praying for you, honey," Her next-door widow lady friend told her. She had lost her husband four months ago to COVID. A 55+ community sees death far too often. Tessie went into her home and collapsed in her plaid recliner. "I had hoped this day would never come," she thought. But it had.

Tessie began the calls with her oldest daughter. "Hi dear, I hope you were up. I needed to let you know that Daddy was just taken to the hospital. He had a high fever and was starting to have a cough." Tessie felt a relief getting the first phone call over with. Her daughter was kind enough to offer to make the rest of the calls to her siblings. Tessie had assured her that she was doing alright and there was no need for any of the children to come. She did not want them to catch COVID if that was what it was. They wouldn't be allowed to go into the hospital to visit their father anyways.

Tessie phoned the hospital and spoke to the ER nurse. They had given Earl a quick COVID test, and it was positive. "Oh no, we have been so careful," Tessie thought. "Earl will be moved to a special COVID Intensive Care floor as soon as a bed becomes available. It shouldn't take too long," the nurse told her. "There were not as many COVID patients as there were a few months ago. In fact, we rarely see COVID since the Maye Moon appeared." The nurse assured her that they were taking good care of Earl and they were working on getting his temperature down.

Tessie would wait for Earl to telephone her because she did not want to wake him if he was napping. "I guess I could use a nap myself," Tessie thought. "This stress and worry has me exhausted," Tessie said a prayer for Earl and lay there with her eyes closed, but she could not fall asleep. The place in the bed next to her was empty, and she couldn't help letting her mind wonder what she would do if Earl didn't make it. She couldn't help it, but the tears finally fell like a slow rain. Tessie told herself, "God is in control. He is the Great Physician." It did calm her and gave her peace. Finally, Tessie succumbed to a blissful, restful sleep.

A telephone call awakened Tessie. It was Earl calling to let her know that they had placed him in a room. "Tessie, I want you to promise not to come up here. I don't want you to get sick too. My temperature is down to 100 degrees. They have me on oxygen and fluids but not a respirator. It could be worse."

"Earl, I am so happy to hear your call. I miss you. I want you to know I am doing ok, and I love you," Tessie told him. "We will get through this. Just keep praying for me. I need some more rest. You rest, too. I will telephone you after dinner and before bed. Keep your chin up, old girl," Earl said. "I will, Earl. Love you Most." Tessie hung up the phone. Tears ran down her cheeks again. Earl's oxygen levels and temperature teeter tottered back and forth for the next three days.

Day Four was a rough one for Earl. The nurses were afraid they would have to intubate Earl to help him breath. It seemed that when a patient was intubated, they had a very long hospital stay or did not make it out of the hospital with this horrible virus. Earl made his evening call to Tessie. "I asked my nurse to open my curtains so I could see both full moons out of my window. I am pretending we are on the beach in our lawn chairs, watching the moonrise, and holding hands. We are just a couple of young lovers." "Oh, Earl, that melts my heart. I will go outside and sit in the lawn chair and think about the same thing. We can be together in our dreams," Tessie swooned. Their love was special.

The Appearance of Maye Moon

Earl focused on the Maye Moon and thought about how weird it was that it just appeared out of nowhere. As he looked at it intently, he heard a voice in his mind, "It will heal you. It will heal the Earth. You will be alright." Earl was a little startled. He had never heard a voice in his head like that before. He had such a rough day, and it was a comforting voice. "I believe the Lord has spoken to me," he thought. "I am breathing a little easier." By the time the doctor made his rounds the next morning, Earl had turned the corner and was nearly 100%. "A miracle," the doctor told Earl and his nurse. "If Earl is still feeling better by 2:00 p.m., let's release him."

Earl telephoned Tessie with the good news. "Earl, I had a dream last night that the Lord told me you were going to be ok. An answer to prayer! I can't wait to hear from you after lunch to see if they release you. I need you home with me!" The nurse came into Earl's room and told him that the doctor could not see any reason to keep him any longer.

"Praise the Lord!" Earl exclaimed. "No offense, but I need to get home to Mother." Tessie was waiting for the call and proceeded to the hospital to pick Earl up. Tonight, they will head to the ocean and hold hands and watch the Moon and the Maye Moon rise, just a couple of young lovers on the beach.

Sunday morning, Tessie and Earl headed off to church. Two of their children and their families greeted them in the parking lot.

They decided they wanted to come and see them and see how Earl was doing. They were staying in a hotel near Tessie and Earl's home so as not to make any extra work for Tessie. "What a wonderful surprise," Tessie thought. Tessie just loved filling up the church pew with her family. It reminded her of the days when she and Earl had seven little ones lined up between them. All of their children were saved, and most of them still served the Lord. Tessie and Earl loved their pastor and the church they attended because the Word of God was preached without apology, traditional hymns were sung, and there was such a sweet spirit amongst the people.

During the alter call, their 10-year-old granddaughter Rose walked the aisle after hearing the Roman's Road message and got saved. What a glorious day! She accepted Jesus in her heart, and she wanted to be baptized. The pastor was happy to baptize her right then, so most of the congregants stayed and witnessed it. It was wonderful. The family went out for lunch afterward at a favorite restaurant on the beach. Earl thought about how thankful he was to be there with his family. God is so good!

Chapter 8

After her first interview with SNN, Kathi Calloway was asked to do interviews on various news programs. She felt her first interview with Winston Warren went pretty well and had managed to say nearly the same spiel in each interview after. She felt like many people had accepted this scientific explanation for Maye Moon. The Big Bang Theory just made the most sense. To be perfectly honest, NASA had not come up with any other explanation. NASA had investigated as many video recordings as they could find of the event and Maye Moon had appeared in microseconds, no explosions—no sound. It was just there.

NASA and Space X were nearly ready to man a flight to this beautiful blue-green satellite, and they were anxious to find out what was on the surface and any other important scientific data they could measure. NASA decided to partner with Space X because they had a head start in the race. It would be best for NASA and America. Fortunately, Space X accepted their partnership because it would cut their costs in half. Elon Musk made it clear, though, that Space X was in charge. Since Maye Moon strangely appeared, Musk had not been able to think about Mars or anything else. This mystery must be solved. Calloway and Arlene Turner, the publicist for Space X, will be coordinating what can be said in public about the mission.

The Hubble and Webb telescopes had been picking up a lot of strange behaviour in the universe. NASA has reported that a river of star formations has been seen between galaxies. It appears the speed of the growth in the universe is getting faster. The appearance of the Maye Moon has renewed the interest in the Space Program. People are watching the sky nightly to see if they can witness any other new happenings. The government has been releasing several reports of UAPs and UFOs discreetly, and they continue to be leaked to the news media. The Navy has reported that the reports are real, which has the Pentagon concerned. Reports of UAPs are coming in from all over the country at an unprecedented rate.

Kathi Calloway and Arlene Turner were adversaries and competitors but now were expected to partner. Both were strong, intelligent women who wanted to be in charge. Both had received an email that they were to be at a joint meeting between NASA and Space X to discuss the upcoming mission to Maye Moon.

Calloway and Turner arrived early and almost entered the door of the NASA conference room at the same time. "Good morning." They cordially greeted one another. Each carried their own favourite coffee in hand. The seats of the conference room were starting to fill up with various experts in the space field. Loraine Maxwell, COO of Space X, presided over the meeting.

"Good morning. Thank you all for coming. I want to discuss our upcoming mission to Maye Moon. As you know, man has not stepped on the moon since 1972. We have focused our Space X endeavours on Starlink and transporting to and from the International Space Center. While doing this, we have continued to work on Elon Musk's goal from the beginning, which is for Space X to put man on Mars. For approximately the last 20 years this goal has been worked towards, and we have made great strides towards this goal. That is why I can confidently say that we are the leader in the Space field. The conference meeting attendees clapped.

"Since the appearance of Maye Moon, there has been a renewed interest in the world to see man explore the universe. Many countries have the goal of being the first to land on Maye Moon. Fortunately for Space X, we have the technology to make it happen. We are temporarily putting our Mars mission on hold and using that technology to move ahead on a mission to Maye Moon sometime in late October. We will be conducting several preflight tests to ensure our astronauts will be safe and secure," Lorraine said

"Ten men and women have been training for this mission, and we will soon announce which four will be chosen to actually go.

The other six individuals will be alternates in case they are needed. As always, Space X has made all of the necessary arrangements to be successful. I am confidently declaring now we will be #1 in this space race to Maye Moon. The conference room was filled with enthusiasm and clapping. I want to thank each and every one of you for your contributions to this goal. It has not gone unnoticed. Without each of your expertises, we could not be successful. The next three months will be taxing, but I can assure you the reward will be worth it." Lorraine continued.

"I want to announce that there will be a lot of publicity surrounding this mission, and for security reasons, we will limit the information being given to the public and media. I am ordering that no one speaks to any news media. I will be distributing a memo to each employee indicating that if anyone speaks to the media, they will face immediate dismissal, loss of all benefits, including retirement, and legal action. This is very serious. Failure to report any other employee will result in the same. NASA employees will be given the same memo from their COO. I hate to sound threatening, but this is imperative. We do not want our competitors to know what we are doing."

"I would like to announce that Arlene Turner, our Space X publicist, and Kathi Calloway, Chief Scientist for NASA will have the sole responsibility for the directed publicity for this mission. We do want a lot of celebration, hoopla, and excitement created for this upcoming mission—more than in 1969 when man first walked on the moon. People will be watching all over the world. It will be a moment that people will never forget for centuries to come. The information and research will be important to mankind. You will all be a part of history," Lorraine concluded. At that moment, a roar of applause came from the group and even some tears fell down the cheeks of some of the committee members. They understood this would be the most important event up to this point in history, and it was less than three months away.

Kathi had butterflies in her stomach as she realized she was now the face of the Maye Moon mission. Her schedule for the next three months will be a crazy roller coaster ride. She had already been asked to be on the Tonight Show, SNN, CNN, MSNBC, Fox, The Late Show, The Late Late Show, Purdue University, Florida Institute of Technology, and several others. She had a script to follow for the questions she could answer about the Space X launch to Maye Moon, and she had to follow it exactly. No giving away secrets. Every interviewer will try to get something new out of her, and she must not slip up.

A new Marketing department had been hired to begin producing a wide variety of items that could be purchased in celebration of the Miracle Mission. A Marketing firm was hired to begin an advertising campaign designed to get the world excited about the upcoming event. The launch date was set for the last

Saturday in October. It would be known as Maye Day from then on. Space X and NASA were operating in tandem, and no corners would be cut. Kathi and Arlene had created an interview outline and it had been approved by Musk himself.

Kathi entered Fox Studios and told the receptionist that she was here to see Jess Wanamaker. She decided to wear a modest, solid navy dress under her Space X/ NASA Maye Moon emblemed jacket. It had the new logo for the Miracle Space Mission on it. Jess appeared, looking quite handsome and flashing his million-dollar smile. "Hi Kathi, thank you for coming down to our studio today." "Thank you for inviting me on behalf of Space X and NASA," Kathi answered. "We decided to tape our interview instead of doing it live. You will have the final say-so after editing and producing. I totally understand the need for security in this national matter. I am just thrilled to get to conduct an interview with you," Jess explained while leading her to the studio that they would be taping in. He introduced her to the camera men and producer of the show. "Would you like to have our makeup department freshen your look?" Jess asked. "Sure," Kathi answered. "Why not take full advantage of the experience," she thought. Jess led her to makeup and had his own makeup artist put some finishing touches on his face. He was used to this routine.

After makeup, they went back to his studio to do the interview. They sat down in the comfy tan leather chairs that were arranged to look at each other and face the camera. "Are you comfortable?" Jess asked. "Comfortable, but a little nervous," she answered. "Don't worry, I don't bite. This will not be a high-pressure interview. Just two friends discussing the upcoming mission," he said. The camera man proceeded to count down the taping and yelled, "ACTION."

"I would like to welcome Kathi Calloway today to our studio. Kathi is the Chief Scientist from NASA, and she will be telling us about the upcoming mission to Maye Moon." "Thank you, Jess, for having me," Kathi said. "Kathi, can we start by asking, were you taken by surprise when Maye Moon appeared?" "Very surprised. NASA had no warning that this would happen. We found out at the same time as the rest of the world. One minute, it wasn't there, and the next second, it was. Nothing like this has happened to Earth before."

"What about in other parts of the universe?" Jess asked. "I believe so. As our telescopes become larger and stronger we are able to see more and more going on in the universe. It is really amazing how much more that we know compared to 20 years ago. The universe is rapidly changing," Kathi explained. "Do you support the Big Bang Theory as being responsible for the Maye Moon and these changes?" Jess asked. "Yes, I do. Science has proven that the origin of the universe started from the tiniest of hot molecules inflating and stretching into the universe, a fireball that exploded 13.7 million years ago, and the universe is still growing today," Kathi explained.

"Kathi, a lot of people all over the world contribute to the creation of the universe to God. Do you think that God had anything to do with this? Do you ask yourself, what was there before this Big Bang, and Who caused it?" "Jess, I do question what was before the Big Bang and have come to the conclusion that nothing was before the Big Bang. I base my beliefs on Science that can be proven." Kathi said. "Kathi, how do you explain how everything in the world really seems to fit together just right?" Jess pondered. "I mean, just take the human body, for instance, it is so amazing how everything just works together." "I would have to say that we weren't always so perfectly made, but through the millions of years, we have evolved into a more perfect human body," Kathi replied. "Hmm. you know, a lot of people would disagree with that." Jess stated.

Jess continued, "What can you tell us about the upcoming mission to Maye Moon?" "I can tell you that it is going to be manned by four highly qualified astronauts who are training as we speak. The launch will take place on the last Saturday in October. We are planning a huge celebration for the entire world to witness through live coverage. Most people in the world will be watching. We are hoping that every community in the U.S. will participate and organize parades and activities to celebrate. The U.S.A. will have won the race to Maye Moon!" she said with some phoney excitement.

"Can you tell us the name of the four astronauts?" Jess asked. "Right now we have ten candidates that have all been training together. Four will be on the actual flight. As far as I know, they have not chosen or announced the four." Kathi answered. "If your viewers visit our website, www.mayemoonherewecome, they can find out the latest detailed information about Space X and NASA and the launch. There is also a really great online store where you can order Maye Moon commemorative collectable items. I brought you a Maye Moon jacket, Jess." "Wow, this is really cool. Thanks," Jess smiled. "Can I be your date for the launch, Kathi?" Jess asked. Kathi blushed and immediately became tongue-tied. "Well, Jess, we will see what we can do," she giggled like a school girl. "Be serious, professional," she immediately thought.

Chapter 9

T wo hundred sixty-two applicants applied to be one of the first men or women to walk on the surface of Maye Moon. For most of them, it has been a lifelong dream. The list was narrowed down to 10 astronauts who will train for the mission. Of those ten, only four will be making the trip. The other six will remain alternates until the mission is complete. They will train side-by-side and be ready at a moment's notice. With COVID still lurking around, it was necessary to have alternates ready to go if needed. The four astronauts chosen will be announced next week.

Beyond having skills in leadership, communication, and teamwork, an astronaut must have completed a minimum of a Master's degree in a STEM program – Science, Technology, Engineering, and Mathematics. Additionally, they must have attended a test pilot school. Preferably, they have spent time at the Space Station. It is a rigorous process that very few can complete. It is not for the faint of heart. For the rest of their lives, they will be known for the mission they made to the Maye Moon.

The Appearance of Maye Moon

Cora Collins longed to be one of the astronauts on the first mission to Maye Moon. She understood that since it was totally unexplored and no one had made such a long journey for years, it was dangerous. Cora had enough courage for ten men. She came highly qualified. She had spent six months at the Space Station. What she feared she lacked was strength compared to men applicants. She immediately ramped up her exercise regimen to gain as much body strength as she could. When Cora learned that she was one of the ten astronauts training for the mission, she was so excited. It motivated her to work harder. Depending on the conditions on Maye Moon, it could be physically taxing. She would be ready. She would eat, drink, and sleep during the Maye Moon training.

Finally, Cora received the call she was waiting for. Arlene Turner and the Maye Moon Mission management wanted to meet with the ten chosen astronauts in the morning. Cora was afraid to get her hopes up too high because she knew each candidate was as qualified as she was. Even though she was exhausted, she could hardly sleep.

Cora arrived early and took her assigned seat. "Good morning," she cordially greeted each person who entered the room. Each astronaut tried to appear cool, calm, and collected, but Cora knew they were each a ball of nerves inside. "Jones, are you ready for this?" Cora asked the man sitting next to her. "I am so ready I could take off this morning," he answered. "How about you?" "Got my fingers and toes crossed. I know we have all worked really hard to be here, and anyone chosen is deserving," Cora said. Arlene finally arrived.

"Good morning, crew. I know you are all eager to know who made the cut, but I have to say first that each one of you is top-notch and worthy. I wish I could allow each of you to go to Maye Moon, but as you know only four can go. I would like to announce that Bob Hutchinson, Ben Jones, Larry Lowe, and Cora Collins will be representing the U.S.A., Space X, and NASA in this historic mission. Let's give each of them a round of applause," Lorraine reported. Applause filled the room and some disappointed looks, but everyone understood. "The other six of you will be alternates, and we will not rank you in any certain order. If you are called upon to go, it will depend on the continued hard work and expertise needed. I want to thank you for coming. This information will be released later today to the news media." Lorraine concluded.

Cora was ecstatic, but she wanted to maintain her composure. She felt like screaming and jumping up and down, but not here. Six others who also had worked so hard were disappointed. With plenty of high fives, fist bumps, and congratulations to go around, she finally made her way to the doorway. Tomorrow, the intensive training begins, and in 4 weeks, they will head to Maye Moon.

Chapter 10

"Come in, Come in. We've been waiting for you. Did you have a good flight? We really could have picked you up from the airport. That traffic on I-95 can be treacherous at times. What have you been eating, boy? You have grown a foot since I last saw you," Tessie gushed. Earl teared up and kissed his youngest daughter, Jenny, and shook hands with his grandson, Thomas. "Thomas, why don't you put your and your mother's luggage in the guest room," Tessie said. Thomas was obedient. It would take a few minutes to warm up to his grandparents since he only sees them once or twice a year. It is always a little strange at first.

"Come and sit down, Jenny. Can I get you something cold to drink?" "Sure Momma, you have any sweet tea?" Jenny knew she would be spoiled this week at Momma and Daddy's. She was ready for a rest from her busy life in Chicago. She worked far too many hours as an accountant and having a teenage son kept her even busier. Thomas participated in all of the sports at his private school. She was expected to attend every home game, although she generally missed his away games due to her work schedule. Her husband, Peter, rarely made it to anything. He left the raising of their son to Jenny. "How about you, Thomas? I bought some of those sports drinks that you like?" "That would be great, Gram," Thomas replied. "Are you hungry? Do you need a snack? I made some chocolate chip cookies this morning," Tessie asked. "Sure," Thomas replied. Tessie would have to get used to the fact that Thomas had grown up. "Where did the years go?" she thought.

"Are you still a White Sox fan, Thomas?" Earl asked. "Still watching baseball?" "Yes, sir. We went to an exposition game, and hopefully, I can catch some home games. I mostly watch it on T.V.," Thomas answered. "We will check and see if the St. Lucie Mets are playing while you are here. I could use a baseball game and a hotdog myself," Earl patted Thomas on the back. His youngest grandson is taller than he is now. "Gram, these cookies are delicious," Thomas said. "You eat all you want, Thomas. I can always make some more." She smiled.

"So Jenny, tell me about yourself. How's the job going?" Earl asked. "Same old, same old. Things don't change much in the numbers business. I have been at it for 18 years now. I have been made a department head over six other accountants. I just have a few more papers to file. They do their work and really don't need to be managed," Jenny answered. "Really quite boring," she laughed. "I am thankful for a job that I could work at home during COVID. We are finally back at the office." "What would you like to do while you are here?" Tessie asked. "See you, of course, and rest," she smiled at her mother.

"We wish Peter could have come too," Earl said. "Oh, you know it is always one case after another. The life of an attorney. He hasn't taken a vacation for a couple of years now. He usually drags in around 8:00 p.m., eats dinner, and heads to bed. His job is his life," Jenny sighed. "He will regret that one day; that is all I will say," Earl answered.

"Thomas, we have a launch this evening. Let's all go down to the beach and watch it. It is at 9:43 p.m., and the skies will be dark, and it should be clear. Gram and I try to catch all of them that are at a reasonable hour. We've been known to go to some of them in the middle of the night," Gramps chuckled. "There have been a lot of launches lately because they are testing and preparing for the mission to Maye Moon."

"I would really like that, Gramps," Thomas answered. "How about we go a little earlier, and Thomas can swim for awhile. I will pack some sandwiches and drinks," Gram said. "I promised Thomas that I would take him to Ron Jon so he could get some new beach gear. He says he has outgrown his boogie board and needs some better equipment," Jenny explained. "I would like to take you to lunch in Coco, and I'll drive," Jenny offered. "That sounds like a plan. Maybe I will get a new boogie board, too," Gram teased. Thomas couldn't help but laugh because he could picture Gram on a boogie board.

It was about a 20-minute drive to Ron Jon Surf Shop, and Thomas picked out several things. He got his best friend a souvenir shirt from Ron Jon Surf Shop and his Dad a cool pair of sunglasses. Gram even found a pair of sandals that she couldn't live without. Jenny was happy to buy them for her mother. Afterward, they found a fun, beachy-themed restaurant for lunch. Who couldn't resist fresh seafood?

"Dad, I am so thankful you have recovered so fully. You had us all worried," Jenny said. "Jenny, the Lord healed me by the Maye Moon," Gramps declared. "The Maye Moon?" Jenny looked puzzled. "Yes, the Maye Moon. He whispered to me to open the curtains in my room and look at the Maye Moon. He said that I would be healed, and it would heal our nation. I immediately began to feel better, and by morning, the doctor was amazed. It was God, Jenny." Gramps looked as serious as a heart attack.

"Oh yes, Jenny. God healed your father by using the Maye Moon. I give God all the praise, glory, and honor for doing that. I don't know what I would have done without Daddy," her mother agreed. Jenny just said, "Wow!" She did not know what to think. She was a believer, but to think that God spoke to her Dad and healed him with the Maye Moon was a little much for her to comprehend. Actually, this conversation made her a little uneasy. "How's your shrimp and scallops, Thomas?" she dodged.

Tessie told Jenny about what was going on in their neighborhood and the upcoming events at the clubhouse. She and Earl were thinking about joining the water aerobics class for some exercise. Thomas told his grandparents of his plans for the summer and how he planned to umpire the summer Little League. Earl seemed pretty quiet and he sat there and intently listened. His mind kept drifting off to his encounter with God. "I wonder if others might think I am crazy if I tell them about it. I don't think Jenny believed me," he thought. They finished their wonderful lunch and were ready to return home.

"I think I am going to take a nap when we get home. I am stuffed," Tessie exclaimed. "Thank you, Jenny, for taking us out to lunch." "If you don't mind, I think I will go and sunbathe at the pool for a while, while you are doing that. I want my co-workers to know that I went to Florida," Jenny laughed. "What's your plan, Dad?" "I guess I will sit in my recliner and watch Fox News until I fall asleep, too. It usually puts me to sleep," he amused. "Gramps, do you mind if I borrow your golf cart and ride around the community?" Thomas asked. "I don't mind as long as you don't get a speeding ticket," Gramps answered. "Thomas just can't wait until he gets his license. He begs me to practice driving all the time, and he does a pretty good job. He is scheduled to take driver training in the fall and will have his license by Christmas," Jenny said. "Great, we all have a plan for our afternoon," Tessie said.

At 7:00, Gramps and Gram, Jenny, and Thomas all piled into the SUV and headed for the beach. Thomas grabbed his new board and headed for the ocean. "I swear he is part fish," his mother sighed. Jenny grabbed the picnic basket, small cooler, and her beach chair. Gramps grabbed the other two beach chairs. They made their way down to the beach. This was their happy place. Earl and Tessie always brought their children here for a two-week vacation every summer. Jenny wishes she lived here instead of in Chicago, but Peter does not like the heat of Florida. He has a fantastic job that pays really well, but she will always be a beach baby.

"Gram, Gramps, look," Thomas called as he handled a wave like a pro. They both clapped with enthusiasm. "He is so happy to be here. At home, it gets lonely. Most of his friends have plans for the summer, and his father works all the time," Jenny explained. "I would let him stay, but he has already committed to umpiring." "I believe it is good parenting to make him keep his commitment," Earl said. "Shapes him into an honest man."

"So Jenny, what do you think of the Maye Moon?" Tessie asked. "I guess I side with God; that was the way I was raised," she answered. "It is crazy, though. Who would have dreamed something like this would ever happen." "Your mother and I were sitting on this beach the night it appeared. We were in shock at first, I would say. The more I thought about it I realized that God has a purpose and plan for this. I am excited to find out what will happen," Earl said. "We plan to watch the Maye Mission launch when it goes off. That is really exciting. I would love to be at Cape Canaveral but I am sure that the traffic would be too much for us. People will probably arrive a couple of days early and camp out. I would if I was younger," Earl sighed. "That would be a great time. Historical. Wish I could get Peter to come down," Jenny said. "It would be something Thomas would never forget."

Soon, it was time to watch the launch, and the group turned their chairs facing north. They listened to Space X on Twitter for the latest updates and count down. Take off! They all watched as the bright, fiery ball appeared in the distance. "It is beautiful!" "Cool," "Awe," "There she goes!" they all gasped. Its tail got longer and longer as it streamed across the sky. "This doesn't cease to amaze me," Earl exclaimed. "Thanks, Gramps, for bringing us down here. This is so cool!" Thomas declared. They all watched until it left their sight. "Guess we should pack up and head home. Tomorrow is another big day. I think we should do some fishing in the morning, Thomas," Earl smiled.

When the family arrived home they flipped on Fox News and saw the announcement of the four astronauts going to Maye Moon.

Gramps replied, "This is so different from the Apollo mission because we have information 24/7. I remember watching intently with my college roommates around a small black-and-white television box during the first moonwalk. We were amazed and glued to the TV. Those astronauts were heroes. People were patriotic and proud to be Americans. I sure hope that the Maye Moon mission has that effect on people." "We have already seen a lot of space missions through Star Wars, Star Trek, and lots of other sci-fi movies," Thomas replied. "I mean it is neat and everything, but I feel like it is no big deal." "No big deal, son? Those are all movie props and camera tricks. This is the real deal. This is exactly what I feared about this generation; it will take a lot to impress them. They have had a computer at their finger tips and think they have seen it all. No sense of reality," Gramps said with disappointment in his voice. "Dad, I know you have lived through so much, and Thomas did not mean to disrespect you," Jenny said with concern in her voice. "I know that, Jenny. It is just sad that the younger generation thinks everything is so easy when it is not. I was just two years older than Thomas when I went to Viet Nam. I was just a kid, and I saw so much death and things I can't even talk about. When the youth of today see war, they see it on TV, and the soldiers look like they are at summer camp." Gramps replied.

"What did you think when you saw the Maye Moon Thomas?" Gramps asked. "I thought it was cool," Thomas answered. "Did you wonder where it came from?" Gramps asked. "I guess so," Thomas replied. "Where do you think it came from, Thomas?" Gramps inquired. "I guess it came from the universe somewhere else, showed up from another planet," Thomas was feeling uncomfortable. Gramps was making a point that kids see so much make-believe on television that the real thing does not impress them. They are lacking a real belief that God can do anything. "Where do you think it came from, Gramps?" Thomas asked. "I think that God put it there to do something very good for this planet. God loves us and does not want to see the sin and hatefulness going on in the world today. He gave us something to bring mankind all together. This space launch will be watched all over the world at once. I believe that something very good will come from this space mission. Mark my words. I love you, Thomas. Do you want to go down to the D.Q. for some ice cream?" Gramps asked. "Sure, Gramps, that sounds great. I love you too." Thomas replied. Gram and Jenny were happy that their deep conversation had ended on a good note. "Hey, bring us back a couple of strawberry shakes, Dad."

Chapter 11

P astor Scott had seen an increase in church attendance despite the negative publicity from a group of science lovers protesting outside his church. Evidently, people see the Maye Moon's appearance as an act of God more than the scientific explanation provided by NASA and Space X. The mob group effort to call Christians "Moonies" did not work either. The Lord has a plan going on. Pastor Scott preached several messages recently tying into Maye Moon, but he still did not have a clear understanding of why God would place Maye Moon in the Earth's orbit.

"What have been the positive outcomes since Maye Moon?" he thought. "COVID has nearly disappeared. That is a big one. COVID took so many loved ones and shut down the country for a while. It really hurt church attendance, and some churches shut down completely or used online broadcasts. Attending church online is like trying to bowl online. It hurt the economy and made millions of people depressed and suicidal. Many businesses went under due to supply chain shortages and loss of employees.

The Appearance of Maye Moon

Maye Moon appeared, and suddenly, people were healing physically and mentally. That is a miracle," he thought. "People are recognizing God's power. Creation was hard to believe for some people. Even though they claim to be Christians, they do not fully believe everything in the Bible as truth. My Daddy always said if there is one jot or tittle of the Bible that is not truth, then the whole Bible is a lie. To be honest, I have doubted some of the Bible myself, even though I would not admit that publicly. God knows my heart, thou."

A strange feeling came over Pastor Scott, and he felt like he was going to get sick. Suddenly, Pastor Scott felt compelled to get down on his knees and repent and ask God for forgiveness. He knew in his heart his ministry was based on a lie. He knew that if he were to die that day, he would most likely go to hell because he had a head knowledge of Christ, not a heart knowledge of Christ. He was in the ministry for his own glory and recognition, to live a lavish lifestyle, and to hobnob in upper-class circles with "important" people, not God's people. The numbers were important to his pride. Many people were attending, how much was in the offering plate, how many missionaries they supported, and how many outreach programs they had; all the numbers made him feel significant. He liked feeling important and being well-known. "God, please forgive me," he cried out. "I know I am a sinner, and I need you in my heart and life. I am asking you, Lord Jesus, to forgive me of my sins and save my soul." That day, Pastor Scott was saved by the blood of Jesus and His grace.

The tears poured from his eyes as he knew everything in his life needed to change. The Holy Spirit spoke to his heart about his lavish lifestyle. "I must use my money for God's work and not for my luxury." He called the church treasurer and told her that he was transferring $7 million dollars he had earned writing books to the church fund, to be split between the General fund, Homeless program, and the Missionary fund. She asked with surprise, "Are you sure?" "Most definitely," he answered. "Make sure it is anonymous."

Pastor Scott felt a heavy weight lifted from his shoulders. He had been doing God's work all along, but his motives were wrong. His personal life was not right. He was not a murderer, but he was just as bad--a lost sinner headed to hell before he accepted Christ into his heart. "What should I do next? Call in my deacons and trustees and admit I have been lost. Tell my congregation? I will pray for God's direction."

"Thank you, Lord Jesus, for putting Maye Moon in the sky to show me your power. Thank you for showing me that the Holy Bible is your inspired Word. Thank you for being the creator of all things, big or small. Thank you for giving me the opportunity to lead your congregation. Show me what I should do next. From now on, everything I am and everything I own belongs to you," Pastor Scott prayed. "Let me help others to recognize that the Maye Moon is your gift to mankind and to help people see the purpose in it. Amen."

Pastor Scott awoke in the early morning before the sun came up and decided to go out to the garden of his home and talk to the Father. This was extremely out of character for him. He went out and sat on a cement bench that possibly no one had ever sat on before. He saw the two full moons fading away with the morning light. It was a sight to behold. "Father, I want to do your will. I need your guidance in telling my congregation the truth. I need them to know that I was a fraud, standing before them and preaching about salvation when I needed to be saved. Even if I am fired or asked to resign, I need to be honest. Someone else might be fooling themselves about their salvation and letting pride get in their way of the truth."

Both moons disappeared for the day. Pastor Scott felt that the Lord wanted him to address his congregation with the truth on Sunday morning. He left the garden and headed for his study to begin the hardest sermon of his life. This was another miracle of Maye Moon.

Sunday morning arrived and Pastor Scott met his members and guests in the foyer of the church. He shook as many hands as he could and welcomed them all. A lot of "God Bless You" and "Good

Mornings" were shared. This was not his normal practice. On a normal Sunday, Pastor Scott would make a grand entrance to the pulpit for all to be amazed.

After the hymns, the solo, the choirs' performance, and the scripture reading, Pastor Scott began his sermon for the day. "I come to you this morning a changed man. This is probably the hardest sermon I have ever delivered, but the Lord has asked me to deliver it to you. Last Sunday, I was a lost and broken man. I was headed to a devil's hell and did not even realize it. Well, I probably knew it deep down if I was ever honest with myself," Pastor Scott shared with tears slowly making their way down his cheeks. "I do not preach this message to anyone in particular. It is about me. But I urge you to take a look in the mirror and examine your own self to see if anything applies to you also," he continued his message.

"I was thinking about the Maye Moon and asking myself-- Why would God put the Maye Moon in the sky—what would be his purpose? I thought about the good that the Maye Moon has already done. Maye Moon has offered hope and the realization that God is still in control. Maye Moon gave us something positive to focus on instead of the horrific, grim conditions of the world today. God gave Adam and Eve a perfect sinless garden to dwell in. Sin entered in, and today we can't open the newspaper or internet without being totally appalled," Pastor Scott continued.

The Appearance of Maye Moon

"Since Maye Moon, COVID has nearly disappeared. For several years, COVID has sickened our world and left many victims in its path. Can you think of anyone you know who has not been affected by COVID in some way? COVID made us fearful to touch our loved ones. People isolated themselves in their homes for weeks. Many people lost their jobs, their homes, and loved ones to suicide. We have come to think of a mask as protection from COVID instead of remembering God is our protector. I am not saying you were wrong to wear a mask. We had to do anything and everything we could to not get COVID, but God is always our first source to go to for protection," he continued on. "Amen," sounded from around the sanctuary.

"Social problems have been on the rise. Our youth have been angry and prevented from getting an education. They have rebelled by taking their anger to the streets and destroying other peoples' property. Children have murdered other children in their schools. Many have felt hopeless and have taken drugs to ease their pain. So many have felt so hopeless that they took their own lives, feeling suicide was better than life. It breaks my heart. I think it breaks God's heart too. Maye Moon gave us something to talk about other than our problems," Pastor Scott preached in the spirit. "Amen!" many shouted.

"Maye Moon put an end to the war and fighting between Ukraine and Russia. We feared Ukraine was just the first of Russia's causalities. We thought the worst—that Israel would be the eventual victim. Israel, God's chosen people. For now, Russia has retreated. I believe that the appearance of Maye Moon played a part in that. Palestinian and Israeli relations have improved also. Let us always pray for peace." "Amen" was shouted in agreement by many throughout the congregation.

"Maye Moon has revived the church. People were told to stay home during COVID. Our church, like many across the world, went to online services. People could watch from home in their pj's and put their time in with God. We got complacent. We got out of our routine. We lost our worship. We tried to multi-task while attending church and did not pay attention to the messages. We should always give God our full, undivided attention. For several weeks we had less than 25% of our regular church attendees coming. We had to spread out. We couldn't hug or shake hands with our friends. Instead of smiling faces there were masks everywhere. Many just decided not to come or even watch YouTube services at all. The more you miss, it gets easier and easier and pretty soon you are not thinking about God at all."

"Another miracle that Maye Moon caused – it caused me to examine my own faith. Friday morning, I was going about my usual day, and I began thinking about Maye Moon and the miracles that had happened. I thought about how God is still in the miracle business. I got down on my knees to pray, and suddenly, I became convicted that while I confessed to being a Christian, I had a head knowledge of God but not a heart knowledge. I was a sinner headed to hell." A gasp could be heard across the sanctuary. "I prayed at that moment, confessed my sins, and accepted Jesus as my Lord and Savior. I felt convicted and that I needed to be totally honest with you today. I never did intend to deceive or mislead anyone about my salvation. I just had to get real with myself," Pastor Scott explained. As he looked through the pews, he could see some looks of disappointment and sorrow. He could see others who, like him, were gently weeping. "I am so thankful that I realized it before it was too late."

"I have given God my body, soul, spirit, and everything I own. I vow to rid myself of my lavish lifestyle and give my wealth to this church and its important ministries. I understand that I was prideful and sought after worldly things. Some of you may be in the same condition that I was in. I encourage you to come to the altar while the music is playing and make it right with the Lord," Pastor Scott smiled and held out his welcoming arms. Many people made their way to the altar. Tears continued to flow.

"If you have never accepted Jesus as your Savior and the Holy Spirit is speaking to you, come now." Several people left their seats and came forward. "If you have a head knowledge of Jesus, but not a heart knowledge, come now. Let's see a revival and a movement in this church as never before! Don't be afraid, please come." The music played softly in the background, and Pastor Scott said, "If you do not know how, it is a very simple prayer, Dear Jesus, I accept you as my Lord and Savior. I know I am a sinner condemned to hell. Please forgive me for my sins and wash them away with your precious blood. Save my soul so someday I can spend eternity with you. Come into my heart, Lord Jesus. In Jesus' Precious Name. Amen. Friend, if you meant business, you are a Child of the King and are saved forever more," Pastor Scott professed. Pastor Scott walked down the aisle so he could be at the door when his parishioners left. He was greeted with hugs and handshakes, tears and joy.

Chapter 12

Kathi Calloway arranged a press conference to announce and introduce the four astronauts who were going on the mission to Maye Moon. The press room was packed with all of the major news organizations, newspaper reporters, and magazine reporters. She definitely had butterflies in her stomach. Lorraine Maxwell, Space X COO, was at the podium with her, sharing the spotlight. Lorraine began, "We would like to thank everyone for attending this joyous announcement today. The Space X and NASA team would like to announce that the Mission is on target for launch on October 28th to Maye Moon and will be called Miracle 1. We feel the name describes the arrival of Maye Moon perfectly. This whole mission has been a miracle and was never planned. The speed of organizing, building, and executing a space flight to Maye Moon has been miraculous. Space X and NASA will have outperformed and won the Space Race by years, I believe." Clapping and cheers could be heard throughout the room. "I would like to introduce Kathi Calloway with another special announcement."

Kathi approached the microphone and podium and smiled at the crowded room. "Thank you, Lorraine. I have had the pleasure of speaking to many of you over the past few months. I believe I have been asked the same question in every interview—who is going on the space mission? The four astronauts who have been chosen may now be revealed. They are Bob Hutchinson, who will serve as Lead Command, Cora Collins, Larry Lowe, and Ben Jones. Each of these outstanding astronauts has worked on the Space Station in different capacities and will make an exceptional team to go on the Miracle 1 Mission." Each astronaut appeared on stage when their name was called, dressed in their official Maye Moon Miracle 1 training suits. The clapping and cheering was deafening.

"These four heroes will be available for questions for a few minutes. We also want to let you know that you may pick up a press packet before you leave the room. There is a bio included for each astronaut chosen. The countdown is 30 days from today. Please join us online on Twitter, YouTube, Facebook, and, as always, on the NASA channel. Our CEO, Elon Musk, has prepared a special video outlining the mission and what Miracle 1 means to him. He regrets not being here in person, but his busy schedule would not allow it. I am turning the microphone over to Bob, and you may respectfully ask some questions for 30 minutes. We don't want to wear them out before their mission."

The Appearance of Maye Moon

Bob Hutchinson stepped forward and said, "It was an honor to be chosen for the Miracle 1 Mission. There were many fine candidates, and I feel blessed to be chosen. I look forward to exploring the unknown and making history on this voyage." A CNN reporter was the first to speak out, "Could you tell us what your research will hope to find when you reach Maye Moon?" Bob answered, "With this being the maiden voyage to Maye Moon, we will be measuring a lot of different things like distance, temperature, atmosphere, gravity, soil samples, air quality, etc. We will be taking a lot of photographs of the Maye Moon's surface. We will be looking for any type of life. We will be looking to see if there is any water on the surface. A lot of exciting stuff."

The next reporter was from MSNBC. He asked, "This question is for Ben Jones. How does it feel to be the first African American to take part in a lunar mission?" Ben stepped forward and answered, "I am happy to represent African Americans, but I want to represent all Americans, and I don't think I was chosen because of the color of my skin. I have worked very hard to get where I am today, and I will continue to work hard in the space exploration field."

The ABC reporter asked, "Larry, will you be walking on Maye Moon?" "Yes, sir, we all plan to take our turn making a walk on Maye Moon. This is another giant leap for mankind. I wasn't even born when the last moonwalk took place. We are a team, and we will all work together to make this mission a success."

Fox News was represented by none other than Jess Wanamaker. This was one of the best assignments he had ever received. "Could you tell me, Cora, how did it feel to be chosen out of so many potential candidates?" Cora smiled at the handsome reporter, "It felt like a dream come true. I worked hard, and it paid off. I love what I do and can't wait until the launch. Team U.S.A.! Could I give a shout-out to my Mom, who is watching in Biloxi, Mississippi? Hi Mom, I love you." The team all chuckled.

"I am sorry to cut off, but the astronauts have early bedtimes. We appreciate your participation in our news conference and hope to speak to each of you at a later time," Kathi ended the conference promptly. She was happy with the outcome of the press conference. "Good Job, Kathi," Lorraine said on the way out. "Do you want to grab a cup of coffee before heading home?" "Sure. I could really use a cup." The two ladies headed to the nearby coffee shop to de-stress.

Chapter 13

P resident McIntosh watched the press conference about the Miracle 1 Space Mission in the oval office. "I wonder why I wasn't invited? I would have liked to have had some input on the Mission name. I do like the name Miracle 1, though." "I am sure they did not mean to offend you, Mr. President," John Stafford, Senior Advisor to the President, answered. "Do you know if any progress is being made on the Maye Moon Summit? I think we should call it the Maye Moon Miracle Summit now," President McIntosh said. "Yes, there has been some progress; however, it was decided that we should wait until after the Miracle 1 Mission to proceed with the planning," Stafford answered. "What? Who approved that?" McIntosh was visibly angered. "The committee did. The committee felt that it would be better to know the outcome of the Miracle 1 Mission before proceeding," Stafford answered. "Why wasn't I at this committee meeting? I explicitly told the Cabinet Secretary of Energy that I wanted to be informed about all things Maye Moon. I think I learn more about it from the TV than my own people," President McIntosh grumbled.

"On a positive note, Congress approved the extension of the tax rebate for going solar unanimously. That is a definite win," Stafford stated. "Are more people going solar?" McIntosh asked. "Yes, I believe so. We are running PSAs announcing the extended tax rebates and also that Maye Moon has increased solar production," Stafford answered.

"I want to see all the minutes from the committee meeting on the Maye Moon Summit. I can go along with waiting until the Miracle 1 Mission is complete. That is a good strategy. I want to be in Cape Canaveral for the launch. Make sure that is on my schedule. I want to have a special press conference scheduled that day. People need to know that I am an important part of the Mission," McIntosh ordered. "Yes, sir," Stafford answered.

"The EPA is reporting that the new data they are collecting suggests that air quality has improved drastically since Maye Moon. Greenhouse gases have decreased. It is not conclusive at this point, but the Center for Atmospheric Science is conducting tests to figure out what is happening," Stafford explained. "We have put a lot of regulations in place throughout this year. They are working, and my administration is responsible for it," McIntosh replied. "Sir, the EPA is reporting this is happening globally," Stafford replied. "Interesting. Keep me informed. Any other good news?" McIntosh asked. "The EPA is reporting that water supplies are up and temperatures are down this summer. It looks like this is going to be a very good year for farmers. Also the World Health Organization reports that there have been no new COVID cases whatsoever in the past week. This is considered a miracle," Stafford stated. "Yes, and if Maye Moon could just fix the economy," McIntosh sighed. "What do you know about the Miracle 1 celebrations taking place? We need to get people pumped up for the biggest event in modern history." "I believe there are celebrations planned all across the country. I will have my staff prepare a detailed list for you," Stafford answered. "If that is all, sir, I have a meeting to attend." "Yes, go to your meeting. I have a luncheon to attend," McIntosh answered. "Mrs. McIntosh gets cranky if I am late or I stand her up."

Stafford was chauffeured to his meeting with the United States Ambassador at the United Nations. Natalie Steubens had been the Ambassador to the United Nations throughout the last three administrations. Being bi-partisan and highly qualified, she maintained her position. "Thank you for meeting with me, Ambassador Steubens. I appreciate your time," McIntosh said as he shook her hand. "Fortunately for you, this is a slower time of the year. Sometimes, I don't see Washington, D.C., for weeks on end. What would you like to discuss?" the Ambassador inquired.

"Madam Ambassador, I am here to represent a committee that has been developed to work on a project for the President. He would like to host a Summit for the members of the United Nations to get support for the United States making Maye Moon a U.S.

territory," Stafford stated. "Do you know how crazy that is? I heard about the President making that statement during a Press Conference. Has he lost his mind? Respectfully, of course," the Ambassador asked. Stafford answered, "I am just the Messenger. I am really in a predicament. I have tried to discourage the idea and have managed to stall the committee by telling him that the committee decided to wait until the Space Mission is complete. He wants to move forward on this, and it will destroy his Presidency."

"So, did you come here so I could talk some sense into him?" the Ambassador asked. "I came to find out what you thought the repercussions would be if we preceded. How would other U.N. Ambassadors respond to this?" Stafford asked. "As serious as this could be, I would say that the U.S. could become an enemy to the other members of the United Nations. This is absurd. I could not support this Summit or the idea that the U.S. lay claim on Maye Moon for their own. I would have to resign if I were made to be a part of this sham. You are right; it would definitely destroy his Presidency. Surely, Congress would start the impeachment process or question his sanity. I am glad that you stalled this. How much time do we have?" the Ambassador asked. "Less than a month, unfortunately. He is asking for updates every day. He wants to control any resources that are found. I think he believes this could be the answer to our waning economy," Stafford stated. "Well, he hasn't considered the repercussions from a move like this. I can understand his concern for the economy with double-digit inflation," the Ambassador replied.

"He must not know that I came to you for help. He will consider it a mutiny, not a concern for his Presidency," Stafford requested. "I understand politics, John. I guess I think the best way forward is a private meeting between the President and me, and I just lay it all out. Tell him that I have heard rumors at the United Nations that he is considering this contest for Maye Moon. I will tell him the ramifications of doing so. I am sure he will listen to reason," the Ambassador smiled. "He's not crazy, is he?"

"You don't know how much I appreciate this. I owe you a steak dinner at Bobby's," Stafford said. "I will be grateful to you if we can head this off before getting all the way to the U.N. I can't imagine how catastrophic that would be," the Ambassador replied. "I will call for an appointment right away."

Ambassador Steubens returned to her office and asked her secretary to telephone the President's office and make an appointment for a private meeting with the President as soon as possible. Being the Ambassador to the United Nations held a little weight so she received a meeting time for the day after tomorrow. "Good," she thought, "That will give me a little time to think this over and develop a strategy. Presidential power has gone to his head.

Seriously, making a moon a territory of the United States? Does he think the U.N. would bow down to him?"

Chapter 14

The corporate powers-to-be have been impressed with Jess Wanamaker, and he has been receiving a lot of air time on other Fox shows as a sub when hosts are on location, vacationing, or sick. "This is great," he thought. "I get to show them what I can do. One day I will be the featured Prime Timer for the biggest news organization in the world. For now, I am willing to pay my dues. I think it is time I call Kathi Calloway and cement our plans for the Space Launch. I hope she knows I was serious about wanting to be her date for the launch. Flowers – What girl can resist flowers? Something exotic," he thought.

After researching several flower shops on the Space Coast, Jess found one that would fit the bill. They promised to create an arrangement that would blow her mind and his wallet. He went through his phone directory of an enormous amount of names and found Kathi. "Let's make the call," he said with confidence.

As the phone rang, he suddenly felt a little nervous. After all, she was a celebrity, and he was asking a pretty big favor. "Hello," she answered softly. "Kathi, this is Jess. Jess Wanamaker. I hope I did not wake you," he said. "Jess, oh yeah. No, I was just lying here. I had a really late night last night. I flew in from Orlando pretty late. I am in New York for a couple of interviews and will be back out to Orlando tomorrow night. They have me on a crazy schedule until the Miracle Mission is over. What can I do for you, Jess?" she asked. "Oh, you are in New York. I am in New York. How about we New York together?" he tried to say as charmingly as he could. "I don't know Jess. I doubt I would be able to find time. I wouldn't be very good company either. I am really exhausted. What exactly do you have in mind?" she replied. "I get it, but a girl's gotta eat, right? How about dinner tonight and an early bedtime? I mean, I won't keep you out late and let you get your beauty sleep. But honestly, I don't think you could get any more beautiful if you tried." He knew he was smooth. "I should finish up by 6:00, but you are right. I have to make it a short visit. Tomorrow is a very early day. Where should we meet?" she replied. "How about The Garden at 7:00? I promise to have you back to your hotel by 9:00."

"How did you know I was staying at the Four Seasons?" she thought. "Can we make it 6:00? I will cut my appointment short. I really need to be asleep by 9:00. The Garden would be great," she answered. "Perfect, it's a date," Jess said quickly. "A date?" she asked. "I didn't realize that you were asking me out on a date," she said with surprise in her voice. "You can call it whatever you like. In fact, why don't we wait until 'it' is over and decide together what we want to call it, okay?" He was smiling big as he said it. "I will meet you in the lobby at 6:00, and we will walk in together." "Okay, Jess, I will see you at 6:00 in the lobby at Four Seasons. Thanks for calling. Bye now." She hung up the phone. "That was unexpected," she thought.

"Smooth Operator," an 80's tune by Sade, started playing in Jess's head. He was quite pleased with himself when he was interrupted by the Fox Program Manager. "Jess, there is a spot for you tonight on The Five." "Sorry, Lew, I can't. I have some important plans at 6:00. I can't change them. I would love to if I could, but it is just not possible," he answered. "I thought you wanted air time, dude?" Lew sighed. "I do, I do, but this is kinda big business and could lead to something really big for Fox and for me. I would tell you about it, but it is top secret. Ask me again next time. Sorry Lew, forgive me," Jess replied and looked disappointed. Lew walked away, shaking his head.

Jess arrived at the Four Seasons at 5:45 p.m. It was important to be punctual. He texted Kathi and let her know he was there, but no pressure to hurry. She appeared on the elevator at 6:00 sharp. She looked great, having had a day of interviews. "Hi Jess, great to see you," she said. "I made us a reservation for 6:00, so I am sure they can seat us now," Jess answered. They walked into the beautiful restaurant and were led to a wonderful seat. Jess pulled out the seat for Kathi like the perfect gentleman. "So Kathi, tell me about your day. Did Everything go well?" Jess asked as they looked over the menu. "Pretty well. Lots of time in the green room reading magazines. I interviewed with Kelli Mark and Rachael Ray today. I wish I had more to tell them, but every interview goes about the same. I am very limited about what I can talk about due to the confidential nature of the Mission. I try to add some humor, but frankly, I am not very funny," she blushed. "Hey, I have seen your interviews, and they are all very good, entertaining, and genuine. People are attracted to you because you seem like someone they could be friends with. That is important," he smiled.

The waiter brought menus and water. "I am not a big drinker, Jess," Kathi said. "Me neither," he replied as they looked over the menus. "How did your day go?" she asked. "Well my day was spent doing a lot of prepping for upcoming shows. In two days I get to go to Atlanta for a few days. I will be interviewing Pastor Scott Morales, who is the pastor of the Atlantic Berea Baptist Church. The interview will be on my Friday night segment in a couple of weeks. When I return to New York, I will be filling in on the 2:00-3:00 p.m. slot for Bernie for a week. Flexibility is key in this job. I love that about my job, and every day is different. What about you?" he asked.

"Well, normally, I live a pretty mundane life. As Chief Scientist, I am managing other scientists at NASA and reviewing their projects and studies. I get to have my hand in a lot of projects at once. Science, you know. This entertainment gig just fell into my lap, and to be honest, I will be glad to be back in my old position. I don't really enjoy the airport-to-hotel room or city-to-city life. But I was asked, so I did it. I am more of a geek, really. Science Nerd," she answered. "There is no way you are a geek or nerd. I don't see a pocket protector or a bandaid holding your glasses together," he smiled.

Actually, Jess hadn't stopped smiling since he saw her get off of the elevator. "Well, they changed some lingo and call it STEM nowadays, and a lot more women are employed in the Science field today. I guess we need to upgrade our names for the Science babes," she laughed. "I love Science and Math, things that can be proven through experiments. I especially love the study of the Universe. I was a star-watcher as a child. My parents bought me a huge telescope, at least it was huge for a kid, and would take me to planetariums on vacations. Space camps in the summer. They really guided my journey to becoming an Astrophysicist and Scientist," she answered.

"My parents wanted me to become a lawyer or doctor. They were terrified when I told them I wanted to be an entertainer or actor. I started college and found I really liked Politics so I majored in Politics and Communications. Fox News seemed the perfect fit for me," he explained. "I think I am going to have the salmon." "That sounds good. I will, too." The waiter returned with two iced teas and took their order. Then he brought one small loaf of bread with herb butter for them to share.

"My parents were horrified when I joined Fox. They are progressive Democrats, and our politics clash at times. They would rather see me on a different network. I am happy at Fox, and they have given me lots of opportunities to climb the ladder into a better time slot. For now, it is where I want to be," Jess explained. "To be honest, I have not watched a lot of news shows, especially not Fox. I work pretty long hours, and when I get home, I eat, bathe, and crash. Sometimes, I turn on the NASA channel for fun," she smiled. "I am a reader, too. I have so many Science journals to cover to keep up on what is going on in the Science community. You never know what might lead to a breakthrough in something we are working on in our department. If it is on TV, it is probably outdated," she explained. "The world moves so fast; that is the way it is in politics, too," Jess answered. "One day, you are on top, and the next day, they are trying to impeach you."

Jess was surprised that Kathi was so easy to talk to. The waiter brought their entrees, and they looked delicious. They continued their conversation and enjoyed the meal. "You will have to show me your telescope someday. I am amazed at the vastness of the universe. The appearance of Maye Moon was a real surprise. I mean, it seemed to appear out of nowhere," Jess said. "I know, it took us by surprise at NASA, too. We have no explanation of how it appeared so quickly. We have watched as stars develop in other galaxies, but nothing is instantaneous. This will be studied long after I am gone," Kathi said. "Do you wish you could go to Maye Moon on the Miracle 1 Mission?" Jess questioned. "No, not really. I would rather study it, and I am looking forward to the specimens that they collect. That research will be an important part of the mission. Hopefully we discover how it happened and something beneficial for all of mankind," she said. "Now, that is exciting," Jess replied. They decided to order coffee and dessert.

"Where did you grow up, Kathi?" he asked. "Atlanta, in Buckhead. My father was in Finance and my mother was a teacher. I am going there next weekend to see them." She replied. "Hey, I will be there too. Would you join me for dinner Saturday evening?" Jess inquired. "That sounds nice, Jess; I would like that," she answered. "Why don't you pick the spot and let me know where and what time to pick you up," Jess said.

"Things must be going ok," he thought. "Isn't that crazy that we will both be in Atlanta at the same time? I am a New Yorker through and through. My parents live in the Forest Hills, Queens area. My father is a dentist, and my mother is a stay-at-home Mom," Jess said.

"Any siblings?" he inquired. "Just a sister, Kate. She is a stay-at-home Mom also. Very 'Susie Homemaker'; the complete opposite of me. I love going and staying at her home, though. Her five children adore me, and she likes to spoil me when I am around. How about you? Any sibs?" Kathi asked. "Well, I am one of three boys. One older and one younger. My older brother became a lawyer, and my younger brother is just finishing dental school. I am the black sheep," he chuckled. "Ahh, but you are famous. I am sure your parents appreciate that," Kathi surmised. "Well, if they do, they don't tell me. I guess they want to keep my head normal-sized. We boys were all pretty athletic and kept my mother pretty busy. When we get together, we still wrestle and argue, but we always have each other's backs," Jess explained.

"Jess, the dinner was lovely, and I really enjoyed getting to know you better. Unfortunately, I have a very early morning show appearance and then fly out late afternoon. I will message you with the details for Saturday. I am really looking forward to it," she smiled. "Me too. I will walk you to your elevator. I promise to be a gentleman," he said. "That is quite thoughtful of you," she replied. They walked across the hotel to the elevators and stopped and said their goodbyes. "Thank you again for a wonderful dinner, Jess. Oh, and the dessert was so delicious. I will let you know the details for Saturday," Kathi said. "That will be great. Thank you for coming to dinner with me. I had a fabulous time. What floor are you on?" he asked. "Eight," she replied. He pushed the button, and the elevator door immediately opened, and Kathi entered. Jess watched as the doors closed. This dinner date went better than he had dreamed.

Chapter 15

Natalie Steubens had a scheduled 9:00 a.m. meeting with President McIntosh in the Oval Office. She arrived at 8:50 and was directed to take a seat. "Would you like some coffee, tea, or a bottle of Evian?" the receptionist asked. "A bottle of Evian would be great." She replied. "It shouldn't be much longer. You are his first appointment of the day," the receptionist said. Her telephone buzzed, and she said, "The President is ready to see you."

Natalie prayed a silent prayer as she entered the office. She was nervous about the outcome and hoped that this meeting would go well. "Good morning, Madam Ambassador; please have a seat and make yourself comfortable." "Thank you, Mr. President," she replied. "Madam Ambassador, you called this meeting, so I am anxious to find out what is on your mind," the President stated.

"Mr. President I have been hearing some chatter around the U.N. that there is deep concern over a statement that you made in a press conference regarding the United States claiming Maye Moon as a U.S. territory. Is this true?" she boldly asked. "Yes, Natalie, I did say that, and that is my plan. I probably should not have said that in the press conference. I should have kept it confidential until a more solid plan was formed. I believe that the United States should be the owner and distributor of the resources that are on Maye Moon because we invest the most capital in the space exploration program. I want to beat the other countries to the draw, as they say," The President responded. "I am here to warn you, Mr. President that is a very divisive plan that could cause very bad repercussions with the other countries that are members of the U.N. They may hear it as a declaration of war," replied the Ambassador.

"My plan includes hosting a Summit called the Maye Moon Miracle Summit, where I will provide the U.N. members with sound reasoning as to why the United States should control Maye Moon as a territory. I have been advised to wait until we know more from the Miracle Mission before proceeding, but I want to be ready to move forward as soon as possible. I have a feeling that Maye Moon is going to possess important mineral resources that we can mine and use in crucial advancements in technology in the future. Who knows? We may be able to colonize Maye Moon sometime in the future," President McIntosh stated.

"Why do you think the other countries would go along with that? I happen to know they would not. Maye Moon is a large natural satellite, and we do not even know if these resources exist. It is irresponsible to start a war over this," Ambassador Steubens replied sternly. "Irresponsible? A war? You are way off base. We are the leaders in the Space field. The other countries will see that this makes logical sense." The President proceeded, "With you helping to gain allies, we will be successful."

"Woah, stop right there, Mr. President. I cannot support this move. I cannot be a part of any plan such as this," the Ambassador answered firmly. "What do you mean? You serve at the pleasure of the President. You can be dismissed at any time I wish," the President's voice rose loudly in anger, "I can ruin you." "You will ruin yourself if you go forward with this charade. Congress will impeach you. You will lead this country directly into war, and your Presidency will go down in history as a failure. I know I am taking a huge risk saying these things, but Mr. President, I am trying to protect you. Please think these actions through very carefully. The Chinese, Koreans, and Russians are all actively planning their own missions to Maye Moon. The U.S. may be first, but these three countries will not be far behind. They will not bow to the U.S. in this matter. How would you feel if any of these three countries tried to claim ownership of Maye Moon? Maye Moon is a sovereign natural satellite. It is no different than laying claim to the Moon or Mars," Ambassador Steubens retorted. "If it means my position as Ambassador of the United Nations, so be it."

President McIntosh was stunned at her rebuttal. He was not used to anyone going against him since becoming President. After a few moments he caught his breath and said, "I will take your objections into consideration and speak with the Speaker of the House and the Senate leader and see what kind of support that I have there. This meeting is adjourned." He turned and walked briskly out of the office.

Ambassador Steubens had lost control of her emotions and had crossed a line that she hadn't intended to cross, but it was necessary to get President McIntosh's attention and make him see that this was an irrational plan. She gathered up her things and made her way out of the oval office and down the halls to the exit. The White House interns who passed greeted her, and they could see the shock still on her face. Out in the fresh early fall air, she inhaled like she was hyperventilating. She was so happy to be out of there! "This was much harder than I thought, and it didn't really go the way I planned. I don't know, maybe President McIntosh has lost it. I have done my job by warning him. I will resign if he plans to go forward," she thought. "The line has been drawn in the sand."

President McIntosh returned to his office when the coast was clear. He called his Senior Advisor, John Stafford to his office. "John, I need to somehow set up a meeting with the Speaker and the Senate Majority leader about a sensitive matter. I need complete confidentiality. I met with Ambassador Steubens, and she is totally against the idea of making Maye Moon a U.S. territory. She has no vision. I want to gauge my support from both sides of Congress to see if they will support the idea. I need to make sure that the news media is not aware of this meeting," the President said. "She met with him. My meeting with the Ambassador was successful," Stafford thought.

"Maybe we could say the meeting is about the improved solar data. Start the meeting that way and then dismiss the news media and get down to the real business of the meeting," Stafford suggested. "I think that idea might work. We can prepare press releases with the latest numbers and get additional PR for our solar rebate program. Great idea, John!" the President remarked. "Please handle the details and schedule the meeting as soon as possible. I do not want this opportunity to get away from us." John Stafford was dismissed.

"Now, hopefully the Speaker and the House Majority Leader have more common sense about this absurd idea of his. I hope that the President lets them know the Ambassador is not on board," Stafford thought.

Chapter 16

T essie and Earl went down to the beach to watch both moons rising this evening. It had been awhile since they had been down here because of the traffic. "I think people have gotten used to having two moons now. There are not as many people down here, Dad," Tessie said. "I think you are right. I am happy that there are not as many people around – makes it a little more romantic, Mom," he replied. "Oh, you old sweetie!" she exclaimed. They set up their chairs towards the waves. The waves were clapping loudly this evening, and the ocean water was a beautiful azure blue color. They sat down and held hands. Tessie thought about how blessed they were to still have one another. God has been so good to them.

"Tessie I was thinking, how about we go visit our son Paul and his wife Monica for a few days. We could drive down there by the back roads, take our time, and see those grandkids. It has been awhile," Earl inquired. "Are you feeling up to it, Dad?" she replied. "Sure, I feel great. It will be a good time to get out and stretch our legs. I talked to Paul the other day, and he asked if we would come down," Earl answered. "I think that is a wonderful idea. I am thankful Paul lives on the south side of Atlanta, and we are at his home before the traffic gets too bad," Tessie said. "We will be sure and time it so we do not hit the rush hour. I am sure we will be alright, Mom," Earl answered.

"I think about Paul and his family a lot. I hated to see Paul give up on attending church after he graduated from high school. His children know very little about the Lord and have not had the advantage of having good Christian friends from a church," Earl said. "I know, Earl. I pray that he and his family will get in church some day. It is so important that they have that Christian fellowship with other believers. I don't know what we would have done over the years without our church family," Tessie agreed. "Paul is a good man and does a lot for his community, but that doesn't get you to heaven. I wish I knew for sure that he was saved and that his family knew the Lord," Earl sighed. "The hardest people to witness are our own children. We love them so much and do not want them to make them uncomfortable or angry. I pray that Jesus gives me the right words to say to them while we are visiting. May I have the wisdom to speak to Monica about joining a Bible-believing church," Tessie said.

The two moons began to creep up from the ocean horizon. The glow on the water was beautiful and breathtaking. "It looks like a lighted path across the water. Maybe someday we will be able to walk right across it like Peter. Who knows what we will be able to do in heaven? Sometimes, I think about who I want to see when I get there. Jesus will be first, of course. I can't wait to see baby Melissa, whom we lost before she was born. I wonder if she will be a baby or will she have grown up into a woman?" Earl said. "I didn't know you think about that. I think about her often, and it used to make me sad. Now it makes me happy because I know I will see her before too long," Tessie said with a smile. "I bet my Mamma has helped take care of her. I am sure she told her all about us, and she is waiting on us, too."

"We will have the rest of eternity to fellowship with other believers. I plan on taking off and running when I get there. These tired old legs haven't been able to get around for so long," Earl said. "I love to think about the Homecoming—seeing all the loved ones in heaven, meeting all the people we read about in the Bible. What a glorious day that will be!" Earl continued. They both started humming the church hymn "What a Day That Will Be." When they finished, Earl said, "I love you, old girl." Tessie replied, "I love you, my handsome boy." They gazed at the moon and Maye Moon and sat quietly for a few minutes, still holding hands. "Why do you suppose the Lord placed Maye Moon in the sky?" Tessie pondered. "I think he wanted to give us a sign of hope. Things seem so bleak in the world today. It looks like the devil is winning. Evil abounds. For Christians, this is the worst it will ever get. For the unbeliever, this is the best it will get. Maye Moon is like a nightlight of hope, a reminder that God is still in control and that He is coming again. Some unbelievers need proof, even though becoming a Christian is based on faith. Maye Moon may be enough proof that they will turn to God and become saved," Earl explained. "Let's pack up and head home, Mom. I love you most." "No, Dad, I love you most."

Chapter 17

Jess received a text from Kathi that suggested a restaurant near her parent's home and the address where she could be picked up. She thanked him for the flowers that had arrived in Orlando before she left for Atlanta. She said they were "amazing". He had changed his flight and hotel reservations so he could be in Atlanta a couple of days early so they could have dinner together Saturday night. Fortunately, Fox did not have a problem with it because he was working on the interview with Pastor Scott Morales.

Jess arrived early Friday evening and rented a black sedan for the days he would be in Atlanta. "He would work in his hotel room and get a good night's sleep so that he would be ready for their dinner tomorrow night," he thought. He took a long, hot shower, ordered some room service, and got comfy. His cell buzzed, and he saw that the call was from Kathi. "Did your flight go well?" she asked. "Not too bad. It was a little bumpy landing, but I am here in one piece," he laughed. "How is your visit going?" "Wonderful! I have been on a rollercoaster for the last couple of months and it is so good to be home with my parents and be spoiled a little. Something about sleeping in your old bed in your parents' home feels so safe. My mother has been cooking all of my favorites. Today, my father and I played tennis at his club," she gushed. "Tennis? Ok, who won?" he asked. "I let him win, of course," she laughed.

"What I called about was to make sure you still wanted to have dinner tomorrow night?" she teased. "It's not too late to back out." "Absolutely, you are not getting rid of me that easy," Jess answered. "My parents are looking forward to meeting you. I am sorry, but I couldn't let them down. I feel like a schoolgirl going on my first date. They want to check you out," she laughed. "That's great; I would love to meet them. I will arrive a few minutes earlier so that we are not rushed," Jess replied. "Sounds great, Jess. I will see you tomorrow night. Goodnight." she said softly.

Jess worked on his upcoming interview with Pastor Scott Morales. However, his mind kept wandering off to his date with Kathi. She was so different than he thought she would be. She was so easy to talk to and so down-to-earth. It had been years since he met any date's parents. He chuckled. Around 4:00 p.m., he began to get ready so that he would be early for their date. He stopped at a nearby flower shop and picked up a single red rose. The Atlanta freeway is always bumper-to-bumper this time of day, and he did not want to be delayed.

The Appearance of Maye Moon

He arrived at Kathi's parents' home at a little before six. It was a beautiful two-story brick with a circle driveway in a gated community. Kathi had texted him the gate code. The neighborhood had lots of wooded areas and could pass for a park. Jess felt his pulse racing and was definitely a little nervous. He went to the door and rang the bell. Kathi's father greeted Jess with a "Welcome, welcome, welcome. Hello Jess, I am Charlie, Kathi's father. Please come in and make yourself comfortable. Can I get you something to drink?" "Maybe some water, if you don't mind," Jess replied. Kathi's mother, Kim, entered the room, and she was very attractive. Jess could see where Kathi got her good looks. "Hello Jess, we are so pleased to meet you. We are big fans. Kathi is almost ready." Charlie brought Jess a bottle of water, and Jess thanked him. "So Jess, Kathi said you have some work here in Atlanta this week," Charlie said. "I do. I will be interviewing Pastor Scott Morales of Berean Baptist Church. Despite COVID, his membership has grown exponentially, and he is Pastor of the largest church in the South," Jess answered. "I am very familiar with Pastor Morales. I have watched his service on television a few times. I have found him to be quite knowledgeable," Charlie stated.

"Jess do you do a lot of traveling? Kathi has been traveling so much the last few months she doesn't always remember what city she is waking up in," Kim laughed. She and Kathi laughed the same. "I do not travel that often. I seize the opportunity when they let me.

I like mixing it up a bit," Jess answered. "Most of the time, you will find me in the New York City Fox studio. This was a special assignment," Jess explained. "Well, we are happy that it worked out for you to be in town at the same time as Kathi," Kim said. Kathi entered the room and looked so classy and stylish. "Hey Jess, I see you have met my parents. I hope they did not interrogate you," she said with a smile. "Kathi, you know we were being very friendly and polite," her mother smiled. Jess leaned over and gave Kathi a hug and handed her the rose. "Thank you, Jess, that was very thoughtful," Kathi said sweetly. He followed her to the kitchen so she could put the rose in a bud vase.

"Jess, I think we better go so we don't miss our reservation. Mother, don't wait up for me. I am a big girl," Kathi smiled. "Have a good evening. It was a pleasure to meet you Jess," Charlie said as he shook Jess' hand. They left the home and headed for the rental car. Jess had splurged on a beautiful black Beamer, and he opened the door for Kathi like a gentleman. "Now, that was awkward. I never dreamed I would go through that torture at my age," Kathi laughed. "I think they loved it," Jess agreed. "It was cute. I really enjoyed meeting them."

They drove to the restaurant, a quaint Italian restaurant called Connie's. The restaurant owner greeted them and treated them as celebrities, giving them the best seats in the house. Jess was becoming used to being recognized occasionally in public. Here,

Kathi was also viewed as a celebrity now that she had been doing so many television interviews; she was the hometown girl who made it big. The ambiance of the restaurant was perfect for a romantic dinner. The waiter brought the menus, and they were both very careful to make the right choices-nothing too messy. They decided on a stuffed mushroom appetizer with warm Italian bread and herb dipping butter for starters. For the main course, they choose chicken rigatoni arrabbiata and fresh grilled asparagus.

"I would have loved the spaghetti, but I get pretty messy when I eat spaghetti," Jess laughed. "Me too. Italian is probably my favorite food, but I try not to eat anything too messy in public now that I am a celebrity," she laughed. "Were you able to get some work done today?" she asked. "I did, I did. I drove by the Berea Baptist Church and scoped out the place. I decided I needed to attend the service tomorrow morning to see Pastor Scott in action. I want to know what makes his church service so special when so many other churches closed down completely during COVID-19."

Kathi got a little quiet. "Do you have a church that you attend when you are home in Atlanta?" Jess asked. "Eh, no. I haven't been to church since I was a kid. Sure, I went when I was little because my parents made me. By the time I was a teenager, I protested and they quit making me attend. I was deep into studying science and you could say I was an unbeliever. The whole idea that a supreme being could know what everyone was doing, thinking, every hair on your head thing did not seem plausible. As I learned more about Astronomy and how the universe was really created, I could not buy into the whole God thing," she stated with a very serious look on her face. "How about you, Jess?"

"I was raised in church, and I would describe my family as the typical Catholic family. We never missed mass. My mother still calls every Sunday and asks, 'Did you go to mass this week?' She is happy as long as I go to one mass and confession each week. The church I attend has plenty of service times so I am able to get there sometime during the week. She says confession is good for the soul." Jess realized they had just found the first thing that they were polar opposites on.

"Hey, I got an idea. How about you come to Pastor Scott's service tomorrow with me? I am going there to do research for my interview more than attending a church service. I could use another set of eyes and a different view of what is happening. After the service, we can grab a bite to eat and head over to the Atlanta Planetarium, and you can strut your stuff—explain everything that is going on in the universe to me. I would love that," Jess asked. "Hmm, give me a little time to think about this. I don't know if I could make it through a church service. I would be really uncomfortable because I think it is untrue. I am used to being around science people who think like I do. I don't know…" she answered. "I don't want to pressure you, but we would only be doing research

116

for my interview, and I bet you could help me think of some really good questions to ask Pastor Scott," Jess looked at her with his 'puppy dog' eyes. "That is true, I guess, since it is research. Okay, you got me." They enjoyed the rest of their meal.

"What is for dessert, Kathi?" Jess asked playfully. "They have an Italian Cream cake that is to die for. I would love a cup of coffee with that," she answered. "That sounds amazing. You picked a wonderful place. I think Connie's is the best Italian restaurant I have ever been to—or maybe it is the company."

Sunday morning, Jess picked Kathi up for church, and she did not look happy. "You know, I dread this. I am only going to be a voice of reason when you are developing your interview questions," Kathi said. "I know, and I love that you are willing to help me. It will be so much more fun with you along," Jess said. They arrived a little early to get a good parking spot and to find a close place to sit. Jess grabbed Kathi's hand and led her into the sanctuary. Her hand was cold and clammy, and he could sense that she was nervous. "Nothing to be nervous about. No one will call on you. We will just blend in," Jess assured her.

They both were amazed at how big this gold and purple sanctuary was. There were many greeters situated throughout the sanctuary to welcome them. Everyone was friendly. Jess found a spot for them on the 4th row towards the center. He should be able to see and hear everything going on from there. "Are you sure that you don't want to sit at the back so we can make a quick getaway if we need to?" Kathi asked. "Trust me, we will be good," he answered.

The sanctuary filled up quickly, and eventually, there were no more seats. They had a second service starting right after this one, so parishioners who came late would have to wait. A song leader led the congregation in a couple of hymns, and then the choir took their places and sang, "Our God is an Awesome God." Next, a male vocalist sang "How Great Thou Art" with the choir backing him up, and it was beautiful. A little boy came forward and read a Bible Scripture, and Pastor Scott approached the pulpit, thanked the little boy, and let him know he appreciated his courage to get up there.

"Thank you all for coming this morning. It is a beautiful day in the Lord. If you are a guest today, please sign one of our guest cards and place it on the offering plate when it is passed. We appreciate our visitors and hope that you find Atlantic Berea Baptist is a church that is friendly and is solid and sold out for the Lord. Be sure and pick up one of our brochures when you leave that outlines the many ministries that we offer, and maybe there is something available to help you if you are in need. We all have problems in our lives. A Christian friend can help with those burdens," Pastor Scott said.

The Appearance of Maye Moon

Pastor Scott preached that day from 1 John Chapters 3 and 4 about love. He explained that you must have love for your brother, neighbors, and fellow man or you do not have the love of God in you. "You must examine your own heart, not the person sitting beside you." He explained the four different types of love: Eros, Philia, Storge, and Agape. He explained how the world only focuses on romantic love between two people, and Hollywood has made it sleazy and dirty. The Agape love of God reaches deep down in our soul and is greater than any other love. "Agape love is unconditional and moral and is charity for our fellow man. When you experience God's love, you no longer feel alone. Jesus made the ultimate sacrifice for each and every one of us by dying on the cross to save us from our sins." Kathi looked over to Jess and could see he was buying into all of this. She noticed a cute older couple that held hands throughout the service and wondered what it would be like to still be that much in love after all those years.

"I have had several questions regarding Maye Moon, and I would like to address one today. Many people have asked, 'Is Maye Moon referred to in the Book of Revelation as the New Jerusalem or the New Earth?' No, I don't believe Maye Moon is in the Bible at all. After much prayer and thought, I think the Maye Moon is a symbol God placed in the sky, kind of like the rainbow. I think God is telling us, I am here, I have always been here, and I am going to help heal you and your planet because I love you. What have been some outcomes that show his love? The temperatures this summer have helped farmers to grow record crops. Violence is on the decline. Our air quality has improved; the water quality has improved; solar power has increased; COVID has disappeared, and we haven't even explored the surface of Maye Moon yet. Who knows what they will find there to improve the quality of life here on this planet? Most importantly, people are returning to God. I believe that people feel this miracle is something very special from God. It gives them hope that we can recover from the social decline that has permeated our world the past few decades."

"I like to always share my testimony for our visitors. I have been the pastor of this church for many years. Until recently, I did not realize I was a lost soul going to hell. I thought I was a good person; just look at the wonderful church I ministered at. Look at all of our programs that help children, the poor, the drug abusers, and many others. But the Lord tugged at my heart one morning when I was thinking about Maye Moon and told me that my works and righteousness were as dirty rags. I did not mean to deceive anyone. I, myself, was deceived. I had become worldly and desired money, fancy cars, and fancy homes. I wanted to be in the rich, popular crowd."

"That morning, I got down on my knees, confessed I was a sinner, and asked the Lord to forgive me of all my sins. I experienced God's agape, forgiving love. If you have never turned your life over to Jesus and asked Him to save you from your sins, you are going to hell. That is not what I say, and I am not your judge. That is what the Bible says. You may be the best person here on Earth, the Mother Theresa of your community, but if you have not accepted Jesus and His gift of eternal life, you will be sentenced to hell by the only righteous judge. That is Jesus, who knew no sin." Amens, Hallelujahs, and Praise the Lords broke out throughout the sanctuary.

"If you feel Jesus and the Holy Spirit tugging at your heart… if you long for sweet peace… if you want to know Jesus as your personal Lord and Savior, please pray this prayer with me: Lord Jesus, I accept you as my Lord and Savior. I know I am a sinner condemned to hell. Please forgive me for my sins and wash them away with your precious blood. Save my soul so someday I can spend eternity with you. Come into my heart, Lord Jesus. In Jesus' Precious Name. Amen. Friend, if you meant business, you are a Child of the King and are saved forever more," Pastor Scott professed.

Kathi did feel something in her heart telling her that she needed to get saved. "Would that mean that everything I have believed up to this point has been a lie? I must think this through before I commit. Can Science and Christianity co-exist?"

Pastor Scott continued, "I want you to know that the King James Bible is the infallible, inspired word of God. Maybe you do not believe the Bible. Let me reassure you that the Bible is the Word of God. It will give you the answers to all of your questions. Our Lord is so good, and I feel the Holy Spirit working here today on so many hearts. It feels so good to lay your burdens at Jesus' feet."

An altar call was offered to those who needed prayer, new converts, and those who wanted to talk to the Lord. "Just As I Am" played softly in the background. Many people moved to the altar and bowed their heads to pray. The older couple sitting beside Kathi went forward and prayed together, still holding hands.

After the altar call, Pastor Scott said, "Ushers, please come forward at this time." A prayer was said by one of the ushers. Jess had filled out his visitor card, but Kathi did not. He placed it in the offering plate along with a check for $500.00. "I wonder if Jess did that to impress me?" Kathi thought. A final prayer was given, and the congregation was dismissed. The Welcome Committee took their places at the door and thanked each person for coming. People stood about socializing, but Jess and Kathi immediately headed to their car. "What are you hungry for, Kathi?" "More of the Word," she thought. "It's your turn to pick," she replied.

There was a Pancake House a couple of blocks from the church. Jess pulled in and said, "I think pancakes sound delicious."

"A man after my own heart," Kathi replied. They entered the restaurant and were led to the last table in the house. It wasn't the celebrity treatment they got at Connie's, but that was fine with them. The place was packed, and all the waitresses were really hustling. Kathi looked up and saw the older couple that had been seated beside her had just entered the restaurant. "Jess, maybe we ought to give our seat up to that older couple." Jess left the table and approached the couple. Less than a minute later, Jess came back with the couple following him. "Kathi, this is Tessie and Earl and they are joining us for breakfast this morning, my treat." Kathi smiled a big smile, "Tessie, Earl, it is so nice to meet you. Please have a seat."

"I believe we just sat near you at Berea Baptist. Is that your church?" Kathi asked. "Oh no, we are visiting our son Paul and his family here in Atlanta. We had always wanted to visit Berea, so this morning, we decided to do that. We live in Florida now that we are retired," Tessie said. "I live in Florida, too. I am just visiting my parents this week. I grew up here but I work at the Space Center at Cape Canaveral," Kathi shared. "Well, we are practically neighbors then." Tessie laughed.

"I hate to ask, but you look so familiar. Where do I know you from?" Earl asked Jess. "You may have seen me on Fox News," Jess replied. "That's it, Jess Wanamaker, the reporter on the street. I love your show! I can't believe I am having breakfast with Jess Wanamaker!" Earl exclaimed. "I can't believe I am having breakfast with you either, Earl. We must be the two luckiest guys on the planet," Jess laughed. The waitress filled their coffee cups and brought them menus. They ordered and continued their conversations until the food arrived.

"I am here on an assignment to interview Pastor Scott for a Fox News segment. What did you think of his sermon?" Jess asked. "I thought it was wonderful. He has certainly changed a lot over the past few months since the Lord got ahold of his heart," Tessie said. "Could you explain what you mean by that, Tessie," Jess asked. "Pastor Scott preached at Berea for several years. He developed a lifestyle for riches and fame. One day he was thinking about the changes that Maye Moon was causing in people and wondering why God would place Maye Moon in the sky. The Lord spoke to his heart and convicted him that he was not saved. He knelt and prayed and asked the Lord to save him right there and then. He committed everything he owned to the Lord and immediately started liquidating his assets and giving them to the Lord's work. He thought maybe his church members would leave, but since then, his congregation and grown and grown. The Lord has really blessed him," Tessie explained.

Tessie turned and asked, point blank, "Are you saved?" to Kathi. Kathi got a shocked look on her face and mumbled, "That is kinda personal." "Oh, I am sorry, Kathi. I didn't mean to cross the line," Tessie apologized. "No, it is okay. I have been out of church for many years. Something stirred in me this morning. I want to get saved, but my life has been driven by Science. It is hard to think that everything I believe in is wrong. I have so much to lose," Kathi sighed. "But you have eternity to gain. When you are ready Kathi, I would love to share how to get saved with you from the Bible. We don't live very far from each other, and it would be my pleasure," Tessie said with a smile. "Thank you, Tessie; I will keep in touch. I can always use your prayers," Kathi said.

"Earl, I have been a devout Catholic all of my life. Do you think Catholics are going to heaven?" Jess asked. "Sure, if they ask Jesus to save them. Heaven is not just a place for Baptists," Earl laughed. "That's sure good to hear," Jess answered. "I really enjoyed today's service and it was quite a bit different than a Catholic mass. I learned a lot and I am looking forward to speaking to Pastor Scott. He has accomplished a lot building his ministry," Jess said. "Actually, God has done a lot through Pastor Scott. Be sure and ask him about the missionaries his church is supporting. Thousands are getting saved by the work Berea Baptist is supporting," Tessie said.

Breakfast arrived, and they enjoyed the food and the fellowship. Kathi couldn't believe how easy Earl and Tessie were to talk to. They exchanged numbers and promised to get together in the future. When they all said their goodbyes, Tessie told Kathi, "I will be praying for you, and I believe that God has something in store for

you. You will see how your present and future can work together."
They hugged, and each couple returned to their car.

"Jess, would you mind if we skipped the planetarium and just go to my parent's house and visited? We could watch a movie or play cards or something," Kathi asked. "That sounds great, Kathi. I would really like that, too," Jess replied.

After a full day, Kathi walked Jess to his car and they had their first kiss. It was short and sweet and made her heart flutter. "Be careful going back to the hotel," Kathi sweetly said. "I will be flying out tomorrow afternoon. I will call you when I get back to New York," Jess told her. "I will be waiting to hear from you. I leave on Tuesday for Orlando. We will see each other soon, I hope," Kathi said. "You can count on it, Kathi. Pleasant dreams," Jess answered.

Chapter 18

"John, I want you to be here for the meeting with the Speaker of the House and the Senate Majority Leader today. Do you have any questions about the stance that I wish you to take? We need to be a united front if they are not on board," President McIntosh stated. "I understand what you want, but I am hoping that you will proceed with an open mind. They may have some very good reasons for not supporting your push to make the Maye Moon a U.S. territory," Stafford replied. "And they may have some very good reasons for supporting their President. Why don't you think positively for a change, John? I do have some negotiating power on this issue. Both of them have a couple of pet projects that I have held back on just for a time as this," the President replied. "I want to go down in history as the President who made the most important contribution ever in history." "Or the biggest fool. The President who got us in a war with all of the other countries in the world," John Stafford thought.

The meeting was to be held in the Oval Office at 1:00 p.m. This was a strategic move by the President. "Maybe if the Speaker and the Senator have had their lunch, they will be anxious to conclude the meeting by agreeing and be able to get out of town early for the day," the President thought. "I think I will go to our private quarters and have lunch with my wife. That will make her day."

At 1:00 p.m., the President entered the Oval Office and welcomed his guests. "I appreciate you coming and meeting with me today. I hope you are both doing well," President McIntosh said. "Let's get down to business, shall we? Let's find out what you are up to," the Majority Leader said snidely. "I wanted to find out what your positions are about making Maye Moon a U.S. territory. I need to know if I have your support," President McIntosh said intently. "Speaker, let's start with you. Tell me if you can support my proposal?" he asked. The Speaker looked a little bewildered. "President, you know I have been very supportive of your plans in the past. I have to be honest, Mr. President, this is not something that you can get enough support to pass in the House. Most of the chatter is very negative and a lot of people just thought it was a poor attempt at humor. It will be political suicide to try to get enough votes to get it to pass. I believe other nations will align together to fight this boldly. We may be talking about a war," Madam Speaker explained. "President McIntosh, why in heaven's name do you think a country should claim Maye Moon as theirs?" the Majority Leader asked.

The Appearance of Maye Moon

"Maye Moon may have some very valuable resources that will need to be protected. Whom better than the United States?" President McIntosh stated. "Mr. President, there has never been a reason for the United States to claim the moon; I doubt if there is a need to claim Maye Moon either," the Majority Leader smiled, "Are you playing a joke on us? Is there a hidden camera?" "I am 100% serious. I think this is an opportunity to mine precious minerals on Maye Moon that could pull the U.S. out of an economic slump. Some day, people may want to inhabit Maye Moon and we can control what goes on. I have heard scientists claim that Maye Moon's appearance is so different from the Moon that there may be a lot more than rocks on the surface. I want to be known throughout history as the President that was most successful in the history of the country," the President declared proudly.

"Mr. President, this is an unexplored natural satellite at this point in time. I do not think you want to have people question your mental health. Elections are next year. Isn't it enough to win the race to Maye Moon?" the Speaker asked. "I can see this plan going awry in so many ways, and I have to think of my own political career." "I need you both. You need me. I can recall a couple of pet projects you both have wanted my support on. Maybe now is the time to make those happen. Let's negotiate," President McIntosh said.

The Majority Leader knew what the President was talking about. He had asked him to support a spending bill that would improve infrastructure in his state at a cost of $422 Billion dollars. The state needs bridges, schools, roads, and a new Interstate crossing East to West across the upper half of the state. President McIntosh had told him that he would not approve it. "McIntosh has been holding out for something that he wanted," the Senator thought.

The Speaker had asked for money for the support of the homeless and illegal aliens that had overrun her state. "The drug problem is out of control, with discarded needles and junkies in upscale areas of the cities. People were moving away in droves, and the already high taxes were not covering the costs. McIntosh uses it against me every chance he gets. It has become an embarrassment because my District is the worst in the state. I really need Federal dollars to attack the problem appropriately. McIntosh is ruthless, and nobody gets anything without getting something in return in Washington D.C.," she thought.

"I cannot give you a decision today. I need to speak to some of my advisors. I would also like to speak to Ambassador Steubens about this," The Speaker told President McIntosh. "I can tell you here and now that she has said she will resign if I go forward with this plan, so you really do not need to waste time talking to her," President McIntosh replied.

"I agree with the Speaker. Today is not the day for a decision. I must think your proposition over. My state's needs are important, but I still think your idea is political suicide, and I don't want to be responsible for a war with other countries. Steubens is a very intelligent woman and remarkable Ambassador to the U.N. If she tells you it is a bad idea, I think you should heed her warning," the Majority Leader said.

"I thought you were both Progressives. This is probably the most progressive idea in history, and you are both too spineless to go for it. Let's meet back in a week, and I will give you time to consider the plan and what it could mean for this country," the President concluded. Two weeks until launch.

Chapter 19

Jess and Kathi had been talking and texting several times a day and Jess was ready to pop the big question, "Can I go with you to the Miracle Mission Launch?" He was actually very nervous about it because he did not want to be turned down. "I think she really likes me, but that is like making a public statement that we are a couple," he thought. That evening, when they spoke on the telephone, Kathi suddenly said, "Meet me." "Meet you? How?" Jess asked. "I just flew into New York on a last-minute assignment. Someone canceled on 'Good Morning New York,' and they asked if I could cover. I thought it would be an opportunity to get to see you," she gushed. "That is fantastic! Tell me where you are, and I will come to you," Jess exclaimed. "I am at the RIU Plaza. I will meet you in the lobby. Will a ½ hour work for you?" Kathi answered. "I will make it work. I will be right there," Jess answered. Jess was on cloud nine as he quickly freshened up.

Jess arrived on time, and the two of them greeted one another with a long, warm embrace and a kiss. "Would you want to walk around awhile and enjoy the lights, and we can find a place to grab a bite?" Jess asked. "Sounds great. How was your day, Jess?" Kathi asked. "It was good. I got to fill in for Walter, and I think it went pretty well. The rest of the day I spent preparing for my show on Friday," he answered. "How about you?" "I spent my day preparing for the upcoming Miracle Mission Launch. I checked in on my Assistant in my department at NASA to see how things were going and to see if she had any questions. She is doing a great job covering for me. Lorraine has been covering a lot of interviews, too. That helps. Busy day as usual," she replied.

"Kathi I was wondering, could I be your guest for the launch?" Jess asked. "Fox is sending a team to cover the event and I was thinking I might get an even closer view if I was your guest?" Jess asked with his puppy dog eyes, which he used when he really wanted something. "Jess, I don't think I can have a guest. I will be anchoring the event and will be really tied up," Kathi explained. "I know you will be really busy, but I will stay out of the way and just stay in the background. I promise not to be any trouble," Jess pleaded. "I will think about it and find out if I need any special permission to have you around. My assignment will last throughout the entire launch and even when the astronauts return. I will be so busy. I will need to really rest up before because I will get very little sleep during that time," she explained. "I understand, and I promise not to expect you to pay any attention to me. Trust me, I get it. I am in the business. Duty calls and our jobs require us to make sacrifices," Jess proceeded. "I promise I will see if this can be worked out. I am so glad you understand how it is in this business. That little pub doesn't look too crowded. Would you want to try it?" Kathi asked. "I ate there once, and it wasn't bad. Sounds like a good idea to me," Jess replied.

Jess and Kathi found a cozy seat away from people and talked about so many different things. They were really getting to know each other and feeling very comfortable around each other. The time passed so quickly, and finally, Kathi said, "Jess, I better call it a night. I have a very early morning, and I don't want bags under my eyes." She laughed. "Yes, I have a pretty early morning myself. We better get you back to your hotel. What time is your flight tomorrow?" he asked. "11:00 a.m. back to Orlando and then back out to the Cape," she answered. He held her hand as they walked through Times Square back to the hotel. The lights made everything surreal, and Kathi felt like she was in a fantasy world. She had finally met someone she enjoyed being with and seemed to understand her. They enjoyed a long lingering kiss before entering the hotel.

"Text me and let me know you made it home," Jess said. "I am going to miss you, Kathi. Hope you have a good interview and hope you have a safe flight home tomorrow morning. Promise you will text me and let me know when you get back to Orlando," he said. "I will. Goodnight Jess, and be careful," she gently said. They shared one last kiss.

Chapter 20

“**J** ohn, I have been patient. So far, I haven't heard anything back from the Speaker or the Senate Majority Leader. I want to know what is taking them so long!” President McIntosh yelled. “Get them in here for a follow-up meeting. I want to talk about this when I am in Cape Canaveral for the Miracle Mission.” “Sir, I don't think that is wise. I don't think you should take the nation's attention away from the biggest event in the history of the United States,” Stafford told him. “I guess you're right. I am just anxious to get this deal done and declare the Maye Moon territory officially ours. I say we plant a U.S. flag on Maye Moon like the Apollo astronauts did on the moon,” President McIntosh said boldly. “I imagine that NASA and SpaceX will go along with that if you do not make claims of the Maye Moon being a U.S. territory. They might not want to get in that dog fight,” Stafford warned.

“Stafford, you are spineless. You tiptoe around like something bad might happen. I am the President! The buck stops with me. I make the rules that everyone else follows. Don't forget it!" he shouted.

John Stafford arranged a follow-up meeting between President McIntosh, the Speaker of the House, and the Senate Majority Leader for the next day. President McIntosh invited them to have a seat in the Oval Office. "I asked you here today to find out if you are going to support my decision to make Maye Moon a U.S. territory. I hope you have thought about what it could mean to the United States in the future. The field of Space Exploration is exploding. Who knows what the next 5 or 10 years might bring?" President McIntosh stated.

"Mr. President, after I have weighed all considerations, I cannot bring myself to support this agenda. The chance of war with other countries is too great. We have worked very hard to improve international relations over the years and have greatly improved our relationships with other NATO nations. The NATO members may feel you have drawn them into a war. This would enrage other countries, especially those who have their own space program," the Senate Majority Leader said. "That is the purpose of a summit. I will be able to convince them there are advantages of having Maye Moon become a U.S. territory," President McIntosh whined. "If I thought that was possible, I would agree. Have you spoken to any leaders and gotten their support yet?" the Senate Majority leader asked.

"No, I want Congress's approval first," he answered. "Then my answer is no. A solid no," the Senate Majority leader said sternly.

"What about you, Mrs. Speaker?" the President asked. "With the right deal, I will support you. I want your original offer, but I would also like to include 2% of the profits going directly back to my state indefinitely. Additionally, my husband's company needs a new contract with the Department of Defense," she said firmly. "You know how to play hardball," the President replied. "I will approve this if it gets to my desk. Making the Maye Moon a U.S. territory will be the boldest move in history. I know that we can make it happen."

"What about Ambassador Steubens? I spoke to her in detail and she is not going along with this. She feels it will be a declaration of war. She doesn't feel that we have a single ally in the United Nations in support of this issue. We cannot initiate a World War III. Our military is not strong enough. The economy is in shambles already. How can the U.S. afford to do this?" the Senator asked. "Our military is strong. We will have to tighten up. Americans will have to pay a little more, but the future will be much brighter. We just have to look ahead," McIntosh answered. "I haven't changed my mind. I really think you have become mentally impaired to risk so much. I think you can count on an Impeachment," the Senator exclaimed. "There will be no impeachment as long as I am Speaker of the House!" she said sharply. "You are a sellout! You have no scruples, Mrs. Speaker!" he shouted as he stormed towards the door.

"He will be back in time. After he considers the fallout for not cooperating, he will crawl back," the President responded. "The Miracle Launch takes place in a week. There will be festivities all over the country, and people's patriotism will be at an all-time high. We must move quickly through the House. Work on your constituents in the Senate. I will work from my end to organize the Miracle Maye Moon Summit and invite the United Nations members to attend. I really believe we can get some cooperation from most countries. The ones with major Space Exploration programs of their own will be against us for sure. Unfortunately, they are the ones that will want to go to war. We will be ready to move into action once we know the Miracle Mission launch is a success," the President instructed. "Just don't forget, we have a deal," Mrs. Speaker responded.

Chapter 21

E mceeing the Miracle Mission with Kathi Calloway was sure to be the most important gig of Warren Winston's skyrocketing career. SNN's popularity had exploded with the appearance of Maye Moon. He and Kathi would be covering the mission nearly non-stop until the spaceship returned to Earth and even a few days after. "I like Kathi and she will make a great co-host. Thankfully, we will have a lot of help from writers and producers to make the conversations flow comfortably. A lot of interesting guests are lined up also," he thought as he packed his bags to head to Cape Canaveral, FL.

Kathi decided to make the call. "Hello beautiful, how is your day?" Jess answered. He was always so upbeat, and she loved that about him. "Hey Jess, my day is fabulous, especially now that I have you on the phone. I wanted to call and let you know that I got the final approval for you to be on the set of the Miracle Mission broadcast. There were several hoops to jump through, but it was approved. The only problem is that you will have to stay off-camera and out of the way," she explained.

"Oh my gosh, this is awesome. I convinced my boss to let me come down as a host on some of the Fox segments, so this will work out perfectly. When I am not on camera I can be hanging around your set. I promise to stay out of the way and not be a demanding boyfriend," he answered. "Boyfriend? Are we an official couple?" Kathi thought. "Just remember, I will be extremely busy for the next few months. It may seem like I am trying to avoid you, but I can assure you that is not the case. When the astronauts return, I will begin the work in the laboratory, and research and testing will take a long time. Are you sure that you are up for that?" she asked. "I totally understand, Kath; I am here for the long haul. We will make it work," he assured her.

Tessie hung up the telephone and had a big smile on her face. "Jennifer, Peter, and Thomas are coming for the Miracle Mission launch. They will be coming in a few days and will be staying until the spaceship returns. I can't believe that Jennifer was able to talk Peter into coming," Tessie exclaimed. "That is great news, Mom. We will have to drive up to the Cape to see it closer. Thomas will remember this for the rest of his life!" Earl answered. "I would love to go to the parade, too. The traffic will be horrible, but I am sure Peter would be willing to drive us all there," Earl said excitedly. "I have to get the beds ready, go to the grocery, and clean the house. Peter just found out he was able to get away," Tessie explained. "Don't overdo it, Mom. I will help," Earl said.

"Mother, are you sure you and Daddy don't want to be here for the launch? NASA and SpaceX will provide an escort for you, and you will be treated like royalty. You will literally have the best seats in the house. They will take care of everything. I have a couple of days off to rest and be with family before the launch takes place. I was really hoping y'all would be here with me for this," Cora implored. "No, Cora, we won't be coming. We will be watching on the television, though," her mother answered. She sounded weak and tired. It broke Cora's heart, but she understood that her mother was not in any shape to make the trip.

"I have a special announcement to make before we leave today. We will be having a special prayer service for the Miracle Mission here at Atlantic Berea Baptist. We will have the launch streaming on our mega wall screens, so you will be able to watch it with your brothers and sisters here at ABB. Our children's ministry and teen ministry will be having special activities in the gyms and will be watching too. Following the launch, there will be a celebration with refreshments in our fellowship hall. We encourage you to invite your friends and neighbors to celebrate what God has done for our world," Pastor Scott Morales announced to his congregation. "I have been asked to pray at the Prayer breakfast for the astronauts and the televised Miracle Mission launch. I plan to use this prayer to give God the praise and glory for the appearance of Maye Moon."

The Appearance of Maye Moon

"Mr. President, you will be a special guest at the Prayer Breakfast for the astronauts the day before launch. You will have approximately 6 minutes to speak. You will be seated at the head VIP table with the astronauts, SpaceX and NASA executives, the Governor of Florida, State Senators and State Representatives, and Pastor Scott Morales of Berea Baptist Church of Atlanta. There will be a parade later that afternoon. Do you want to ride in the parade?" John Stafford asked the President. "Of course, I want to ride in the parade. I need visibility. This is going to be watched by people all over the world. If it were not for me, the Miracle Mission would not be taking place," President McIntosh responded. John Stafford accidentally rolled his eyes. "I will let the parade committee know. I will arrange the details. Security has determined that you should stay on Air Force One at the Kennedy Space Center instead of a hotel," Stafford explained. "That will be fine. The First Lady will be going with me. Just make all the arrangements. This needs to go smoothly. I have some work to do, so please leave," President McIntosh ordered.

Natalie Steubens confirmed that she would be attending the Miracle Mission Space Launch and be seated in the special United Nations section. She would be giving a Welcome speech to the delegation. Most U.N. ambassadors will be attending. She had also been asked to be on the Live show and be interviewed by Warren Winston and Kathi Calloway. She hoped to have an opportunity to stress that she was not supportive of making Maye Moon a U.S. territory. She had been quietly discussing the matter in one-on-one meetings with several other ambassadors who also saw the danger of making such a move.

Launch time is 12:03 p.m. in two days. All tests have been successful. The weather report is 100% favorable for the next three days. The most important historical event is a GO!

Chapter 22

K athi had her alarm set for 3:00 a.m. She was to be at work on the set at 4:00 a.m. Fortunately, all she had to do was take a quick shower and jump into something comfortable. She would have her hair, clothing, and makeup done on the set. Today, at 6:00 a.m. began the marathon Miracle Mission coverage with Winston Warren. People all over the world would be watching. She still couldn't believe that she had gone from a respected NASA Chief Scientist to a news commentator. "I really can't wait to get back to my normal life in the lab," she thought.

As she entered the set, she saw Warren and waved. She was glad he was her co-anchor. He was very knowledgeable about the Space program and was easy to talk to. He would have some intelligent questions to ask their guests, which would make it easier on her. They would be breaking away to cover a lot of parades across the country today.

At 5:45 a.m., she and Warren were ready to go. Their first guest would be Arlene Turner, the Space X publicist who has been doing a lot of the interviews across the country and managing the whole Marketing program that has been going on for months. This morning she is sharing parade details across the country. She will be bringing along the Miracle Mission mascot, a loveable bulldog dog in a spacesuit who will be riding in parades across the United States. The interview is scheduled for 15 minutes and will break away to a NASA weather update and this morning's headlines. Arlene will be taking her place at noon so she and Warren can take a quick break, eat a quick lunch, and return to their places by 12:30 p.m.

"That was fun," Warren stated when they went to commercials. "Yes, I enjoyed the segment. Arlene is really good at her job. Initially, I thought we would be competing for top dog, but we really needed each other, and she has become a good friend. I respect her work, and she inspires me," Kathi said. The next guest was a NASA engineer who helped design the Miracle. He was going to explain how the spaceship operates. This will be a more technical interview with illustrations. It would be generic enough that no secrets would be given away to foreign countries or corporate espionage. Kathi was supposed to include some marketing at the end of the segment and tell the viewers that there are 24" models that you can purchase from the online store. ("I really hate doing this," she thought.)

"For our viewers that have never visited NASA Kennedy Space Center in Merritt Island, Florida, make the sunny coast your next vacation spot. Explore the attractions and be inspired. Hear about the space pioneers who made Miracle I a possibility. Watch the voyage into space on the giant IMAX screen. Take the Kennedy bus tour and see the operational space flight facilities. Kennedy Space Center is home to the actual space shuttle Atlantis. Check our website, www.nasa.gov, for hours and dates," Kathi recited her lines perfectly. "Warren, tell us about our next guest."

The interview with the NASA engineer went well and was quite interesting. After his segment, the show went to Orlando to hear about the work that went into putting on the Miracle parade that would be starting at noon. Disney partnered with Space X and NASA to create a parade that would capture the heart of anyone 0 to 100. The Grand Marshalls of the parade are none other than President McIntosh and the First Lady.

Kathi felt blessed that Jess had been watching her from the sidelines all morning. He stayed back as he promised, but it was so nice to know that he was there. "I will get a chance to spend a few minutes with him during my lunch break, but I must focus on listening to the producer and making this show a success," she thought.

Another weather update and Headline news update. "Our next guests are here from the Midwest state of Indiana. They are homeschoolers who are here to watch the Miracle launch and explore Science from a hands-on approach. Please welcome

Matthew, Hannah, and Adam," Kathi smiled and greeted each child with a hug. Kathi and Warren spent 5 minutes interviewing the kids. It was a heart warmer. An affiliate covered another remote segment from Houston, Texas, where a Texas-sized parade was taking place today. The Johnson Space Center was waiving the admission fee to get in to visit today. The day was passing by fast!

"I remember visiting the Johnson Space Center as a child. I am sure that influenced my love of Science," Warren told the audience. "I was too afraid of heights to become an astronaut," he laughed. "I was also a Buzz fan." "Buzz Aldrin?" Kathi asked. "No, silly, Buzz Lightyear. 'To infinity and beyond,'" he answered. Kathi laughed and said, "If you liked Buzz Aldrin or Buzz Lightyear, you will love our next guests. We would like to welcome our Miracle Flight team, astronauts Cora Collins, Bob Hutchinson, Ben Jones, and Larry Lowe. The Dream team who are heading to May Moon tomorrow at noon." The team entered the makeshift studio, and a large crowd of fans clapped from the sidelines.

"We are so happy to have you. I know you are busy with last-minute preparations for this historic mission. People all over the world are watching and praying for your safety. Bob, what is it like leading a mission this important?" Warren asked. "This is like a dream come true. Just seven months ago, this big, beautiful satellite suddenly appeared in the sky, and I immediately thought, I want to be the first man to walk on its surface. Tomorrow, we will begin our journey to Maye Moon," Bob answered. "Are you nervous?" Warren asked. "No, sir. NASA and SpaceX have taken all precautions to make this a safe voyage. We have been training for months, and many, many tests have been performed to ensure our safety," Bob answered with confidence.

"Ben, are you ready for this adventure?" Kathi asked. "I was born ready, Kathi. This is what I have spent my adult life training for. I want to tell all the kids out there watching, if you have a dream put in the hard work and don't give up. NASA did not put a "Help Wanted" sign on the door, nor did we wander off in the street and ask for a job. We spent years hitting the books and preparing for whatever may happen. Amongst the four of us, we probably have over 50 years of training for this one mission. Make your dream a reality," Ben told the audience. "That is such good advice, Ben. You have had an amazing career and now you are part of a team who will go down in history as being the first to ever explore Maye Moon in person. It gives me chills," Kathi exclaimed.

"Larry, you are the youngest of the team. None of you were born when Apollo 11 and the first astronauts, Neil Armstrong and Buzz Aldrin, landed on the moon, and Michael Collins piloted the mission. Do you think that there is still public interest in the space program?" Warren asked. "I do. I do, but it takes a lot more for the youth of today to get amazed by anything. This generation grew up watching Star Wars and other space movies, and they sometimes get caught up in the special effects. In reality, this is a historic moment in time. To travel that far from Earth in a manned flight has taken NASA and SpaceX a lot of time and money. Who knows what we may find on the surface of Maye Moon and how it could influence scientific discovery in the future?"

"Cora, we have saved you for last. We want to congratulate you for being such a fine role model to the millions of young women across the world who want to make Science their career. Cora, did you have a female role model that you looked up to and motivated you to enter the field of aerospace engineering?" Kathi asked. "My mother was my main role model in life. She was an Astrophysicist and taught at Ole Miss until she had to end her career due to Multiple Sclerosis. She is my biggest fan. I love her very much and she taught me so much more than science. She is my hero. I was also influenced by Christa McAuliffe, a teacher who lost her life on the Challenger. Christa was the first American civilian to go to space. Her bravery has always been an example I have tried to emulate. The Challenger explosion took place when I was three years old, and it is the first national tragedy that I remember watching on television. My mother had met Christa and was deeply saddened by the loss," Cora said as she wiped a tear away. "Tomorrow will be a successful mission that I will dedicate to both of these great ladies." "Thank you, Cora, for sharing that with our audience. You are an amazing woman," Kathi said, and the program broke away to the Weather and Headlines update.

Kathi and Warren thanked the astronauts for coming and being guests. Kathi gave Cora a special, heartfelt hug and told her that she would be praying for her. It was finally time for Lorraine Maxwell to replace her so she could take a quick break and have some lunch with Jess.

Jess had bought her a wonderful grilled chicken salad and had it waiting on her so they could spend as much time as they could together. He was so thoughtful, and she loved being with him. As they say, he is a keeper. "Kathi, the show has been going so well. The guests you have lined up have been so interesting, and you are a natural. I am sure that Fox would love to have you," Jess gushed. "I don't think so. I am a scientist at heart. I am anxious to get back to my real job as the NASA Chief Scientist. Thank you so much for the salad. I didn't realize how hungry I was," Kathi replied. "Wow, to be able to interview the Miracle Mission astronauts the day before they enter outer space—that will win you some kind of award," Jess beamed. "I can imagine people all over the world glued to their television sets or computers, watching every minute of your show."

"Thank you again for getting me on the set. I wouldn't want to be anywhere else in the world but right here watching you," Jess said as he leaned over and kissed her. "I love you, Kathi." Kathi blushed. The cat is out of the bag. She hadn't discussed her "relationship" with Jess with her co-workers and friends, but now it is pretty obvious. Jess used the "L" word. Suddenly without thinking, she replied, "I love you too, Jess."

Chapter 23

H er lunch break had flown by, and Lorraine had covered the spectacular parade in Orlando. Disney had done a fantastic job of making the parade very special with the most beautiful floats she had ever seen. For the next hour, she and Warren joined Lorraine in covering the parade. The President and First Lady were the parade Marshalls, and tomorrow morning, she and Warren would be interviewing President McIntosh in person. Kathi hadn't told Jess because she didn't want to brag and secondly, she wanted to surprise him. Kathi wasn't aware of the President's plot to make Maye Moon a U.S. territory.

Kathi and Warren also checked in with the Washington D.C., Chicago, Atlanta, and Houston parades. Major cities and small towns were having parades of their own today. Today was a day of celebration and anticipation of tomorrow's Miracle Launch.

"Let's welcome our next guest who came here from Atlanta to be with us today, Pastor Scott Morales, pastor of Atlantic Berea Baptist, one of the largest churches in America," Warren said. "Pastor Morales, could you tell us a little bit about your ministry and how it relates to the Miracle Mission," Warren continued. "Thank you, Warren, for having me. Our church is a place for everyone. Each Sunday, we have three services, and our sanctuary seats 7,000 people. People attend because they want to hear about the gospel of Jesus Christ. Jesus came on this Earth to seek and save those who were lost. People today are seeking answers to the critical questions in their lives, and they find the answers in church. We have lots of options for our members to serve others through our outreach ministries. We have a preschool, elementary school, middle school, and a high school. We are in the process of building a university for those who want to enter the ministry. We have youth groups, athletic teams, a homeless shelter, a senior citizen center, a food pantry, a free clothing shop, and many other outreach opportunities. One of our most important outreach ministries is our Mission board where we send missionaries throughout the world, taking the gospel to other countries. We have more but I would take up the rest of your show. We serve Atlanta as best as we can. I will be delivering a prayer tomorrow before the Miracle Mission. Maye Moon holds a special place in my heart because it changed my life. I was a lost man pastoring the largest church in Atlanta. When Maye Moon appeared, I was convicted to change my ways; I got saved and turned my life around.

"I am from Atlanta and was fortunate enough to visit your church when I last visited my parents. I would have to say it is something to see. So large and so beautiful," Kathi stated. "I want to be sure and say that I am not bragging on my accomplishments at Atlanta Berea Baptist, but what God has done. I am nothing but a tool in His work."

"What is the number one question that people ask you, Pastor, about the Maye Moon," Warren asked. "I would have to say that people want to know if the Maye Moon is a sign from God that the End is near. I tell them the Bible does not mention Maye Moon, but it does say that there will be signs of His coming. The one thing I can guarantee is that Maye Moon was put there for God's purpose in His time."

"Do you think that the Big Bang may have produced this new Maye Moon?" Warren asked. "No, Warren, I am a Christian. I believe that the Bible is the Word of God and that everything in it is 100% true. The Bible explains in Genesis that God created the Earth, Moon, and Stars in 7 days. I believe He was talking about seven Earth days because He is God, and He can speak it into existence. Maye Moon appeared in less than a second. For me, Warren, it would take a lot more to believe that a couple of microscopic atoms bumped into each other and created the universe than a Supreme GodFather created it," Pastor Scott smiled. "I give God the praise, honor, and glory for all things."

"If any of your viewers want more information about Salvation, the Creation, or a whole host of other topics, please visit our website," Pastor Scott said. "Kathi, God wants you to leap out in faith. Thank you for having me," Pastor Scott continued. "Thank you Pastor Scott, and we will look forward to your benediction tomorrow at the Miracle Mission launch," Warren concluded.

Kathi had a few minutes while the program went to Space coast weather and headlines. She followed Pastor Scott off to the side where they could talk. "I don't have but a couple of minutes Pastor. I wanted to tell you that I believe and I want to be saved but I keep letting my lifelong love of Science from making a commitment." "Kathi, you can still love Science. You just have to believe that all things are from God, and he gives each of us special talents to do His work, whether you are a Chemist, a doctor, or a bus driver," Pastor Scott explained. "I want to do it right now and commit to Christ," Kathi said. "I will gladly help you. Kathi, Romans 3:10 **tells us,** "As it is written, 'There is none righteous, no, not one." **God knows everything about each and every one of us. He knows we are not perfect, but we need a Saviour. Romans 3:23** states, **"For all have sinned, and come short of the glory of God."** The standard to follow is Jesus Christ, for he is the only perfect one. We all fall short. **Romans 6:23** explains, **"For the wages of sin is death; but the gift of God is eternal life through Jesus Christ our Lord."** Without God's free gift of dying for our sins, we would be destined to spend eternity in hell. Sin cannot enter heaven. **Romans 5:8** says, **"But God commendeth his love toward us, in that, while we were yet sinners, Christ died for us."** His death and shed blood gave us eternal life. **Romans 10:13** states, **"For whosoever shall call upon the name of the Lord shall be saved."** We must ask Jesus for His gift of life. **Romans 10:9-13** says, **"9 That if thou shalt confess with thy mouth the Lord Jesus, and shalt believe in thine heart that God hath raised him from the dead, thou shalt be saved. 10 For with the heart, man believeth unto righteousness; and with the mouth, confession is made unto salvation. 11 For the scripture saith, Whosoever believeth on him shall not be ashamed. 12 For there is no difference between the Jew and the Greek: for the same Lord over all is rich unto all that call upon him. 13 For whosoever shall call upon the name of the Lord shall be saved. 1 John 5:13: "These things have I written unto you that believe on the name of the Son of God; that ye may know that ye have eternal life and that ye may believe on the name of the Son of God."**

"Kathi, do you believe these scriptures?" Pastor Morales asked. "I do with all my heart," Kathi answered. "Then Kathi, pray this prayer with me. Heavenly Father, I believe in my heart and confess with my mouth that Jesus is your Son, and He died on Calvary that I might be saved. I know I am a sinner, and without your free gift of salvation, I would be destined to hell. I repent of my sins and ask you to please forgive me of my sins. I believe the Bible is your holy word. I ask You to come into my life and save my soul. Change me, mold me into what you would have me to be, Lord. Fill me with your Holy Spirit. In Jesus' precious name. Amen.

"Kathi, you have been born again."

Chapter 24

K athi felt a lightness, freshness, and happiness in her soul. She could not keep from smiling. She was looking forward to sharing her wonderful news with Jess this evening. Even Warren noticed that Kathi had changed after the interview with Pastor Scott. "Should he ask her about it? No," he thought. "She will tell me if she wants me to know. It really is not any of my business. Besides, I know her pretty well, but not in a personal way." The following guest is the President of the Kennedy Space Museum. Lots of museum shots in this segment. "Have you been to the Kennedy Space Museum?" Kathi asked Warren. "Only about a 100 times. Sometimes, I conduct interviews there for the show. It really doesn't get old, and I usually get to go behind the scenes and see things the public never get to see, like the alien space bodies," he laughed. She looked shocked at first, then laughed along with him.

The next guest was Astronaut Judith Hines, who spent six months in 2021 at the International Space Station. "Judith, we are so happy to have you as our guest," Warren stated. "You are one of a few people who have had the opportunity to live in space. Would you do it again?" "Absolutely. It was the most exciting experience of my life. Traveling there on the Crew Dragon was a journey that took 29 hours. Getting to live with a Russian cosmonaut and Japanese astronaut for six months was quite an experience also. I hope I get the opportunity to return in the future."

"Could you explain some of the projects that have been conducted at the International Space Center," Kathi said. "As you know, Kathi, I am not at liberty to speak about some sensitive projects, but I can share that the ISS scientists have made advances in medical scanning technology and created new drugs. We have made advances in robotics. Advances have been made to lower heat in cities and track water sources, and we get to look at the vastness of space. It is very spectacular and exciting!" Judith explained. "I know Judith. As the Chief Scientist at NASA, I get to take your experiments and have teams of scientists replicate the results and do additional testing. Mankind will greatly benefit from the work we are doing there," Kathi added.

"Judith, were you a candidate for the Miracle Mission?" Warren asked. "Yes, I was, but sadly I was not chosen. I believe we have a very competent crew going, and I wish them all a safe journey. I look forward to learning about what they discover. Hopefully, they will solve the mystery of the appearance of the Maye Moon," Judith answered. "Are you one of the scientists that believe Maye Moon appeared as part of the Big Bang?" Warren asked. "No, Warren, mathematically, that doesn't make sense to me. I am a follower of the intelligent design theory of the creation of the universe. It is a topic that most scientists refuse to discuss and could be argued and debated for hours. Maybe the Maye Moon Miracle Mission will provide some answers," Judith replied. "Interesting. We will have to have you as a guest on my show sometime so we can hear more about what led you to this conclusion. Thank you, Judith, for being our guest today," Warren concluded.

Break time. Kathi followed Judith offset and stopped her to talk to her for a second. "Judith, I followed the Big Bang Theory explanation of the universe throughout my adult life. I officially became a Christian today. I guess that puts me on the side of intelligent design also," Kathi stated. "Expect some lashing out from those on the side of the Big Bang Theory. Kathi, I have felt that God and Science can co-exist if we are open-minded. I may become a Christian also, but I have not quite got to that decision," Judith said with her head down. "Maybe we could meet for lunch after this mission returns," Kathi said. "That would be great, Kathi. I would like that," Judith replied. "I will definitely give you a call. Take care," Kathi answered. "Thanks Kathi, you take care also," Judith said as she turned and walked away. Kathi thought, "Am I guilty of ridiculing fellow scientists who are believers or believe in intelligent design?" Kathi was told by the producer in her earpiece that the next guests were a couple who saw the Maye Moon rise. The couple came out and took their seats and it was none other than Tessie and Earl. Kathi jumped up and gave each of them a hug. "What a surprise! It is so nice to see you!" she said joyfully. "You will never believe what happened. I got saved this morning! Pastor Scott was our guest, and I just felt the Lord telling me I needed to get saved right then and there." "Oh, Kathi, we couldn't be happier for you. We have been praying for you, and God answered our prayer," Tessie exclaimed. Warren just stood there with his mouth open. The producer told Kathi in her earpiece that everyone needed to be seated immediately.

Everyone found their seats, and Kathi introduced Earl and Tessie. "I would like to welcome my friends from Cocoa Beach, Florida, Earl and Tessie Hawkins. They are here today with family to enjoy the Kennedy Space Center and to watch the Miracle Mission take off tomorrow. I want to start by asking Earl to tell us what happened the night they first saw Maye Moon." "Tessie and I enjoy watching the full moonrise from the beach when we can. We were enjoying the ocean and holding hands like newlyweds. It was a beautiful sight seeing the big yellow moon arise from the ocean. Most of the other people on the beach had packed up and left. Suddenly, I said Mom, look over there. What is that? A big bluish-green glowing ball crept up over the ocean's horizon until it was fully in the sky. Suddenly, Maye Moon appeared out of nowhere,"

Earl explained. "I was speechless," Tessie added. "While it was beautiful, it was also a little scary because we didn't know what it was."

"Did you hear any weird or strange noises?" Warren asked. "No, sir. It just rose up in the sky," Earl said. "What did you think it was?" Warren asked. "To be honest, we didn't know what to think. We decided to go home and see if there was anything about it on the news, and news people were going frantic over it," Earl answered. "So, Earl, why do you think this moon suddenly appeared?" Warren asked. "Well, Warren, I have thought a lot about it. I was reading my Bible one day, and a verse spoke to my heart. **Habakkuk 1:5 says, "Behold ye among the heathen, and regard, and wonder marvelously: for I will work a work in your days which ye will not believe, though it be told you."** I believe that Maye Moon is a work of God, and God will reveal His purpose very soon. This Miracle Mission may reveal what God has for His children very soon. I am excited!" Earl said earnestly. "Me too! I am so excited!" Tessie said, nodding in agreement. "Praise be to the Lord, the Maker of all things!"

"Tessie and Earl, you are a delight. I am so happy to see you and hear about your beach experience, and I am sure our viewers enjoyed it too," Kathi said as she hugged them both. "Now for a Miracle Mission weather update." When off camera, Kathi said, "I am sure that Jess wants to say hello. Please don't mention to him that I got saved this morning. I want to surprise him with the news. I wish I had more time to visit, but we have such a tight schedule. I am just happy I got to see you both!" "Mumis the word Kathi," Tessie said. The sweet old couple headed over to where Jess was sitting.

After checking in with a few more parades taking place in various places in the world, the last interview of the day was with U.N. Ambassador Natalie Steubens. "Ambassador Steubens, thank you for allowing us time out of your busy day to come in for our show. It is an honor to have you," Warren said. "Thank you for having me, Warren. Tomorrow is a major day in history and I am so proud that the U.S. has moved forward with the next step in space exploration," the Ambassador replied. "Could you tell us about the delegation in the U.N. tent and what your role has been?" Winston asked. "I was asked to give the opening welcome speech to the delegation. There are 193 sovereign countries in the United Nations. One hundred twenty-seven countries are represented here today. They are sending their best wishes for a successful mission tomorrow. Our meeting is mostly social, but there has been a lot of chatter of how to precede when the Miracle Mission is over and how to protect the sovereignty of Maye Moon once the mission has concluded," the Ambassador replied. "No single country cannot own Maye Moon. If there are natural resources on its surface, they must be shared proportionately by all nations of the world. We cannot allow any one country to get greedy and controlling." "I would say that makes perfect sense," Warren answered. "I would hope that is not even an issue," Warren said with concern. Steubens continued, "We have to be prepared for this. The United Nations is a little over 75 years old, and our goal is to keep peace throughout the world and help nations that are combating hunger, illness, and poverty. Any one nation that would claim Maye Moon would cause a huge upheaval at the United Nations, and rightfully so," the Ambassador explained. "Let us pray that nothing like that would ever happen," Kathi said.

"We hope that your delegation is enjoying the NASA festivities and will have a wonderful view of the launch tomorrow," Warren transitioned to a happier conversation. "Oh yes, tonight we will have a closed formal ball in honor of NASA and SpaceX's success," Ambassador Steubens smiled. "I managed to get Elon Musk to give a brief welcome to the U.N. delegation this morning." "That is impressive. He is such a busy man," Kathi stated. "What was the most important message that Elon shared?" Kathi asked. "Elon explained that he was doing this for mankind. He felt that the sustainability of the human race was important and that his goal had been getting to Mars and opening the door for future generations to build communities there. Still, maybe Maye Moon is where future human habitation will go to sustain," the Ambassador replied." "Wow, that is huge," Warren said with amazement. "I don't think that Elon Musk has given up his goal of going to Mars. Maye Moon is a new mystery, and he wants to solve that space puzzle first," Ambassador Steubens shared. "Thank you for this enlightening interview. We wish you a successful trip here to the Space Coast," Warren said. "Thank you for speaking to me today, Warren and Kathi," Ambassador Steubens replied.

"I am beat...and hungry," Kathi said to Jess. "Let's grab a bite to eat and then I got to get home to bed. I have to be here at 4:00 a.m. again. Anything near your home open?" Jess asked. "We have one 24-hour joint on the way," Kathi said. "I am not going to be picky this late. Maybe I will get some pancakes." "Mhmm sounds good," Jess answered. They walked hand in hand to the car nearby.

"Kathi, you have been amazing all day. You are really made for this job. You have an honesty that your guests trust. I am so blessed." "You are blessed?" Kathi questioned. "Well, yes, we haven't discussed it, really, but you do realize that you and I have a special relationship. I feel like we are a little old to call it boyfriend and girlfriend, but I hope you do realize there is no one else for me. You are the one, the only one," he leaned over and kissed her in the pancake house. "I love you, Kathi," Jess said, looking deep into her eyes. "I love you too, Jess." The waitress arrived with the pancakes and interrupted their romantic moment. "I am famished." She then bowed her head and said a short prayer for her food. Kathi dug into her pancakes.

Jess had grabbed food throughout the day, so he wasn't really that hungry. He noticed an older woman sitting in a nearby booth. She looked so familiar. "Where did he know her from?" he thought. Suddenly, it came to him, it was a woman he had interviewed when he was doing his 'Man on the Street' interviews in New York City. She had given him the "heebie jeebies" (having no better term for it.) What was her name? He thought hard and mentally went through the alphabet "A, B, C, M, Martha. That was her name. So weird she would be here also." Suddenly, Kathi got his attention.

"Jess, I have waited all day to tell you something important. I got saved this morning!" Kathi exclaimed. Jess's mind shifted gears. "What?! How did that happen? Jess asked, knowing this was a huge deal for someone so invested in Science." "When Pastor Scott was our guest, I just got this overwhelming feeling that I needed to get right. I asked him to speak to me privately after the interview and told him I wanted to get saved. Of course, he wanted to share with me how to get saved. He shared with me scriptures in the Book of Romans and the Book of John. He prayed with me, and I accepted Jesus as my Savior. A major burden was lifted from my heart. I have been thinking about this since we visited his church in Atlanta. The Holy Ghost has been tugging at my heart, and I am so blessed to have the opportunity to talk to Pastor Scott today. My first thought after getting saved was, I can't wait to tell Jess."

Jess had tears streaming down his face. "Kathi, that makes me so happy! I can't think of anything that would make me any happier. This is an answer to prayer." Jess knew that God had made a way for him to find the right woman. He had been so intensely focused on what Kathi had told him that he forgot about Martha. A few minutes passed and he looked over where Martha had been sitting, and she was gone. Strange.

"Kathi, we will celebrate this when you have all of this Miracle launch business finished. I want to do something exceptional." "Jess, I was thinking about this too. I thought maybe we could meet in Atlanta for a few days. I would like to tell my parents and my sister in person. I know they will also be happy for me. I want to get baptized by Pastor Scott at the Atlantic Berea Baptist church. I am pretty sure that he would do that." "Kathi, that is a great idea. I love it! We will do that as soon as we can. Just say when, and I will be there. Today was a totally amazing day. I love you so much!" Jess said as he beamed.

Chapter 25

T here was a soft knock at the door. "Sir, you have an interview at 9:00 a.m. Would you like anything special for breakfast?" John Stafford said. "Stafford, I will take an egg white omelet, wheat toast, and grapefruit slices. Coffee will be fine. I am getting in the shower," the President replied. Few people knew the President as intimately as John Stafford. Sometimes, Stafford believed he knew President McIntosh better than his wife. He had worked for McIntosh for the past 18 years. McIntosh had fired him nearly a dozen times, but he never really meant it. He couldn't manage without John Stafford. John was his voice of reason and he had given his life lurking in the shadows so George could be in the spotlight.

Stafford ordered the President's breakfast and laid out his clothes. He had prepared briefings on the top headlines in the news today and the questions that the interviewers were going to ask. Today, the U.S. makes history, and McIntosh wanted to be as well-known for the Miracle Space launch as the astronauts themselves. Kennedy had managed to remain known for the Race to the Moon and the first moon launch under his leadership, and McIntosh wanted nothing less.

The procession of black vehicles headed to the temporary studio on the grounds of Kennedy Space Center. "Time for a name change. McIntosh Space Center has a nice ring to it," he thought. "Great idea staying in Airforce One, Stafford." "If that was a compliment, I will take it, Sir," Stafford said with a straight face. "Already, traffic is backed up for miles. People everywhere are anticipating the most monumental event since the birth of Christ maybe even bigger," President McIntosh said. When they arrived at NASA, the Secret Service security detail surrounded the President and walked him into the outdoor studio. "Hair and make-up this way," the Producer's Assistant said as he led the way. Just a quick touchup. Warren and Kathi were already on the show set and had been discussing various facts about the Miracle Launch for a couple of hours.

"Good morning, Mr. President. You will be seated here," the Producer said. President McIntosh took his seat and was greeted by Warren and Kathi. The Secret Service detail surrounded the set and were watching every movement very closely. President McIntosh didn't seem to even notice they were there. "We are thankful to have you here with us this morning, Mr. President. Is there anything special that you would like to talk about this morning?" Kathi asked. "No, I was briefed on the questions you have prepared. I think we will be fine," President McIntosh answered, "I wouldn't want the interview to look too rehearsed." "Ready on the set in 30 seconds," the Producer yelled.

"We have a very special guest this morning, President George McIntosh. Welcome, Sir," Warren said nervously. "Thank you, Warren; it is great being here with you and Kathi on this beautiful Florida morning," the President replied. "Mr. President, we watched you and the First Lady in the Miracle Parade in Orlando yesterday. I am sure that the Parade committee was honored to have such a distinguished Marshall of the parade," Kathi said. "I was honored to be in the parade. I am not usually able to attend events like parades, but this was such an extraordinary event that my security went to a lot of trouble to make it happen. Mrs. McIntosh felt like a Disney Princess," he chuckled.

"Mr. President, did you think that NASA and SpaceX were going to meet the end of the year deadline to launch a mission to Maye Moon?" Warren asked. "Absolutely, I had no doubt. We have the greatest space program in the world. Once again, we won the race. When the Maye Moon appeared, I reached out to NASA and said, 'I will supply the money; you supply the brains and brawn. Let's get it done for the world,'" the President boasted. "I was thrilled that SpaceX decided to partner with NASA, so we had the most brilliant minds in Astroscience working together on the project." "Yes, I would agree that we have exceptional Space

Science and Astrobiology geniuses working together. I was thrilled to be a small part of that," Kathi replied with a little smirky smile. ("Stop it, Kathi," she thought. "This arrogant man doesn't know that Astroscience is the study of Astrology.")

"What are you hoping they will accomplish on this Mission?" Warren asked. "I am hoping that we find resources that will benefit the whole world. Unlike our U.S. Ambassador Natalie Steubens, I believe that Maye Moon will need the leadership and monetary resources of the greatest nation in the world to manage those resources. I am proposing that Maye Moon becomes a territory of the United States," President McIntosh said. Warren and Kathi both dropped their jaws and were speechless. "Now, he has gone and done it," John Stafford unconsciously said aloud.

"I have spoken with some important scientists who believe that Maye Moon may have many natural resources on it that can be of great benefit to us. Since the appearance of the Maye Moon, our solar recovery of energy has gone up 25%. Did you notice that the terrible COVID-19 virus disappeared? I am hoping that Maye Moon will help the Earth with the problem of Climate Change and renew our atmosphere completely. I believe it is already happening," the President continued. Kathi was finally able to breath. "I have also seen some very promising statistics of air quality improvement. But do you really think it is possible or wise for the United States to claim Maye Moon for ourselves? I just do not know how that could happen," Kathi said. "I know, Kathi, it may seem far-reaching, but the United States is the most benevolent country in the world. It just makes sense that we would control and distribute the resources as we determine each country's need," President McIntosh said with an evil smile.

"What if the rest of the world does not go along with it?" Warren asked. "I think the other World Leaders have no choice but to go along with it for the good of the world. They would not want to enter into a war over it," President McIntosh continued. "A war? Mr. President, have you fully thought of the ramifications? Just suggesting this could bring on a war that would defeat all of the world peace that has happened since Maye Moon appeared," Kathi stated with concern and disbelief. The Producer cut to a break. "Kathi, we need to tread carefully. Pull yourself together. He is the President of the United States," Kathi's producer said in her earpiece.

"Mr. President, may we pivot to talking about the celebrations that are happening across the country today. For both of our sakes, we need to get off of the U.S. territory topic," Kathi soberly said. "Kathi, you have helped me to break this news to the people of the world. Every newsperson wants a 'breaking news story' of this magnitude. You and Warren got very lucky today." Kathi walked off of the set. The Secret Service watched very closely to see what she was going to do. She walked over to a trash can and began vomiting profusely. "Warren, I think you are going to have to finish this interview on your own," the producer said in his earpiece.

"Mr. President, where will you be watching the launch today," Warren asked. "I will be in the Mission Command Center. Best seat in the house," the President replied. "I would like to thank you for coming today to speak to us. I know you have a busy schedule, and we are honored to have you. This is a day that will go down in history," Warren said. "You are right about that, Warren; we are making history today," the President answered. Little did President McIntosh know that a motion would be made in the House of Representatives later today calling for his impeachment on the grounds of diminished mental capacity and high crimes and misdemeanors.

Chapter 26

Kathi pulled herself together and returned to the set. The show had switched the LIVE feed to the NASA control center and was listening to the preparation of the rocket for take off. Kathi and Warren broke in occasionally to explain in layman's terms what the command center was talking about. Everything seemed to be going as planned, and the weather was 100% favorable. The anticipation was building. The astronauts had entered the spaceship, and the fueling had begun. It was estimated that the rocket would reach Maye Moon in three days, two hours, and fifteen minutes since it was further in distance than the Moon.

"This rocket will travel faster than any rocket has ever traveled. There are only twenty minutes until the countdown begins. It is estimated that 8 million spectators have gathered here on the Space Coast to witness this Miracle Launch. People all over the world are glued to their televisions, computers, and phones to see this stream LIVE," Warren said. "After months of careful preparation, the day has finally arrived," Kathi added. "If you were one of the astronauts sitting in the spaceship, what would you be thinking right now?" Warren asked Kathi. "I would be praying that the Mission is successful and that I would return to my family and friends. I would pray that I was able to make a positive impact on the world for mankind," she answered as a tear dropped from her eye. "I am sorry. It is hard not to be emotional," she said, looking into the camera. "That is what we all love about you, Kathi—you are real."

The final fueling began at the two-minute mark. Suddenly, the command center began the countdown—10, 9, 8, 7, 6, 5, 4, 3, 2, 1 takeoff.

A loud rumble drowned out everything, and the ground began to shake like an earthquake. A bright, fiery light rose up in the sky. The Miracle had successfully lifted off! People were cheering, and the sound was deafening. Kathi had been present for a lot of rocket launches, but none were as powerful and loud as this and never had such a crowd of people cheered so loudly. It was so exciting to be a part of that. The Command Center scientists and engineers were going crazy, too! Streamers were dropped, and everyone was hugging, crying, and high-fiving each other. The beautiful blue cloudless sky provided the perfect backdrop for the rocket to be seen for hundreds of miles. Kathi and Warren continued to view the Command Center, and a split screen showed the rocket climbing up in the atmosphere. A voice from NASA explained what was happening as the rocket continued to rise.

The Appearance of Maye Moon

"I have goose bumps and chills! I have never witnessed such a perfect launch, Warren. And I have watched at least a hundred launches from Cape Canaveral. The weather couldn't be better for a launch," Kathi said. "NASA.gov will provide a LIVE webcam feed that you can watch what is happening during this Mission the entire time," Kathi said. "I am sure millions of people across the world will be watching," Warren added. "This group of astronauts are now American heroes." "Warren and I will be turning the show over to Lorraine Maxwell, who is the COO of SpaceX. She will be able to tell you about the important part that SpaceX played in today's launch. We will be joining you back later this afternoon."

Kathi walked over to Jess and nearly fell into his arms. "Let's find someplace private," she whispered. "Sure, babe," he replied. Kathi knew of an employee picnic table about a five-minute walk away. Fortunately, no one was around. She began to cry. Her emotions were strained and at a breaking point. "Jess, you should have seen the evil in that man's eyes," she said. "What, man?" he e asked. "The President. President McIntosh. It was pure evil," she answered. "Hey, the man seemed crazy, but I could see some of his points..." Jess said, looking surprised. "No, no, no, Jess. You can't own Maye Moon. It is a natural satellite in space. Next, he will be claiming the moon, Mars, and the rest of the universe. It is not possible. He thinks he is God or greater than God if he believes at all," Kathi exclaimed. "I had a horrible sick feeling in the pit of my stomach just sitting near him. He is wicked and immoral. He must be stopped."

"Elon Musk tweeted out that the man was insane. Millions of people are tweeting the same thing. I really doubt if he has any support on this issue. Lots of people are claiming he is a narcissist," Jess told her. "I think you should calm down, and we will see what happens. God is in control." "You're right, Jess. It is scary having someone like that in his position. You know what to say to make me feel better," Kathi answered.

The couple walked to the studio food tent and picked out some sandwiches and fruit and found a table to sit at. "I was amazed at how loud the launch was and how it made the ground shake," Jess said. "I forgot this is your first launch to see at Cape Kennedy. This rocket is the most powerful one launched up to this point. It was really loud. Normally, I would be in the Command Center during a launch. That is very exciting in itself," Kathi explained. "I would walk you over there, but with the President in the Command Center, there will be extra security, and I might not even get in." "That's okay. I am just enjoying spending this time with you before you go back on set," Jess smiled and gently kissed her forehead. "I can imagine that the people that are in the Command Center are loathing that he is in there and taking turns throwing rotton tomatoes at him," she said with a smile. Jess laughed until he cried. "Oh my gosh, I can picture that!" Jess said after catching his breath. "Maybe Elon will show up and kick him out on his keister." "We can dream," Kathi said with a smile. The two finished their lunch and walked over and sat closer to a big screen TV that was set up in the food tent.

The program was set to show the inner cockpit with the astronauts in their seats traveling toward the Maye Moon. Occasionally, you would hear the conversation between the astronauts as they talked about what they were seeing or system controls within the cockpit. As they watched, Kathi noticed there was a fifth person in the cockpit. He was not wearing a spacesuit but a long, white flowing robe. "Jess, are you seeing what I am seeing?" She asked. "What are you seeing, Kathi?" he responded. "I am counting five people in the cockpit. There are only supposed to be four." "That is what I am seeing too. You would think that everyone would be going crazy over this! Do you think they can see the 5th man?" Jess asked. "Surely they can. The astronauts don't seem to notice him either," Kathi said, looking puzzled. Kathi's phone buzzed, and she looked to see who was calling. It was Tessie. "Kathi, did you see Jesus? Jesus is in the cockpit. Not everyone can see Him, but Earl and I can see him. Can you?" Tessie excitedly exclaimed. "Tessie, I am with Jess, and we can see Him also. Do you know why this is happening?" Kathi asked. "Not really, but it is part of His plan," Tessie answered. "We will find out in His time. Praise the Lord! Earl wants to say something."

"Hi Kathi, I want to read a short scripture to you from Daniel 3:23; 23-25 (KJV).

23 And these three men, Shadrach, Meshach, and Abednego, fell down bound into the midst of the burning fiery furnace. 24 Then Nebuchadnezzar the king was astonied, and rose up in haste, *and* spake, and said unto his counselors, Did not we cast three men bound into the midst of the fire? They answered and said unto the king, True, O king. 25 He answered and said, Lo, I see four men loose, walking in the midst of the fire, and they have no hurt; and the form of the fourth is like the Son of God.

I was reminded of this when I saw Jesus in the cockpit. The Son of God is going on the Miracle Mission," Earl exclaimed. "I wonder who else is able to see this?" In his excitement, Earl just hung up the phone without saying goodbye. "I guess we aren't the only two that are crazy," Jess laughed. "Seriously, I wonder why we have been chosen to witness this?" Jess said. "I have to get back on the set. I wonder if God wants me to tell the world that I see Jesus in the cockpit?" Kathi asked Jess. "Boy, I don't know Kathi. I guess I would wait for a clearer sign that He wants you to tank your career and be hauled off to the looney bin. Don't worry; I have your back and will help you escape," Jess smiled.

They walked back to the set, holding hands and silent. Both of them were thinking about what they had seen in the cockpit. "I'll be over here the whole time, babe," Jess said softly. "That makes me feel better," Kathi replied. "I hope I am strong enough to do God's will." They shared a kiss before she walked away.

"So you and Jess Wanamaker are a couple?" Warren asked. "Yes, we have been seeing each other for a few months," Kathi answered. "I saw him over on the sidelines and wondered how he got in, now I know. I guess he is an okay guy, but I really wouldn't have thought he is your type," Warren said. "My type?" Kathi frowned. "Yeah, you know, I would have thought you would have been interested in someone smarter and better looking, kinda like me," Warren smiled. "No, Jess is exactly my type. I love his sense of humor and playfulness. He is warm and kind, and I happen to think he is very handsome. He is very smart, but he doesn't try to impress people with his intelligence," Kathi replied. "Ouch," Warren said.

The producer told them to get in their places, and they continued showing footage of the Miracle launch. She could tell by peoples' faces that no one could see the 5th passenger. She and Warren continued to do short interviews with those people responsible for the Launch. They also were able to speak with the astronauts and hear what the experience had meant to them. She and

Warren went off the air at 6:00 p.m., and a regular host from SNN took over.

"How about we pick up some dinner down at the beach this evening? It is getting dark around 7:30, and we can watch the moon and Maye Moon rise. It is a full Harvest moon," Jess suggested. "That is a wonderful idea. We can stop by my place and pick up a couple of beach chairs," Kathi replied. They left quickly and arrived at the beach in a nick of time to see the moon rise first. It was a huge orange ball that slowly peeked up over the horizon. Within a few short minutes, the Maye Moon ascended up over the horizon, shining with a glorious blue-green glow. "It is hard to believe that four astronauts are only a day away from landing on that beautiful glowing ball of wonder," Kathi surmised. "Did you notice how both moons dance around the ocean, making beautiful shadows in the waves? The ocean is one of my favorite places to be. I have to return to New York City the day after tomorrow to the non-stop noise and the hustle and bustle of the city. I wish this moment could last forever," Jess said, gazing into Kathi's eyes. They sat there for nearly an hour, holding hands and saying very little. They were just happy, enjoying the peacefulness of their time together.

Kathi suddenly said, "Jess, there is something I've been meaning to speak to you about." He looked at her with concern in his eyes. "Jess, I am not a perfect angel. I have had relationships with guys that ended up intimate. I want you to know that. I am so happy that you have never pressured me to have a sexual relationship. I haven't been in any relationship for quite a while now. I decided that when the special man came along, I wanted to wait until we were married so that it would be special. I know I can't go backward and be a virgin, but I can go forward and be celibate until marriage. I believe that is what God wants me to do." "Kathi, I feel the same way. When I was younger, I also was active sexually, and the girls didn't mean anything to me. It was just a way to prove to myself that I was cool. I haven't been with anyone for over three years and planned to wait until marriage. I am really glad we had this talk and that we are on the same page," Jess agreed as they embraced.

Jess then said, "Maybe we should go and get dinner. Is there any place that you like on the beach?" "The Boardwalk is supposed to be good," Kathi replied. "The Boardwalk it is," Jess said and helped Kathi out of her beach chair and carried the chairs back to the car. "Kathi, you are the most beautiful woman in the world, inside and out."

Chapter 27

Today is the landing of the Miracle Mission on Maye Moon. Kathi is so happy because she is ready to return to the lab at NASA, and this puts her one step closer to doing that. She fixed a pop-tart, made a cup of coffee, and sat down at the kitchen table and read a devotion. Kathi pulled on some sweats and a t-shirt and headed to the SNN set. On the way there, she talked to God and prayed for the safety of the astronauts as they landed on Maye Moon. She also prayed that everything she said today would be pleasing to God and honor Him.

As she pulled into her parking spot, she saw Warren, and he waited for her to walk with her. "Were you talking to yourself in your car, Kathi?" Warren teased. "No, Warren, I talked to God. We had a wonderful conversation all the way from home," she answered. Warren laughed, and then he saw by the look on Kathi's face that she was serious. "Warren, I am a Christian, and a lot of my beliefs have changed. I am a new Christian, so I am still learning a lot, but I no longer believe in the Big Bang Theory and Evolution and believe that God was the creator of everything. Maye Moon got me thinking a lot about it and it really makes a lot more sense than the Big Bang is responsible for Maye Moon appearing," Kathi told him. She felt like a big weight had been lifted off of her chest.

"Wow…I sensed something was different with you. I would have never guessed that you joined the 'other side' though," Warren responded. "I still am a Science geek, but I believe God is the creator of all things, and we can study to find out how He made everything so perfect," Kathi said with a smile. "But this changes everything. Kathi, your career will be in jeopardy if this gets out," Warren warned. "I am not going to be ashamed of my faith and of God, Warren. I think Maye Moon has caused a lot of people to question what they believe. Haven't you wondered why Maye Moon suddenly appeared out of nowhere?" Kathi asked. "Hey, we better get to wardrobe and makeup, or our audience is going to see the real Kathi Calloway," he quickly changed the subject.

They went to their separate dressing rooms and got ready for their last show together. Warren couldn't stop thinking about what Kathi had told him. "How could someone so intelligent and gifted in Science believe such a fairy tale?" He questioned everything he knew about Kathi. "The Space community would disown her if they found out. It could be death by association for me, too," Warren thought as he made his way to the set.

Kathi could see by Warren's face that everything had changed between them. He couldn't make eye contact with her and was aloof. "I hope he can put on a good act for the camera," Kathi thought. The Director called, "Ready on the set," and suddenly, they were on LIVE television. Warren put on his television persona as she had hoped.

Suddenly, Breaking News interrupted the show, and a Special News Political reporter explained that the House of Representatives had just voted to approve Impeachment proceedings and would be holding a hearing to impeach President George McIntosh. The Special Report showed footage of President McIntosh's interview on Warren and Kathi's show and cited that President McIntosh was planning to make Maye Moon a U.S. territory. President McIntosh had shared a plan to bypass Congress and, thus, put the United States at a security risk by inciting war. Many in congress questioned McIntosh's mental capacity to continue his presidency.

When the show returned back to Warren and Kathi, Warren asked "Kathi, what do you think of the President's proposal to make Maye Moon a U.S. territory?" "Warren, I think that it is very irresponsible of the President to think that the U.S. should control any moon or planet beyond Earth. If there are natural resources on Maye Moon that would be beneficial to our planet, the cost of transporting them back to Earth would be ultraexpensive. If his thought is that man can inhabit Maye Moon in the future, well we don't know what Maye Moon's atmosphere is like yet for sure. If it was possible, then there are lots of potential problems that would have to be considered and I believe that it would be decades away."

"I totally agree, Kathi. There are theories being discussed in the Science community that the world is underpopulated due to low birth rates. Is there a need for starting sustainable communities on Maye Moon or even Mars?" he asked. "Warren, I know that NASA and SpaceX have both been working on space habitats, but it is a plan that is decades away. So many scientific questions would need to be answered first. Let's check in with NASA and Space X with some live coverage of the Maye Mission."

The space craft had been traveling at incredible speeds toward Maye Moon, and the landing was expected at 10:07 a.m., just three hours away. There was a lot of excitement in the Control room as the time neared. Kathi could still see the 5th man in the space capsule. He appeared to be standing in the corner observing the other astronauts. She could tell they were not aware of His presence.

NASA reported that the Miracle spaceship had already entered Maye Moon's atmosphere. This seemed peculiar to Warren and Kathi because our Moon has a much denser atmosphere than Earth. The Earth's atmosphere reaches as much as 10,000 kilometers above the Earth, which would indicate that Maye Moon has a greater atmosphere than the planet Earth. The gravity pull was also greater than Earth, and the space ship had to adjust for this. The astronauts are reporting that an extremely high oxygen content has been present for most of the trip compared to previous missions to the Moon. "Interesting. How can this be?" Kathi thought.

As the spaceship neared the surface of Maye Moon, the astronauts reported that they were looking for a place to land the ship that was level and clear, and they were having trouble finding such an area. Suddenly, an area appeared out of nowhere. "Maye Moon has landed!" the four astronauts shouted together.

Many tests would have to be conducted before anyone could leave the space ship. The Command Center asked the astronauts what is their initial impression of the surface of Maye Moon. Bob Hutchinson, Lead Command, answered, "NASA, it is covered with trees. Huge, full-grown trees! Trees are everywhere! The outside temperature is 60 degrees Fahrenheit. I can't tell what kind of trees these are, but they are very tall, like the giant redwoods in California. We will begin our testing to tell you more information soon."

Warren looked at Kathi as if to say—Explain that. Kathi whispered, "How can that be? If Maye Moon just appeared out of nowhere, it couldn't have been created from the Big Bang, could it?" Warren slowly shook his head no. "Maybe there is life on Maye Moon. If there are trees, it is possible," Warren whispered back. The two of them were in a state of shock. The NASA Command Center was quiet for once. This defied Science!

The SNN Network decided to cut the show and play some earlier guest interviews. The Directors were dumbfounded and weren't sure what to say about this new discovery. Kathi and Warren could not continue their show because they were both in a state of shock and weren't sure what to say when there was no explanation. "Report to the set tomorrow morning when we have had time to think how this strange phenomenon could be," the producers told them. "We will continue the show on LIVE NASA feed."

Kathi walked over to Jess and told him she was free to go. Jess was supposed to board a later flight back to New York, so she was feeling blessed to have the extra time with him, but she knew that they would be discussing this discovery during their precious time together. She hoped that Jess could help her make sense of this.

Jess, on the other hand, was all smiles and giddy. "Kathi, don't you see. God just provided proof that Maye Moon was His miracle. Maybe millions of unbelievers will turn from their wickedness and accept Jesus as their Savior. People say all the time—We need revival. We need a miracle. I think it is safe to say that Maye Moon is that miracle. I am sure that others have seen Jesus in the cockpit. Maybe those who have seen Him are there to be witnesses to others?" "Jess, why don't you telephone Pastor Scott and ask him if he has seen the 5th passenger on the Miracle and whether he thinks it is Jesus or an angel? Maybe he can explain why we can see Him and why others can't," Kathi suggested. "Yes, that is a great idea. I am anxious to hear if he knows what is going on," Jess agreed. "I think I should make the call someplace more private so I can put it on speaker phone."

"We can go back to my place after we finish eating," Kathi said. Jess had not spent much time at Kathi's home because they both have been careful about putting themselves in situations that could compromise their decision to remain celibate. It was best not to put themselves in temptation's way. "Okay, but I need to go back to my hotel by 5:00 p.m. to pack and prepare for my flight. I really hate leaving Kathi. It has been a great week being at Cape Canaveral and watching the space launch with you an experience of a lifetime. I love you and will miss you so much."

Kathi's home overlooked the Indian River and was on a canal. It was very modern and fresh looking with beautiful views. There was a beautiful lanai overlooking a pool and boat dock. It really didn't stand out in the posh neighborhood where she lived. The inside of the home was so tidy that it looked like nobody lived there. "If she saw my place, she would think that I am a hot mess," Jess thought. "Just bachelor life," he mused.

Jess dialed Pastor Scott's personal number on his cell.

"Pastor Scott, this is Jess Wanamaker."

"Hi, how are you doing, Jess?" he replied.

"Pastor, I am here with Kathi Calloway down here at Coco Beach. I am going to put you on speaker. We wanted to talk to you about something pretty unexplainable," Jess said.

"You see Him too? Isn't it amazing! I have had very few people call me who can see Him, but the calls have come mainly from missionaries from all over the world. Kathi can also see Him? That is interesting. So you called wanting to know what is going on?"

"Well, yes, I was hoping that you could explain this. We haven't heard anyone say anything about it on the news. You know Kathi would have an inside track on that, but nothing," Jess replied.

"I have been waiting to get a message from God to tell me what I am supposed to say or do, but I have had a feeling that it isn't quite yet the time. Those who have called me have not said anything to anyone except to me. I guess they have had similar feelings that God will instruct. You have probably thought about the three Hebrew men thrown in the fiery furnace and did not burn up. Jesus showed up and protected them. Maybe the Miracle space ship and astronauts went through some distress and needed God's protection. I do not know this to be a fact, but that is one scenario that I thought about. I think it is more than that, though," Pastor Scott stated.

"Pastor Scott, this is Kathi. I think I would have heard something from my fellow scientists at NASA if that were the case. They keep me in the loop about what is going on because I am returning soon to be the Chief Scientist. This has just been a special assignment until the Miracle I returns to Earth," she explained.

"So maybe this event hasn't happened yet. Or maybe it is something entirely different. Hmm, I will think about this. Have you heard of any others that see the 5th man?"

"Just an elderly couple we met when we visited your church. Their names are Earl and Tessie. I don't even know their last names, but we ran into them down here also, and Earl called Kathi and told her. They are a very kind old couple who have encouraged Kathi and I. They were chosen to be interviewed on Kathi's show by coincidence," Jess explained.

"I have found there are no coincidences in God's work," Pastor Scott chuckled. "I do not think that we are the Witnesses mentioned in the Book of Revelation, but I am still pondering on that theory. The timing just isn't right. Maybe we will be called to be witnesses in different ways, though. There is no way for me to know how many people are able to see the 5th man. I do not call the man Jesus because He has not identified himself as such. It could be an angel sent by God," Pastor Scott explained.

"Could you please let me know if you receive any instruction on what to do? I will let you know if we find anything interesting or helpful also," Jess said.

"Of course, Jess. Let's pray for God's guidance on this matter." Pastor Scott replied.

The phone call ended, and Jess and Kathi had little time left before having to say goodbye. "I really wish I could stay longer, but my producer is blowing my phone up with messages that I better be at work tomorrow. The show must go on!" Jess smiled. "I understand Jess. I have a lot on my plate, and you have been so patient. I will get a break in a month or two and maybe I can come to New York for a few days vacation. My Mom will want me at home for Thanksgiving, and if you are free, you are welcome to join our family," Kathi said. "I will definitely see what I can do. Maybe we can see if Pastor Scott will baptize you that weekend, that is, if you want that," Jess said. "Yes, I definitely do! I am so glad that it is important to you, too. I can't believe how much I have changed in just a few weeks. God has opened my eyes to so many things," Kathi said with a serious look on her face.

It was time for Jess to go, and they walked to the door. They embraced for a long hug and kiss, and a single wet tear fell from Kathi's eye. "Let me know, Jess, that you made it home ok. Call me so I can hear your voice. I don't care what time it is." "I will, Kathi, no matter what time. You get some rest. I know you need it." They kissed one more time, and he walked to his car.

Chapter 28

"**D**oes anyone mind if I pray for our Maye Moon walk before we exit the spaceship?" Ben Jones asked. Only three astronauts would be making the first moon walk: Bob Hutchinson, Cora Collins, and Ben. Larry Lowe would be monitoring the controls and making sure everything was going well. If there is any emergency, he will be the one to fix it. "I think that is a wonderful idea," Larry said. "We need all the luck we can get." "We need God's providence, not luck. We really don't know what we are facing," Cora replied. Ben prayed for guidance and safety for the group, and the three astronauts triple-checked everything before exiting the spaceship.

Immediately, Larry started getting data on the atmosphere on the moon. "This is interesting; the atmosphere has an extremely high oxygen content. It would not be safe for us to breathe on our own." "These trees are amazing. I don't think there is anything like it on Earth. They are huge. Tons of green and blue-green foliage. I am sure that is why there is such a high content of oxygen. They are nearly everywhere," Ben answered.

"Do you see any signs of animal or human life?" Larry asked.

"No, not yet," Ben answered.

The three astronauts planted the American flag onto the surface just outside of their ship. "As our predecessor Neil Armstrong said, 'That is a small step for man, a giant step for mankind,'" Bob stated. Cora secretively placed a small gold cross onto the pole.

"The gravity is about the same as Earth. What are the humidity readings?" Bob asked. "It appears that there is a lot of humidity. I would hypothesize it is caused by a lot of foliage like in the Tropics," Larry answered. "Yes, it appears the trees are receiving their water from underneath the ground," Bob answered. "This is like a woodland paradise. Perfect-looking trees that are not touched by insects and humans," Cora said.

"Is the surface rocky like the moon?" Larry asked.

"No, not really. We will take some soil samples." The soil sample was a deep, dark black color and looked like it was very rich. The lush green grasses covered the soil. "It really is beautiful. We will be venturing further from the ship to see what else we can find," Bob answered.

The Appearance of Maye Moon

As the three moved away from the ship, they came upon another species of tree that was in a clearing. This tree was fruit bearing, unlike any other tree that was on Earth that they were aware of. The fruit looked delicious. "I do not know if we should touch that tree," Cora said. "Remember what happened to Adam and Eve when they took the fruit from the garden?"

"Oh, that story. Is there a good scientific reason for not taking the fruit?" Bob asked.

"Maybe the fruit is poisonous," Cora answered.

"The lab will take the correct precautions; don't worry," Bob answered as he plucked a piece of fruit off of the tree. The fruit was bagged, and they continued on. "We could call this area the Garden of Eden if you like, Cora," Larry Lowe said through her headphones. "I think that is a great idea," Ben answered.

As the three astronauts navigated their way around, they picked up a few rocks, but there really were not a lot of rocks in sight. "This surface is so different from the Moon, which is mainly dust. So far there has not been any evidence of bodies of water, just the moisture in the atmosphere," Bob stated. "I was hoping we could do a little fishing while we were here," Bob chuckled.

Larry said, "I believe I know why the planet has a bluish-green color. I believe there is aero phytoplankton in the air. Aerophytoplankton are microscopic plants that float in the air. The high humidity waters these plants as they float out to space through the atmosphere. The astronauts continued their exploration for the next 45 minutes, describing what they were observing along the way."

The three returned to The Miracle because they had gotten close to their oxygen time limit. "That was amazing!" exclaimed Ben. Cora repeated, "Amazing. It's like everything I worked so hard for all came true in one amazing hour." "I just don't think anyone could imagine this unless they experienced it themselves," Bob added. "I am going to have to process this all in my head to understand it. You know this changes what we have believed about the Big Bang Theory our whole lives. Full grown trees, grass, plants everywhere in this short of time; it just doesn't seem possible. The whole world is going to expect an explanation of this when we go LIVE. We will need to have an explanation for them. I am going to tell NASA that we are going to need tonight to rest and reflect. No sound to the outside world." "I agree," Larry said. "Going over these readings is going to take some time and reflection, too. They just don't jive."

"Be sure and secure your samples appropriately," Bob instructed. "Hey Bob, this is crazy. The fruit that we gathered from that tree in the clearing is nothing but liquid. No seeds whatsoever. No pulp," Ben said with shock in his voice. "That is crazy. We will try again tomorrow to grab another one. Maybe we will find another tree like that when we head in the other direction," Bob answered.

"Tomorrow is a new day. More exploration and fun, kids. Get your rest and be ready to share your thoughts in the morning," Flight Commander Bob told the group. "I have got to shut down for a while. See you at 6 A.M. Cape Canaveral time." The astronauts followed Bob's directions. Each was happy for a little quiet time to think about the mission and the things they observed on Maye Moon. Bob was right. NASA and the Scientific community would want details, and they would have to be very careful what they said.

After the spacewalk, the internet blew up with all kinds of conspiracy theories and lies. One story claimed that the astronauts were eaten alive by an alien. Another claimed they were being held hostage by space aliens. Warren and Kathi did their best to dispel all of these evil rumors, but much to their dismay, they did not have a lot of information to share with their audience. They watched the team wander around Maye Moon's surface, but it was definitely strange and unlike anything they had ever imagined.

Tomorrow arrived, and the team excitedly suited up to explore Maye Moon some more. "Be sure to pick up samples of everything you find so we can test this moon and find out as much as possible," Bob instructed. The team exited the ship and walked in a different direction than the previous day. They immediately came upon a forest filled with a different species of very tall, evergreen-like trees. "Still no sign of any life other than trees. I wonder if the Earth was that way when it was created and before man could contaminate it with our bacteria?" Larry surmised. "Interesting thought," Bob replied as Larry gathered some specimens.

"Let's dig down and get some deeper soil samples," Bob instructed. Cora got down on her knees, which was really difficult in her spacesuit, and was able to go down approximately 3'. She gathered the samples and found, visually, that the soil looked very rich, like the soil that you would find on Earth. "No creepy crawlers," she reported.

"You know what is missing?" Ben asked.

"Decayed wood of any kind. It's just like these trees were placed here fully grown. The air quality would indicate that they are producing an abundance of oxygen and getting their necessary carbon dioxide from underground," Larry said through the headset.

The group continued to move further away from the ship, but did not find anything that was new or different. "Let's each get a soil sample from different locations and then we better head back," Bob said.

"I'll take over here at the root of the tree," Cora answered.

The Appearance of Maye Moon

They each got their samples and began the journey back to the spaceship.

"We will eat, rest, and go back out in 3 hours. Tomorrow will be our last chance to explore and gather. I am hoping we find something new and different," Bob stated. The team followed his direction, and each picked out their nutritiously, scientifically prepared, freeze-dried meal by NASA. They settled back in their chairs for some much-needed rest.

The time came to explore more of the surface of the Maye Moon. "Let's head south this time. Maybe we will find some new genus of trees or ground foliage," Bob said. The team had not traveled far until they reached a forest of different species of trees. These trees were more of a blue-green color. They had large elephant ear-like leaves on them and were as tall as the other trees. Again, there was no evidence of dead leaves anywhere. The team gathered the specimens and moved on. Smaller plants surrounded the trees with thorns on them. The wood was a bluish color. "Very beautiful," Cora said with amazement. As they moved on, they came to a vast area covered with even taller and larger evergreen-like trees. When they explored the forest they did not find any needles on the forest floor. "It is like these trees do not shed their needles. Interesting," Ben said to his fellow explorers.

"Bob, if Maye Moon was created by the Big Bang, how do we explain all of these huge trees on its surface?" Ben asked.

"We can't. I don't know what to make of it. It defies all we have ever believed," Bob answered. "I guess we wait and find out what NASA wants us to believe."

The three astronauts moved forward and found the surface of Maye Moon to be flat in most places. The ground was soggy, and the soil was a rich dark black. "Let's turn around and return to the ship. I definitely don't want our oxygen to run out. I think we have seen enough for today. Tomorrow, we will complete our last two walks outside, and tomorrow night, our ship will make its return flight. I am open to suggestions about what to explore tomorrow." The light from the moon was making the planet Earth glow an eerie, shadowy glow by the time they got back to the ship. "Now that is a beautiful sight," Ben said. They did not have to take pictures like in the old Apollo days. Each helmet was equipped with a forward and backward camera on the helmet. NASA would go through the footage with a fine-tooth comb, looking to see if the astronauts missed anything important. NASA may have instructions on what they want the astronauts to explore tomorrow. Bob knew tomorrow's outing would be his last chance to discover anything new on Maye Moon's surface.

The Appearance of Maye Moon

The team picked out their specially prepared NASA dinners and returned to their seats to engage and eat their meal together. "These are really not too bad. I picked the Cheeseburger and fries with a chocolate shake. I mean, it's not McDonalds, but it is edible," Larry said. "I am thankful that we have not had any major problems on this mission." "Hey, there is still tomorrow," Ben laughed. "Does it feel like you thought it would feel out there?" "I would say it feels lonely and destitute. Although the trees are very beautiful, it is kinda spooky to know there are no people there. I can't stop asking myself, how can this be?"

"Bob, where do you think Maye Moon came from?" Larry asked.

"I thought about that question a lot. I don't know; maybe it traveled through a Black Hole and landed here. Nothing makes sense. It has made me realize what little we know about our own solar system, let alone the rest of the universe," Bob answered.

"Yeah, never in a million years did I think a moon could just appear out of nowhere. And come to find out, it is covered with full-grown trees and foliage. It goes against logic," Larry stated.

"I am going to bed, men. I need all the beauty sleep I can get for the finale tomorrow. I am going to predict we will find something really earth-shattering out there tomorrow. I just feel it," Cora said.

"I hope you are right, Cora. Good night," Ben said. Cora switched her overhead light off, and the room became a little darker. The others decided to follow suit and hit the hay also. The inner capsule became quiet, and each one quickly fell asleep in their bunks. Goodnight, Maye Moon.

Chapter 29

NASA Command interrupted the astronauts' sleep with a cheery 'Good morning, crew.' "I feel like I just closed my eyes," Cora said. "Eat some breakfast and prepare for our first walk of the day. We will be exiting the ship in one-half hour," Bob Hutchinson commanded. "We want to make the most of our time here." "I hope we find some form of life other than plant life today," Ben said. "Maybe some little green people with big eyes." "Not me; I would show you all how fast I can run with all of my gear on," Cora laughed. Cora enjoyed a package of space pop tarts for her breakfast and a bottle of water. Larry, Bob, and Ben all had pancakes and space bacon. "Not so bad. I've had worse at home." Larry said.

The three astronauts put on their suits and gear and prepared to explore Maye Moon once again. "I would really like to go back to the area we called Garden of Eden again. I have put some formaldehyde in a specimen bag and would like to try to preserve a piece of the fruit from the tree," Cora said. "It is worth a try,"

Commander Bob answered. "We will head there first."

The group exited the ship and headed toward the clearing that was called The Garden of Eden. As they stood in the middle of the clearing, Ben wondered aloud, "This area is so different from the rest that we have explored. I wonder what caused it to be this way. It is like nothing else will grow here except this one tree." "I know. It is like it is showcasing this one type of tree. We need a soil sample also. Definitely a mystery for the lab at NASA," Bob replied.

"Alert team. The monitors have detected movement in the woods to your left," Larry cautioned. The team members quickly turned to the left to see what would have set off the monitors. Suddenly, a man in a glowing white frock came out of the woods about 100 yards away and started walking towards them. He was tan, with shoulder-length brown hair and a short beard. He was handsome and masculine but had very gentle eyes. A beautiful white aura seemed to outline his body. As he approached, he called out, "Do not be alarmed. I come in peace." It was like he spoke to them in their headset and he was speaking English. "I think I am going to pass out," Cora said with such fright in her voice. "Cora, I would never harm you. Breathe deeply," the man replied.

Bob and Ben were prepared to battle and protect if need be. "I am sorry I scared you. I came along on your Mission to help make sure that everything went well," the man said as he approached the group. "What do you mean you came on our Mission?" the commander asked. "I rode along in the spaceship. Wow, such a journey with an amazing view," he smiled. "There is no way you could have been on that spaceship with us. We would have detected you," Bob exclaimed. "Actually, some of my disciples watched the entire time from Earth. They were not sure of my plan, but they had faith that there was a good reason for it," the man answered. "Larry, are you getting this?" "Yes, Commander," Larry answered dutifully.

"Sir, what is your name, and where are you from?" Bob inquired. "I am. But I have been called many names. I am from here," he said as he opened his arms to the heavens. Cora immediately knew who was standing before them and fell to her knees. "You can call me Jesus," he said with a smile. Bob and Ben saw how Cora reacted and fell to their knees, too. "Friends, sons and daughters, you have been chosen for an important Mission from God, the Father. Please stand," Jesus said.

"God loves you and the people of Earth so very much and wants to improve the conditions that are sickening the Earth. Man has corrupted the Earth's water, air, and soil with many pollutants that are making people and animals sick. People have become greedy and will do anything for the almighty dollar. What has been meant for good is now evil. The problem is so heinous that I don't think it can be solved by man alone. God placed this moon here to help clean up the environment of Earth by producing fresh oxygen and a secondary night light source. Mans' minds have been poisoned, and they need to get back to God. Many have surrendered and accepted me as their Savior by the Appearance of Maye Moon, but it is not enough, and they forget so quickly."

"By placing the moon far from Earth, we are hoping that its resources will not be disturbed for the pockets of the greedy. Man has believed in Science over the Heavenly Father, and this generation of children is not being taught about God at all. This moon appeared out of nothing and was spoken into existence, just as the Earth was in the beginning. Man is so busy developing theories to disprove there is a God and prove they are greater than God. This turns their hearts evil and cold. This is the work of Satan. This message must be brought back to Earth to turn men's hearts back to God. Otherwise, mankind will destroy themselves.

A group of disciples on Earth witnessed me in the capsule on the way here. They will help you spread the Good News. A revival will ensue if you all get the message out. It is not time for the End of Times yet." The group of astronauts had been standing there listening in awe. Cora spoke first, "Not my will but thine will, Lord." The men said, "Yes, Lord," in unison.

"Cora, this tree is a Tree of Life. It is for the healing of the Earth. No matter how many times you would pick its fruit, it would immediately die. I will pick the fruit for you, and it will live. Do not allow anyone to eat it, or it will make them sick. It is also for the healing of the Earth," Jesus said. Jesus reached up and picked a fruit off of the tree and handed it to Cora. "Thank you, Lord," Cora replied. "Science has its place to see how things work and create new, improved methods of doing things, but it should not replace God in man's hearts," Jesus explained.

"There are many false prophets and churches out there, and God will punish them. The disciples that were chosen are examples of what is pleasing to the Lord. If man would abide by the 10 Commandments brought down from the mountain by Moses, man would be so much better off. Love is the greatest commandment of all.

"You have to admit, Maye Moon is a beautiful place, a wonderful addition to the Lord's handiwork in the sky. You will encounter haters and enemies in your Science community, but stick together and endure. They cannot prove you wrong.

"Bob, do you trust me?" Jesus asked. "I don't know you," Bob answered quickly without thinking. "That is a truthful answer, Bob.

You have not wanted to be a part of organized religion. You have made Science your God. On occasion, you have declared you are an atheist. Christianity is about a personal relationship with a Savior. The only way to heaven is to trust in me. It is very simple, Bob. If you trust me, take off your helmet now. I will protect you from the atmosphere that could kill you," Jesus requested. "I don't know…I am afraid," Bob said with tears. "Bob, I am here on Maye Moon with you. You do not think I am a ghost or live here on Maye Moon. Trust your logic," Jesus said as he held out his hand. Bob slowly unfastened his airtight helmet and removed it with care. He was astonished that he could breathe without it. "Oh Jesus, I am so sorry I haven't trusted in you before. I was foolish, but please be my Savior now and forever," Bob said with tears streaming down his face. "It is done, Bob," Jesus answered.

"Ben and Cora. Although you have trusted me and accepted me as your Lord and Savior as children, you kept me well hidden in your heart and pulled me out when things got tough and you needed me. Your friends and colleagues don't suspect that you are Christians. You have bought into the lie about the Earth being millions of years old. You have bought into the lie that the universe was created by a Big Bang. You need to let your light shine to all you meet. Let them see Me through you. Remember, if you are ashamed of me, I will be ashamed of you. I need you to step up and lead this Mission, which is more important than any mission you have ever been on. Satan has devoured many poor souls. Earth has become a place worse than Sodom and Gomorrah. Heaven's angels will be fighting right along with you against the evil that has permeated this world," Jesus said directly. "I repent, Lord," Cora said with tears streaming down her face. "Me too, Lord, I repent, and you can count on me," Ben said with his head hung low. "All is forgiven, and my mercy is sufficient," Jesus answered lovingly.

"Larry, dear Larry. You have researched the religions of the world and gathered parts of each that you like and created your own religion that allows everything you want in life. Many others pick and choose what they want to follow. Larry, you need to accept me as your Savior if you ever want to enter the gates of heaven." "Jesus, I will follow you, and you alone, Lord. Please, Jesus, be my Savior and save my soul." "It is done, Larry."

"When you return to Earth and have completed the 21-day quarantine period, contact Kathi Calloway and go and speak to her. She will arrange for you to tell the world about the Good News, that the Father is healing the Earth in a telecast. Explain that the water and air will be cleaner, the food of the Earth more nutritious, and the weather better. Warn the people that I have told you that the minds and hearts of the people need to be cleaned also. This is the hard part because it involves free will, and people will have to give up a lot of worldly pleasures. Remember to explain that this is not the End of Times. This is a restart, a chance at a better beginning for all. Satan will try to detour you every step of the way. Listen to the Holy Spirit, for He will guide you down the right path and help you answer any questions. I love you, my children. It is time to go back to the spaceship and prepare for your return to Earth. I will be with you the whole way, and you have nothing to fear; however, you will not see me. Be strong and of good courage," and with that said, Jesus walked away.

The astronauts returned to the ship and removed their gear and space suits. It was so quiet in the capsule you could have heard a pin drop. They were all in shock from the event. Finally, Larry broke the silence and said, "Are we having a group hallucination?" "Larry, If you had been out there, you would have known that we stood in the presence of God. We are chosen," Bob answered. "Most people trust that he is Jesus, the Savior, without any proof at all. We have seen Him, spoke to Him, on the Maye Moon, which appeared out of nowhere, and we still have trouble believing?" "Sorry, Bob, you are right. This is just so unbelievable, but I vowed to follow Jesus, and I plan to do that," Larry answered. "Let's get everything ready for take-off and be prepared. I want to meditate and pray and seek God's plan on the trip home," Bob replied. The others nodded.

NASA had been watching and broadcasting the entire time, but Jesus did not appear in the footage, nor did the audio work the entire time.

Chapter 30

Kathi and Warren had to improvise a lot over the last three days because the footage of the Space walks had malfunctioned. The sound hadn't worked, and frankly it was pretty boring without being able to hear what was being said and what was really going on. Off-camera, Kathi said, "This is really strange because they check the equipment so many times before taking off, and they use the best audio-visual systems that are available." "Maybe some space junk hit the ship and knocked it out. I am sure we will find out when the astronauts return to Earth," Warren surmised.

"Just three days of traveling back to Earth and this Mission will be over. People have returned to their mundane lives and schedules and virtually forgot about the Miracle Mission. Even the mystery and excitement over Maye Moon has practically vanished," Kathi sighed. "I agree, Kathi. The internet has made this world so fast-paced that nothing surprises us nor gets our attention for long," Warren said. Both of them were very tired from the extreme overtime and stress of covering the Miracle Mission. "It is very tiring trying to sound excited and interested every minute of broadcasting," Warren added.

Jess telephoned Kathi when she got off of work and told her that Pastor Scott had called him and wanted to speak to them. "Can you meet me in Atlanta for a short trip?" Jess asked. "You know I really want to, Jess, but I can't leave for a few weeks. Maybe for Thanksgiving, if I am lucky," she replied. "I really wish I could. I am exhausted and could really use a vacation and a home-cooked meal from Mom, no matter how short." "Yeah, I am pretty busy at work at Fox, too. How about if I arrange a 3-way visual conference call? I will call Pastor Scott and arrange a time tomorrow evening," Jess said. "That's a great idea. I should be home by 6:30," Kathi replied. "I will text you and tell you the time. I miss you, Kathi. Get your rest, dear," Jess said tenderly.

Pastor Scott agreed to meet with Jess and Kathi through a conference call the next day. Jess was able to make the call, and the three were able to see each other while conversing. "I understand why you are so busy right now, but I felt this couldn't wait. The Lord led me to make this call and to explain to you what is happening. The Lord chose to reveal Himself during the Miracle Mission to at least 300 people as well as I can tell. It is a delicate situation because I do not want to influence people to claim they saw Jesus, who really didn't. I believe we need to have a vetting process and then give the person access to a very secure website where they communicate with other witnesses. Each person needs to agree to secrecy until we receive instructions from the Lord on how to proceed. We know that there is a purpose for Maye Moon, the Miracle Mission, and being one of the chosen to be able to see Jesus on board, I am sure this has something to do with it," Pastor Scott explained. "Yes, I feel you are definitely right. Maybe we will have some answers when the spaceship arrives back to Earth. Maybe the astronauts found something on the surface that explains what is going on," Jess agreed. "I will find out what I can and report it back to both of you. Hopefully, it is something I can do without breaking any rules of classification," Kathi said. "We do not want you to breach confidentiality or lose your job. God would not put you into this position to lose your job," Pastor Scott said. "The first step will be to find a computer whiz who can create the website that we need. This must be a person chosen by the Lord. He or she will have witnessed Jesus in the cockpit," Pastor Scott continued. "Let's pray."

As they ended the conference call, the trio agreed to conference again tomorrow night. Jess and Kathi continued their conversation after Pastor Scott hung up. "I only know Tessie and Earl have seen Jesus in the cockpit. I would think that Pastor Scott is more likely to be approached by someone than I am," Kathi said. "I know, I feel that way too. I have a feeling that God will make this come together for his glory somehow very soon," Jess responded. "I am so lucky to have met a man that wants to put God first in his life," Kathi thought. **"This was not luck, Kathi."** A male voice replied to Kathi in her head. This shook Kathi up. "Did God, Jesus, or the Holy Spirit just speak telepathically to me?" Kathi thought. "Did you just hear a man on the telephone, Jess?" Kathi asked. "No, I am the only one here, Kathi," he replied.

As the world watched, the Miracle Mission crew landed off the shore of the Treasure Coast. Interest peaked again, as everyone was anxious to hear about the astronauts' news about Maye Moon. The four-person crew was whisked off to NASA to have medical exams and then enter a period of isolation. Each of the crew members would be poked and prodded by doctors and interviewed by psychologists and scientists. The group agreed on board that none of them would say a word about their Jesus experience before speaking with Kathi Calloway. It was difficult to talk about even amongst themselves. Bob, as crew leader, emerged as the leader of the new Mission they were about to embark on. Because Cora Collins knew Kathi better than the others, it was decided that she would be the first to speak to Kathi about Jesus. It would be several days before she would probably get the chance to talk to Kathi though, because of being in ed isolation.

Jess, Kathi, and Pastor Scott connected again the next evening by conference call. "Pastor Scott, how many people have confided in you that they saw Jesus onboard the Miracle?" Kathi asked. "I have compiled a list so far of 84 people. I came up with the number 300 when the Holy Spirit spoke to my heart. I haven't ever reached out to anyone; these 84 people called me about seeing Jesus in the cockpit," Pastor Scott explained. "I have also had a man contact me and say that he thinks that Jesus wants him to help me on a website." "That is exciting!" Jess exclaimed. Kathi agreed with enthusiasm. "I think we should make your church the headquarters we work from. Would that be ok with you Pastor Scott?" "I think we have a small building on campus that would do the trick," he answered. "I will have it cleaned and set up. I have some extra computers we can use from our school. I want to get this computer guy started right away," Pastor Scott continued. "We will talk again tomorrow night. Have a great evening!"

Meanwhile, at NASA, the Maye Moon astronauts were going through the process of quarantining and readjusting to the Earth's atmosphere. The Maye Moon landing in the ocean was similar to a car crash, and each of them bounced about quite a bit even though they were buckled in. The astronauts were then whisked to a medical facility where they were checked from head to toe. Being weightless, for even ten days, in space wreaks havoc on the body. The astronauts tend to lose muscle mass due to their weightlessness. Also, returning astronauts have a lot of eye issues due to the change in pressure. Medical doctors and physical therapists worked with the team to try to make sure they had no lasting effects on their bodies.

Imagine seeing Jesus and talking to Him on a moon that appeared out of nowhere less than a year ago. Psychologists will examine and interview each astronaut to make sure that there are no psychological problems from being encapsulated on the space mission for so long. The group made a pact not to discuss any of the details of speaking to Jesus when speaking to the doctors. "If we mention it to anyone, we may never leave the quarantine area and may have a free ride to a looney bin," Bob told them. "Funny but true," replied Larry. "Boy, am I looking forward to some real food," Ben said. "Just think a big, juicy cheeseburger with all of the fixins and some french fries will taste like heaven." They all laughed. The crew had been on a very regimented diet before going to space to prepare their body for the trip. "Yeah, count me in for a steak and baked potato," Bob sighed. "I kinda like the diet they have had us on," laughed Cora. The whole quarantine process takes ten days if everything is okay. Before the group can return to the outside world they must get the approval of the NASA Chief Medical Examiner.

Kathi stopped by the grocery to pick up a few things on the way home from work. While waiting in line, she read the magazine covers and saw something startling. On the cover of the *Probe* gossip rag was the headline, "Stowaway in the Maye Moon Rocket Capsule." "Oh my gosh," she thought. She picked up the copy and put it with her things. As soon as she got in her car she opened it up to read it. The story said that an unidentified source saw a man lurking in the shadows of the cockpit while watching Miracle I travel to Maye Moon. "I wonder if this person is one of the 300 chosen people or did _Probe_ just make the story up?" Kathi decided to try to contact the writer to try to get the name of his source.

During the conference call that evening Kathi shared with Pastor Scott and Jess about the _Probe_ cover story. "I had quite a few calls today claiming that they saw the man in the cockpit, and several mentioned the _Probe_. I am sure people would believe that it was a ghost before believing that the Son of God could ride along on the Mission. I guess in a way I understand that," Pastor Scott replied. "We are up to 115 names of people that witnessed His appearance now.

"I interviewed the Computer Coder today, and I believe that this is the person God wants on our team. His name is Aaron Campbell, and he is a believer. He attends church at a Bible believing church and wants to serve the Lord. He is only 23 years old and lives with his parents here in Atlanta. Up to this point, he has not told anyone else that he saw Jesus onboard the Miracle. If we are all agreeable, I plan to get him started right away." "That sounds super," Jess exclaimed. "I really planned to talk to Kathi first, but the timing just seems right," Jess said. "God has laid it on my heart to move to Atlanta, where I can work on this with you. I would like to talk to Fox and see if I can go back to my old gig and do a weekend segment talking and interviewing real people around Atlanta. I can do this part-time on the weekends and find a cheap place to live," Jess explained. "If God wants you to do that, then you must do that," Kathi declared. "Jess, I can help out with a place to stay. We have an empty apartment on campus that a professor used to use before he retired and left Atlanta. It's not fancy, but it is in good shape," Pastor Scott said. "Oh wow, that would be great. I will start the ball rolling here," Jess answered.

The next day, Kathi googled the *Probe* writer's name, Billy Lewis. It was in the *Probe* article, and I found a phone number for him in the magazine. Surprisingly, he was not hard to locate. "Hello, my name is Kathi Calloway, and I am calling about your story in *Probe* about the stowaway onboard the Miracle. I was wondering if you could share with me who your source was on that story." "Kathi Calloway, I know that name. Kathi, you probably know when we write a story we promise anonymity to our sources. Why would you want to know who the source is anyway?" "Well," Kathi thought fast. "I am doing some work for SNN still about the Miracle Mission and I thought the person might want to come on the Winston Warren show." "I see. I don't know Kathi. The person who spoke to me seemed to imply that he wanted to remain anonymous. I guess I could contact him and ask if he would be interested. What would be in it for him?" Billy Lewis asked. "I can't offer any money because

SNN does not pay our sources, but I can offer a television platform to get his story out to a larger audience," Kathi explained. "Can I call you back in a couple of days, Kathi, and give me some time to ask him?" "Oh yeah, that would be great, Mr. Lewis. Timing is everything. Would 48 hours give you enough time?" Kathi said with a determined tone. "Okay, Kathi, 48 hours. I will call and let you know," Billy replied.

After a couple of hours, Kathi's telephone rang. "Kathi, this is Billy Lewis calling you back. I need to confess something to you, Kathi. I thought it over and over. I found myself wondering why a person like you would be interested in a *Probe* story when you have such a prestigious job. I came to the conclusion you must have seen Jesus too. Kathi, I was the one who saw the stowaway on board, but I did not want to say that it was Jesus. I did not want to admit that the anonymous source was me either."

"Off the record, Billy, yes, I saw Him too. No, on the record. If we are ashamed of Him, He will be ashamed of us. Are you a Christian, Billy?" Kathi asked. "Yes, I would have to say so. My mama took me to church for the first 15 years of my life. I got saved, baptized, read my Bible, and never missed church; however, when I turned 16, I got a part-time job and left the church, and never looked back. The guilt is tremendous, and I don't feel worthy of going back to church. I have done some pretty shady things throughout my life." "I understand, Billy. I did not get saved until recently. I denied Jesus is the Savior and was convinced that Science was the only truth," Kathi replied. "God is long-suffering, and His grace is sufficient. Billy, my boyfriend Jess, and I are working with Pastor Scott Morales, the pastor of Atlanta Berea Baptist, and compiling a list of people who saw Jesus in the cockpit of the Miracle. We are going to set up a very private network to be able to talk to one another. We are convinced that Jesus showed around 300 people that He was on this Mission. We haven't figured out the details yet but we are determined to carry out what He wants us to do. Maybe your story in the *Probe* will help bring some of those people forward."

"Wow, Kathi, it is so great to know that I am not crazy. I really feared that something was wrong with me. I decided to write a vague, anonymous story to see if there were any others," Billy said. "Hey, it worked. I saw it and wondered if it was someone like us. At the last count there were almost 90 people who saw Jesus. Where do you work from, Billy?" Kathi asked. "I can work from home, and right now, home is Atlanta," Billy replied. "The Lord works in mysterious ways, Billy. Make a call to Pastor Scott. We need you onboard," Kathi told him.

Chapter 31

K athi arrived at her office at NASA and was anxious to return to her job as NASA Chief Scientist. Her secretary handed her a message that said that the Miracle team of astronauts were requesting her presence at the quarantine facility. She thanked her secretary and told her that she was heading over there now. She was very excited to speak to them personally about the Mission. The lab had already begun to run the tests on the specimens they gathered during the Maye Moon walk. Now is the fun part!

Kathi had to enter the area wearing protective gear so as not to contaminate anything. She was used to wearing these HAZMAT suits in the lab when they were running tests, so she was quite comfortable. The astronauts all looked thrilled to see her and were all smiling huge smiles at her. Cora approached her and whispered, "Follow me into the ladies' room, Kathi." Cora then exited the room and headed towards the ladies' room in the corner. Kathi followed as requested.

Cora looked like the cat who swallowed the canary—she had a secret she was dying to share. "Kathi, this is big. Really big. We are afraid to discuss anything in the common room because they are watching and listening. They won't understand." "Who's they?" Kathi asked. "NASA, the medical staff who are assigned to watch us. They will label us crazy, insane, unbalanced, delusional. They may never let us out of here. But He was there. He really was there. We all saw Him and spoke to Him. He spoke to us."

"Cora, back up and start from the beginning. Tell me what you are talking about," Kathi replied. She had thoughts that something was medically wrong with Cora, the way she was acting. "Right… yeah, right. I will start from the beginning. It was Day 3, and Bob, Ben, and I were going back to an area that we named the Garden of Eden. We named it the Garden of Eden because it had one large beautiful tree in a clearing, and the tree produced fruit. We wanted a piece of the fruit for experimentation. The surface of Maye Moon was covered with large, full-grown trees. Everywhere. Everywhere except this one area that had an open clearing with a fruit tree. I had picked a piece of the fruit on a previous surface walk, but the fruit immediately turned to mush. I had filled a container with some formaldehyde to try to preserve it that way. So we returned to the Garden of Eden."

"Okay, that sounds like a reasonable method. But I am still stuck on the full-grown trees. How could the surface be covered with trees when it just appeared in May? That is not logical," Kathi said with a puzzled look. "No, it is not logical in Science terms. Nothing about Maye Moon is logical, Kathi. Suddenly, Larry told us that an alarm went off in the capsule, and something was approaching. Of course, we were expecting some animal or creature to exit the woods, and we feared we might be killed by it. I mean, some crazy thoughts drove like a freight train through my mind. I knew we were too far from the Miracle spaceship to get away." "You must have been scared to pieces," Kathi affirmed.

"We were all afraid. Terrified. Suddenly, we see a human man come walking out of the woods. He is wearing a glowing white smock and has brown shoulder-length hair and a beard. He kinda waves and looks friendly. He continues across the clearing and calls over to us to not be afraid. Of course, we are afraid. I am surprised that none of us passed out. We were so afraid. He told us that He came along on the journey to make sure that everything went okay on the mission. We soon realized that this man was Jesus," Cora said as calmly as she could.

"Of course, that makes sense," Kathi replied like it was something that happened every day. "I wasn't sure you would believe me," Cora said with surprise. "Cora, when you and your team were traveling to Maye Moon, we watched. I saw a fifth passenger who rode with you all the way there. He stood in the corner and protectively watched over you all. Most people did not see it, but I and approximately 300 believers from across the world did see Him. I recognized Him as Jesus, but I wasn't sure why He was there."

"Jesus told us that He gave the Miracle Maye Moon to Earth to heal it. I believe it is a 2nd chance for people in the world to do a better job. The oxygen levels were extremely high on Maye Moon, and some of that oxygen made its way to Earth. Since the appearance of Maye Moon, the quality of air on Earth has improved. So has the water quality, COVID disappeared, and farmers have had record-breaking food production. Jesus wants to heal the Earth but also wants the nations to heal their minds and hearts. Jesus wants you, Kathi, to carry this message to people with our help."

"Jesus actually told you to tell me to do it?" Kathi said with amazement. "Kathi, He told us that we were to contact you and you would arrange a telecast to give the message to the world," Cora answered. "We want to all talk to you, but we knew we couldn't while in here. I am sure the guys are wondering what is going on in here. We better leave the restroom before the NASA squad comes in to make sure I am alright."

"I will hang around awhile so that everything seems normal. Jess and I are working with Pastor Scott from Atlanta on a project so people who witnessed Jesus can communicate on a secure website. We will arrange to meet before everyone returns to their homes. I am so glad you contacted me," Kathi said. "One other thing, Kathi. Jesus said to assure everyone that this is not the Tribulation period," Cora explained. "The crew 'all got right' with the Lord. We intend to actively help in any way we can. We are not worried about our careers. We just want to serve the Lord." "Amen, sister," Kathi replied as they left the protection of the restroom.

"Gentlemen, I heard a little about the trip to Maye Moon from Cora. Sounds like an exciting trip. Tell me about the surface of the moon. Sounds like it is much different from what we would expect, especially if you compared it to our other moon," Kathi proceeded. "Yes, Kathi. We were shocked to see these huge trees and luscious plant life covering them. We collected samples of everything we could within a reasonable distance from the ship," Bob explained. "It was beautiful," added Ben. "Thankfully, we did not have any problems at all. One warning light went off during the Day 3 walk, but it did not turn out to be anything. We did have some audio issues, but it did not affect us on the Mission," Larry added.

"It is my understanding that the lab has already begun to process the specimens and have begun their testing. I will be going there to join them right after leaving here. Can we all meet again after your quarantine period ends? It will be a short meeting before you all head out to spend some time with your families. I promise not to keep you very long," Kathi asked. "We definitely want to hear your updates, Kathi," Bob answered. "Great. I will contact you with the details. Welcome home!" Kathi replied.

Kathi couldn't wait for her daily evening conference call with Pastor Scott and Jess. She headed to the lab to see what was going on and how the testing was going. Some of the testing had involved the astronauts' physical health and she was pleased to find out that they were healthier than when they left Earth. The medical staff were baffled by it because returning astronauts normally have some lasting effects from being weightless in space. Kathi wasn't surprised at all. After all, these astronauts have been given a mission from God!

Kathi looked over the leaves that had been collected from the trees on Maye Moon. All of the leaves were unlike any here on Earth. "Have you found anything unusual about the leaves?" she asked the lab techs working with the leaves. The leader of the group answered and said, "We have found the leaves to emit unusually high levels of oxygen; in fact, over 1000 times more than trees here on Earth. That would definitely account for the high oxygen levels on the surface of Maye Moon. These leaves would allow burn patients to heal at a very rapid rate of speed." Kathi shook her head in agreement.

Kathi stopped and talked to the technician who was examining the fruit from the Garden of Eden area of Maye Moon.

"Let me remind you that a piece of fruit is very poisonous to humans, and you must be extremely careful with it. It was the only piece, and others became rotten almost immediately when picked," Kathi warned. "Yes, mam, we are being extremely careful," the tech answered.

Kathi left the area and made her way to her office. "Home Sweet Home," she thought. She really was tired of the Space reporter gig. "I am a lab girl," she thought. Her 'In' basket was stacked with mail awaiting her review. This will take the rest of the day. A big bouquet of roses sat on her desk. The card read, "Welcome back, Sweetheart, love Jess." "He really is the most thoughtful man alive," she thought. "And handsome." Finally, after a long, crazy day of getting back into the routine of everything, she left to go home.

On her way home, Kathi began to speak to Jesus and tell Him how thankful she was for the wonderful things in her life: her salvation, her family, her career, and the love of her life. She felt so close to Jesus and couldn't praise Him enough. She told Him she would gladly turn her life over to Him to be used however He could see fit. She was aware that this Mission she was a part of was going to bring some life-changing events in her life and she was ready to do what she was called to do.

Chapter 32

Kathi excitedly answered the conference call with Jess and Pastor Scott. "Hello, wait until you hear what I have to tell you tonight!" Kathi gushed. "I have some pretty big news to share, too," Jess replied. "Who gets to go first?" Pastor Scott asked. "Kathi, girls go first," Jess laughed. "Thank you, my love. Well, I went down to the quarantine area to speak with Astronaut Cora Collins and she hurried me into the ladies' room where we could get some privacy. There, she told me that on the third day of exploring and gathering specimens to be tested an alarm went off in the ship. Larry warned them that something was approaching. A man walked towards them out of the woods. He told them not to be afraid. As he got closer, they could see His glowing white garment, and he had shoulder-length brown hair and a beard. It was Jesus. Cora said that He explained that the team would have a special job to do and they were to contact me when they got out of quarantine. Cora couldn't wait any longer, so she had me come to them. There is more to the story, but I have to wait until they get out of quarantine and we can meet someplace where NASA isn't listening in. Right now, they are being watched 24/7 for signs of mental health and body health issues."

"I guess my news isn't so big," Jess responded. "Oh my Lord, this is amazing. What I would have given to be one of those astronauts. Jesus is awesome! I just knew He had a special plan when Maye Moon appeared. We are blessed! We are so blessed!" Pastor Scott was praising Jesus and shouting Hallelujah! "We are almost finished with the secure website. Maybe tomorrow if all goes right. My list of people who saw Jesus on board is up to 210. We have people all over the world on the list. They learned about us from word of mouth. I still believe there are others out there," Pastor Jeff continued.

"Jess, what is your big news?" Kathi inquired. "I have the approval from Fox to move to Atlanta. I will be working out of the local Fox Network studio. I have also requested to cut my work week down to Thursday through Saturday. That will give me Sunday thru Wednesday to help Pastor Scott and the website and whatever else needs to be done," Jess explained. "That is awesome, Jess! I have the apartment ready for you. When do you plan on moving in?" Pastor Scott asked. "If it is alright with you, I will come in on Monday," he answered. "That is super! This has been a telemeeting that I will never forget. God is so good!" Pastor Scott exclaimed. "Oh Jess, I am so happy for you. If you need anything, don't forget my parents are there in Atlanta and they will be happy to do anything they can to help you move in," Kathi offered. "I really don't have a lot to move. I am going to store some things in New York until I need them. I am sure I will have to make some meetings in New York and will bring a little to Atlanta as I can." "Let's pray for God's guidance and safety as we continue on this journey," Pastor Scott said and he continued with the prayer. "I will talk to you tomorrow kids, and this has been just awesome!" Kathi and Jess remained on the phone as they normally did.

"Jess, I think I can get away for a three-day weekend next week. I would love to come and see you in Atlanta." "Oh Kathi, that is fantastic news. I have missed you so much. We need some time together. It is hard having a long-distance relationship." "I know Jess. I have been thinking about changing my career path and trying to relocate to Atlanta, too. I have been praying about it. I feel like I am living a lie, working at NASA and supporting the message that 'Life on Earth is millions of years old.' NASA definitely would not support the belief in a 7-Day Creation. I just don't think I can continue the lie." "I would love for us to be in the same city, Kathi, but that is a decision that only you can make. I will support whatever decision that you make, honey," Jess said lovingly. "I will plan to be there next weekend, and maybe I will have a better insight into what God wants me to do." "Sweet dreams, baby. I love you," Jess said. "I love you, Jess, and I can't wait until we are together," she answered back.

The Appearance of Maye Moon

The next morning, Kathi got to her office bright and early. She wanted to get as much work done as she could to get caught up. She sent a memo to her staff that she would be out of town the next Friday through Monday. "That should give them plenty of time to approach me with any questions that they might have," she thought. A lot of the experiments from the Maye Moon mission would take months to complete. The rocket readings were immediately available and showed extremely high levels of oxygen in the atmosphere. The next steps would be to gather data on how that oxygen has been benefitting the Earth already. The lab's hypothesis is that the farmers had a bumper crop year. There had been perfect weather conditions in most areas of the Earth. They must show how Maye Moon has provided this result.

One team was examining how the tides were affected by Maye Moon. Another team was looking at the outputs of solar energy in comparison to before the Maye Moon appeared. Additional Scientists have been hired to conduct the various research projects. A couple of top universities are conducting identical research projects to make sure the studies are conclusive.

Kathi received an email that informed her that the astronauts had concluded their quarantine and had passed their medical examinations with flying colors. "Hallelujah!" she thought. "We can get together at my home," she decided. She messaged Cora and asked her to invite the group to an early afternoon informal tea. She provided the address and left work to pick up a few things for the group. Cora returned her message and stated that the group would be happy to attend before heading to their homes.

Kathi headed home to prepare some snacks, and shortly, there was a knock on the door. She answered and excitedly said, "Come in, come in. It is so wonderful to see you all. Please have a seat." "Kathi, we could hardly wait to get to talk to you. The quarantine is the worst part of going to the moon," Cora exclaimed. "I have been playing our 'Jesus experience' over and over in my mind. I can't wait to start sharing it with everyone," Ben agreed. "We have to get a few things in place before we start sharing, I believe," Kathi answered.

"Captain, will you please start and tell me how the mission went," Kathi asked. "Sure, everything went smoothly on the way to Maye Moon. In fact, it couldn't have gone better. We were prepared, the ship operated the way it was supposed to, and the crew worked like a finely tuned machine together," Bob began. "Were you aware that many people, maybe as many as 300 people, could see Jesus in the cockpit with you as you traveled to Maye Moon?" Kathi asked. "No, I was not. None of the crew could see Him. Looking back, though, I could feel His presence and felt very safe and protected throughout the trip – a strange feeling of peace that I couldn't quite understand," Bob continued.

The Appearance of Maye Moon

"The landing on Maye Moon was so smooth, although there wasn't much clear land. We found the perfect spot and had a perfect landing – God's divine providence. Days 1 and 2 were spent exploring the surface and gathering specimens. Larry and Ben took turns manning the ship and watched our gauge readings to make sure we were safe," Bob explained. "The oxygen in the atmosphere was extremely high...deadly," Larry chimed in. We found many different species of trees and plants but no other life. As we explored we came to a perfect clearing with one tree in it bearing fruit. Cora was going to pick and bag a piece of the fruit, but when she picked the fruit it immediately decomposed. Upon returning to the ship we decided to try to put the fruit into a bag of formaldehyde and try to preserve it that way. That became our objective for the next day," Bob continued. "Did you find any other trees with fruit," Kathi asked. "No, just the one. There weren't many rocks on the surface either. Everything was covered in lush green foliage...pristine condition. We returned to the ship to prepare for the next day," Bob said.

"That morning, the three of us returned back to the clearing to try to get another piece of the fruit. When we were there, just a minute or two, we received a message from Larry that a warning alarm went off that something was approaching us. We were ready to run, fight, or do what we needed to do to survive. Suddenly, a man came walking out of the forest and waved over at us. He was dressed in a glowing white robe and appeared human. He called out, 'Do not be afraid.' We were afraid. How did he get here? Cora was the first to recognize Him as Jesus. He handed her a piece of fruit, and it did not spoil. Jesus knew what was in our hearts. I was called out for making Science my god. He had me remove my helmet, and I did not die from the high oxygen levels. I repented and got saved."

"Ben and Cora were called out for hiding the fact that they were Christians. They both repented and made a promise to change. Larry was called out for being a little of this or that and creating his own religion, but he accepted Jesus as his Savior also."

"Jesus then told us that He created Maye Moon to help clean up the Earth's atmosphere and water. The oxygen on Maye Moon is so great that it can travel to the Earth and help repair it. The weather will improve, and the food will become more nutritious. He said that Earth had become like Sodom and Gomorrah. The evilness is everywhere and must change. Satan has deceived so many people, and Satan must be stopped. The four of us and you, Kathi, must use the media to spread the good news thru a telecast. He said the hard part will be changing peoples' hardened sinful hearts," Bob concluded.

"I am sure that we will be ridiculed, but that doesn't bother me. I have already been considering leaving NASA. I just can't continue to present the lie about the Earth being millions of years old any longer. I believe the Lord was preparing me for this ministry when I spent six months doing interviews and broadcasts. Little did I know His purpose. The job just no longer has the meaning that it once did. Jess and I have teamed with Pastor Scott Morales in Atlanta and are establishing an office that will house a computer system that will be totally impermeable to break into so we can have a safe way of communicating with others who saw Jesus in the cockpit on the way to Maye Moon. Jess has moved there already. He is still working for Fox on a shortened schedule," Kathy explained.

"I love working at NASA, and I love being an astronaut, but I understand why you would want to leave. I do not feel NASA is the enemy. After all, it led us to this information. Maybe I can serve as an inside guy, or maybe I will leave also. I have to think it over and pray about it," Bob said. "Yeah, I agree," Ben said. He had been silent through most of the conversation. "Count me in," Cora said. "I am ready to serve. The training and the mission have worn me down and I am ready for something new. I love Science, but I believe Science and the Holy Bible can coexist, and I want to be a part of that. I want to encourage young people to see Science through new eyes and follow the Word of God."

"I met Jesus on the Maye Moon. Now I must serve Him. That's my mission. How could I go back?" Larry said to the group. "You're right, Larry, how can we go back? Count me in, too," Bob agreed. Ben shook his head, "Yes, count me in. We are the Fabulous Four, and we are sticking together to fight a battle against Satan and bring the world back to God." They all joined hands and shouted, "Hallelujah!" "Wake up, World, we are back from outer space!" Bob shouted. The team raised their hands and shouted "Hallelujah!" once again.

"I would like to begin conference calling you every few days, so be sure and write down the best number for that. I will make a call to Jess to see if we can break our story on Fox News. I will also call Winston Warren and see if we can make an appearance on his show. I want to give you all some time with your families, so would two weeks work?" Kathi asked. They all agreed and a plan was started. "Would you pray for us Bob, and I will let you get home?" Kathi asked, and the group joined hands and bowed their heads. They could all feel the Holy Spirit strongly in the room and were brought to tears of joy that they were chosen for this mission. "I am thankful for God's amazing love and grace for the people of this world. Amen," Cora said at the end. Amen.

Chapter 33

"Hey Jess, I needed to talk to you," Kathi said nervously. "What is it, Hun? You know you can tell me anything," Jess answered. "Well, I have made up my mind. I am leaving NASA to return to Atlanta, where I can be of service to the Lord. I want to help Pastor Scott as much as I possibly can, and the astronaut team and I are going forward with giving interviews about Jesus' message about healing the Earth. I do not want any interference from NASA, and besides that, my heart is just not in it anymore." "Kathi, I think that is wonderful. How soon are you going to quit?" Jess asked. "Tomorrow. After I talk to you I will be calling my parents to make sure they do not mind if I live with them until I get settled into a home. I am going to wait until I see them in person to tell them all about the Maye Mission. The team and I decided to wait two weeks before moving forward so they could spend some time with their families. Cora sounded like she plans to leave NASA also," Kathi continued. "She did?" Jess asked with surprise. "She is single and does not feel tied to any place and she wants to be in Atlanta helping also," Kathi said. "I am sure that she can be of help. This plan is all falling into place," Jess said enthusiastically.

"Jess, do you think Fox would let you break our story? I plan to talk to Warren, but I would feel most comfortable talking to you because you are a Born Again Believer. I have gotten to know Warren pretty well, and although we get along just fine, he is very skeptical." "Kathi, I will try. Fox loves exclusive breaking news stories, but because of the nature of this one, I don't know how they will feel. I will try my best to make it happen," Jess answered cautiously.

"Kathi, I love the fact we will be located in the same city. This is all I could ask for. The apartment that Pastor Scott has loaned me is not that far from your parents. We will spend a lot of time together at the church too. I thank and praise the Lord for all He is doing for us. We are so blessed." "I know. And just think how much He loves the World to try to revive our Earth and our peoples' souls. No greater love exists," Kathi said, all choked up.

"Oh, by the way, I think our new secure communication system will be completed by tomorrow or the next day. I will be reaching out to our Witnesses personally and helping them to get logged in and get started. We will be posting daily messages to encourage and inform," Jess explained. "How exciting! Hallelujah!" Kathi responded. "Jess, I hate to hang up, but I am going to write my Resignation Letter. I expect that they will escort me to Human Resources and have me sign 'No Compete' forms and will clear out my personal things due to the confidential nature of my job. It is a humiliating experience, but I understand why they do it." "I know I don't have to tell you, Kathi, but watch everything you sign. Maybe you should take an attorney with you so that they cannot sue you for speaking about the Mission," Jess advised. "That is really good advice. I will call Pastor Scott and ask him if he knows anyone. I am glad you thought of that," Kathy replied.

"Goodnight, sweetheart. Try not to worry. God has this," Jess said lovingly. "I love you, Jess. Goodnight."

Kathi phoned her mother and father. Her mother answered, "Kathi, it is so good to hear your voice, dear. Are you ok?" "Mom, I couldn't be better. Mom, I have an important question to ask you and Daddy," Kathi said. "What is it, dear? Ask away," her mother replied. "Would you and Daddy mind if I came home to live until I can find a house or apartment there in Atlanta? I have an opportunity to move back to Atlanta, and I have decided that is what I want to do," Kathi questioned. "What! My little girl is moving back home! Of course you can! How soon will you be coming?" her mother exclaimed. "I will be packing some of my things, hiring a realtor, and driving up there by the end of next week, I hope," Kathi replied. "Amen! I will have everything in your old room ready! Any other news you have to tell me?" "Oh, Mother, you are just going to have to wait until I get there so I can tell you the other news in person," Kathi teased. "You know I can't wait…but I will try. I will tell your father. He had a men's prayer group meeting tonight. He will be so excited!" "Mom, I hate to cut it short, but I have to go to work in the morning," Kathi said. "I understand. Sweet dreams, sweetie! I love you," her mother replied. "Love you too, Mama."

Kathi's father, Charlie, got home from the men's prayer meeting soon after they hung up. "I have some wonderful news. Guess what it is?" Kim said with a smile. "Let me see, you baked me an apple pie," Charlie said, licking his lips. "No, even better. I will just tell you because you won't guess in a million years. Kathi is moving home! She is relocating to Atlanta!" "What? What is wrong? Did she lose her job? Is she bankrupt? Is she sick?" he asked quickly. "No, I don't think so. I didn't ask any questions. She sounded very happy. I asked if she had any other news, and she told me I had to wait until she could tell me in person. I think Jess has asked her to get married. That is my guess. I can't wait to go shopping for a wedding dress!" "Kim, that may not be it," Charlie said with concern. "I can dream, can't I?" she said, and with that, she gave him a big kiss!

Chapter 34

K athi picked up her cell phone and called Pastor Scott early in the morning. She was pretty sure that he would be at the church already, and she wanted to talk to him before she went to work and gave them her resignation. "Pastor, this is Kathi," "Good morning, Kathi, is everything alright?" he asked. "Pastor, I wanted to let you know I have decided to leave NASA and join you and Jess in Atlanta. My parents live in Atlanta, so I will be moving in with them until I find a place of my own. I have thought it over and prayed about it, and I think I am making the right decision that God would have me make. I just don't have my heart into my job at NASA now that I am a Christian."

"Kathi, I think that is wonderful news, and we would love to have you here," he answered. "Jess gave me some good advice last night about how it may be advisable to have an attorney present with me when resigning. He was concerned that NASA might make some non-compete clause that could prevent me from carrying out Jesus' instructions—or at least give me a legal headache," she explained. "I think that was very sound advice," Pastor Scott replied. "Do you have a recommendation of someone who would understand the problem and would be safe to explain what happened on Maye Moon?" she asked. "I know just the right person, and it just so happens that he is one of the 300 witnesses. Me! I am an attorney, and my license covers Florida."

"That is amazing. God works everything out for His purpose. Do you have time in your schedule?" Kathi asked. "Yes, but unfortunately, I cannot come until tomorrow morning. But I can be there really early, and we can go in together," Pastor Scott answered. "That sounds wonderful. I think I will call in and tell them I am taking a personal day and take care of some last-minute details around here to prepare for the move," Kathi said. "I think that is a very good idea. Is it possible for you to pick me up at the airport?" Pastor Scott asked. "Of course! Just text me your flight information, and I will pick you up at Arrivals." "Great, I will only be staying a few hours because I need to get back to Atlanta," he explained. "Sounds like a plan. Thank you so much, Pastor Scott, you are a lifesaver," she said. "Jesus is the lifesaver, and I just hope to do His will. I will see you tomorrow morning, Kathi," Pastor Scott stated.

When Kathi got off of the telephone she felt like a thousand pounds had been lifted off of her shoulders. She decided to make the call to her secretary and let her know she wouldn't be in today.

The Appearance of Maye Moon

Early the next morning Kathi was up and waiting early to pick the Pastor up at the airport. She waited patiently in the "call area" and received a text, I am waiting at #10. She immediately drove and picked him up. "Kathi, it is so good to see you!" he greeted her. "Pastor Scott, I appreciate your help so much. You are such a blessing to me," she said with a smile.

Pastor Scott and Kathi chit-chatted the hour-long drive back to Cocoa on the 528 toll and arrived at the NASA Human Resources building just as everyone who worked there was arriving. "I better give them a few minutes to get settled in," Kathi sighed. "As your attorney, I suggest that you let me do the contractual talking for you. A lot of people become immediately defensive when you bring an attorney along." As they walked from the parking lot to the office, Kathi felt her heart pumping like a freight train. "Why am I so nervous?" she thought to herself, "Pray for a good outcome, and she whispered a short prayer for courage and strength."

"Good morning, I am Kathi Calloway." "Everyone at NASA knows who you are, Ms. Calloway," the receptionist replied. "I am here to speak to the HR Vice President," Kathi said, trying to sound pleasant. "Do you have an appointment?" "No, mam, I don't, but I am following protocol. I am tendering my resignation this morning," Kathi replied. "Oh, I see. Please have a seat and I will check to see if she has arrived this morning," the receptionist replied a little coldly. "She is here. I watched her enter the building," Kathi answered. With that, the receptionist gave Kathi a rather dirty look.

After a good 10-minute wait, the receptionist finally told Kathi that she could enter the office on the left. Kathi and Pastor Scott stood to go in, and the receptionist said, "Excuse me, but who might you be?" Pastor Scott reached out his hand to shake, "Hello, I am Scott Morales, and I am Ms. Calloway's attorney." The receptionist turned a little flushed at that.

The VP of HR greeted Kathi with a shrewd smile, "Please come in and have a seat. I was not expecting you this morning." "I know I was not planning to disrupt your morning, but I need to resign from my job here at NASA. I brought along my attorney, Mr. Scott Morales, because I assumed that there would be some paperwork for me to sign and I want to make sure it does not hinder me from discussing non-mechanical details of the Maye Moon Mission." Scott spoke up and stated that Kathi had a Public Relations position during most of the Maye Moon construction and during the actual Mission, and she is seeking to not have her speech limited by NASA.

"I see. What are your plans, Kathi?" Kathi looked over at Pastor Scott, and he nodded yes. "I will be leaving the Space Industry. I plan to enter a ministry position in Atlanta. I may be called to be an expert in the Space field from time to time, and I want to be able to speak freely about my experience at NASA. I do not plan to talk about the mechanics used to build rockets or any 'trade secrets' of how the rocket was built," Kathi answered.

"Did you say ministry? That's a rather odd choice, isn't it? With your Science background and experience, I would not have taken you for one of those people," the VP said rather snootily. "Yes, I am one of those people. If you could please prepare the documents that you want me to sign so my attorney has time to go over it," Kathi replied. "Are you sure this isn't about a promotion or a salary increase?" the VP asked. "Oh, I am sure," Kathi said confidently.

The VP left the office and returned with a small stack of papers. "You understand that it is our policy to have you collect your personal things and be escorted by security off of the property." "I do," Kathi replied. "You and your attorney may use the empty office down the hall and go over all of the documents. Kathi, I want you to know that you will be hard to replace, and NASA will be sorry to see you go," the VP said curtly. "Thank you. I will let you know when we are finished going over things," Kathi answered.

Pastor Scott followed Kathi to the small office area to go over the paperwork. "I am so appreciative and I think it was a smart idea that Jess recommended bringing an attorney along. I will sit quietly so you can focus," Kathi said. "Yes, Jess was right," he answered as he began sorting through the paperwork.

"Most of this is pretty straightforward. However, this paragraph could come back to bite us. I will write an addendum to this and clearly spell out what it should say so we can continue our work. It won't take me long. Hopefully, the VP will agree to change it. We are not asking for much of a change, but it should protect you from a future lawsuit," Pastor Scott suggested. "I already removed all of my personal items from my office when I was doing media appearances, so we will not need to go back there to pick anything up. It is intimidating to have to be escorted around by security, but everyone does not leave here voluntarily," Kathi pointed out. "Oh, I definitely understand. You work with a lot of trade secrets we do not want foreign governments to get a hold of. Kathi, do you want me to take these to the VP?" "No, I don't mind. If she has any questions, I will come and get you," Kathi said very independently.

The VP looked over the addendum and did not think it would be a problem to change. "So Kathi, you say you are entering a ministry. Can you tell me a little about it?" Kathi sat down and explained that she got saved recently and just felt that she couldn't continue with the Evolution theory story that is used to explain the universe. "I see. I have to admit that I have questioned that many times throughout my life. I do believe there is an intelligent design to life, but I can't explain how and why everything is what it is. I decided to just trust the intelligence of the Scientists that gave us the Big Bang Theory," the VP said with a sigh.

"Let me explain the truth to you," Kathi said. She proceeded to tell the VP about Jesus and how to get saved while using her laptop Bible to show her the Salvation verses in the books of Romans and John. "It takes faith, but when you know, you know. The Holy Spirit makes things clear as day to you. Will you pray a prayer with me and become a Christian today? I will stay in touch with you and help you to grow as a Christian," Kathi said. "I would like to, Kathi, but I just don't think I can today. I am just not ready, but I would like for you to send me your messages." Kathi was disappointed because she knew that denying Christ was the one sin that would send a person to hell. "Of course, I will," she said as she hugged the VP. The VP had a stunned look on her face that Kathi would still care after she shut her down.

Kathi returned to Pastor Scott with the corrected documents, and he gave his approval for her to sign them. As promised, the security detail escorted them off of the NASA premises.

"I think we have just enough time to eat some lunch before you drop me off at the airport, if you don't mind, Kathi." "Sounds like a plan to me," Kathi replied. She made a right instead of a left at the airport exit, and they found a restaurant that suited them both. "I am so glad that is over," Kathi said with a sigh. "I appreciate having your support this morning." "I was happy to help. We will be working together on getting God's message to the people, and I know you will help me more in the future," Pastor Scott said with a smile. They chatted over a quick burger and fries. "Pastor Scott is so easy to talk to," Kathi thought. They finished their meal and headed toward the nearby airport. "Just drop me over there," Pastor Scott pointed. "It has been a pleasure, and I will see you when you arrive in Atlanta. Big things are coming, Kathi. I feel God working." "Safe traveling mercies, Pastor," Kathi said as she waved goodbye.

Jess picked up Pastor Scott at the Atlanta airport. "Did everything go okay?" Jess asked. "They had to change a little wording, but the VP accommodated us without any trouble. I think it was wise that I looked the papers over. They may have slipped some other language in the contract if I had not been there. Kathi should be able to appear on talk shows without any legal problems now," Pastor Scott said. "Fox News gave me the green light to interview Kathi and the astronaut team. The big boss will look at the footage and make the final approval, but I believe they will be biting at the bit to break the news first. If you can outline what you think we should cover, please pray about it and give me some guidance," Jess said. "I will spend my evening talking to the Lord about it, Jess. May the Holy Spirit speak to my heart with the answers."

Meanwhile, Kathi returned home and collapsed on the bed. It had been a stressful morning, and she just needed some rest before meeting with her realtor in the late afternoon. Within seconds, she was deep asleep. Kathi had a dream that Jesus was saying, "Well done, my good and faithful servant, Kathi. Leave as soon as possible for Atlanta and continue my work to heal my Kingdom here on earth. Rewards await you in heaven." Kathi awoke suddenly with a jerk. She immediately started to pack her clothes into her car along with the things that she needed to survive.

Next, she telephoned a local moving company and made arrangements for packers to pack the rest of her belongings into pods and ship them to her parent's home in Atlanta. Kathi heard a knock on the door and it was the realtor. Kathi showed her around and was pleasantly surprised at the price the realtor suggested that she list her home for. With the recent growth in the value of housing, her home value has nearly doubled since she bought it six years ago. In fact, the realtor has several buyers looking for such a home. Pleased with this information, Kathi signed and listed her home.

"Mom, this is Kathi. I was wondering if you mind if I come tomorrow? Things have been moving right along, and I plan on leaving tomorrow morning?" "Absolutely, Kathi! We can't wait to see you, dear!" After their chat, she thought, "I am so blessed with the greatest parents ever. I am going to bed after talking to Jess and get an early start in the morning. God, thank you for believing in me. Help me be a faithful servant. I ask for traveling mercies tomorrow as I travel to Atlanta to begin this new journey."

Chapter 35

E arl and Tessie were up early, having their coffee on the deck of their home. The coolness and stillness of the early morning were so peaceful, and they loved starting their morning with a Bible devotion. It is something they have done together for as long as they could remember. They sat quietly, holding hands, and prayed to themselves. They felt even closer to the Lord since seeing Him in the capsule traveling to Maye Moon. Since they both witnessed this miracle, they knew they weren't experiencing a joint delusion or dream.

"Next week is Thanksgiving and Jenny has invited us to dinner and for a visit. We haven't been to Atlanta in a long time, and I would love to go," Tessie sighed. "If you want to go, then we will. You know I would do anything to make you happy, even suffer through the Atlanta traffic," Earl chuckled. "We could start out Monday and take our time." "That would be wonderful, Earl. I love helping Jenny get the meal ready and I would really like to go back to Pastor Scott's church. There is such a sweet, welcoming spirit amongst his people. They are the friendliest church I have ever been to, and it is amazing since they are such a large church," Jenny said with a smile. "I will call Jenny after a bit and let her know we will come."

The two of them decided to go inside and have their light breakfast of toasted English muffins and another cup of coffee. Earl flipped on the TV to Fox News and sat in his recliner to watch the news. Everyone was buzzing about the impeachment of President McIntosh. President McIntosh started out being investigated because he wanted to make Maye Moon a territory of the United States, but his list of offenses has grown rapidly to include money laundering, bribery, selling secrets to the Chinese, and may even include hiring a hitman to take out his wife. The latest newsbreak said that the final Senate hearing trial is underway. "President McIntosh could save everyone some time and money and just resign, but I doubt he will do that. He still claims that Maye Moon should belong to the United States since we will be the first country to visit it. Pretty soon, he will try to move this Earth to a one-world government," Earl surmised. "I don't know if all of the allegations are true, but he is compromising the safety of the country by making us look weak," Tessie agreed.

"We need a godly President, not a President who thinks he is God. God had His reasons to have made McIntosh president. Maybe it was so our country would make the journey to Maye Moon. McIntosh had selfish reasons for doing it, but maybe God had His reasons for doing it," Earl surmised. "God is great and knows all things work together for good. Who are we to question His timing and purpose?" "Amen," Tessie agreed. "I am going in the bedroom and prop up my legs and call our baby girl." "Tell them I love them, and I can't wait to see them," Earl called after her.

The trip to Atlanta was getting harder and harder for Earl to make. He and Tessie loved living in their Florida paradise, but they were getting up in years and could use a hand a lot more often. It was hard for their children to get away and come down and see them. They may have to make the hard decision to move back North to be near one of their children someday soon, but not today.

"I am still not sure why God allowed Tessie and me to see Him in the cockpit heading to Maye Moon. I know He will reveal this in His time, but time is running out, and he won't be here very long," Earl thought.

Chapter 36

K athi was driving down I-75 heading towards Atlanta, singing loudly to the Christian station on the radio. She felt ecstatic about the new opportunities that awaited her in Atlanta. "It seems so funny that a year ago, I was a whole different person. All business. All Science. Not interested in relationships. I couldn't see the need for a Savior in my life. I was so unhappy and didn't even realize it."

Suddenly, the telephone rang over her radio. It was Jess. "Hello, my love. Just calling to see how your trip is going?" he said cheerfully. "I am making pretty good time, and the roads have been pretty good. I am about 6 hours out," she replied. "Great, just be safe. I want you here all in one piece. Call me when you get to your Mom's, and I will come over. I just can't wait to see you, Kathi," he said sweetly. "I know Jess. I have really missed you and can't wait either, but just think, we will both be located in one spot. Soon, we can work on God's Mission together." " Just wait until you hear the progress we have made finding the 300 witnesses. I will let Pastor Scott tell you all about it," Jess added.

"Don't close your eyes, Kathi, but I want to pray for your safety before I hang up," Jess said, and he continued to pray for Kathi and their new ministries. "Thank you, Jess. That means a lot. I love you, and I will call you the minute I reach Mom and Dad's," Kathi replied.

Kathi continued down the highway and felt the presence of the Lord with her, guiding her back to Atlanta.

As Kathi pulled into her parent's driveway, the two of them were there to welcome her back home. "Oh, Kathi, it is so good to have you here. I never dreamed you would leave NASA and return to Atlanta," her mother said with tears in her eyes. Her father was at a loss for words, the big sentimental bear. "I know, Mother, God's plan took over, and here I am. Thank the Lord he saw fit to save me when I was leading others to destruction," Kathi replied. "What? You would never lead anyone to destruction," her mother answered, very shocked. "But I did, Mother. Let's go in, and I will tell you all about it." The three of them carried all of Kathi's luggage into the house and placed it in Kathi's old bedroom.

"I will fix some coffee and get us a snack, and you can tell us your story, Kathi," her mother suggested as they all sat down at the kitchen table. "Okay, it started when I came to visit last. I attended Pastor Scott Morales's church with Jess. I had really gotten away from God and really didn't think about God at all. My life had become Science-based since attending college and working as a Scientist for NASA. Everything in my life was based on Scientific theory and what could be proven by Science. However, as Pastor Scott shared how his life had gotten more about himself and gathering wealth, he shared how, after preaching for many years, he finally got saved."

"What? A preacher who had a huge ministry like him, and he wasn't even saved?" Kathi's father, Charlie, exclaimed. "Yes, he realized it was all for himself, not God," Kathi explained. "It resonated with me. The Holy Spirit spoke to my heart and told me I needed to get saved, also. I was convicted but too afraid to go forward and accept Jesus as my Savior. That is only the beginning. The Holy Spirit started convicting me of helping to spread the lie that the universe was created by a Big Bang, not God. I knew in my heart that there really is no proof of the Big Bang happening, but as an Astro-Scientist, I had just accepted it as fact. It completely dispels that God is the creator of the universe, which would make the Holy Bible a lie. When Warren Winston and I interviewed Pastor Scott, I asked him to lead me to Christ and I got saved. I knew I couldn't help to fuel that lie any longer. That is when I decided to leave NASA."

"Don't you think you could have just kept that to yourself and continued to work there?" her mother asked. "No, Mom. The Bible teaches that if we are ashamed of Jesus, he will be ashamed of us. I just can't be a lukewarm Christian. There is much more to the story." "Let's hear then, girl," Charlie smiled.

"During the Maye Moon Mission, Jess and I were part of a group of people who were able to see Jesus in the Miracle's cockpit. He was there three days as the rocket traveled to Maye Moon." "What!! Kathi, are you having a mental breakdown? I watched the flight and I didn't see anything. You must have been imagining this. Did Pastor Scott put you up to all of this? Is he running a cult or something now? Kathi, let Dad and I help you through this," Mom said hysterically and began to cry. "Mom, I am wonderful, never better. Pastor Scott did not put me up to anything. You know that Maye Moon is a modern day miracle by God. God is just using me to help others see that the whole world needs to accept Jesus as their Savior. I came to Atlanta to help Pastor Scott and Jess organize the 300 witnesses of Jesus and to share Jesus' message with the rest of the world. By using my experience as the spokesperson for the Maye Moon Mission, I am able to use some of my connections to make television appearances and tell the world what the purpose of Maye Moon is." Kathi's mother looked white as a sheet and looked like she could pass out at any minute.

"Kathi, this is some story," Charlie said. "It is 100% the truth. I would never lie to you," Kathi answered. "I know you wouldn't, dear. It is just so hard to believe that you actually saw Jesus. Did the astronauts see him, too?" her Dad asked. "No, they didn't know he was there with them. But as they were doing their research gathering on the surface of Maye Moon, Jesus approached them. He came out of the woods and told them they were part of his Mission also."

"Kathi, I know this is a big joke you are playing on us," her Dad said as he began to laugh. "This is no joke, Dad. I am as serious as I can be. Jesus said Maye Moon was created to improve the environment here on Earth and to help show people their need for salvation and the evilness in men's hearts." "Man has certainly become evil," her father replied. "Dad, there will be many people come forward who also saw him. We are keeping it under wraps for now until we can officially announce it." "Mum's the word," her Dad said. "You can always count on me, Kathi," her Mother replied.

"I need to call Jess and tell him that I have arrived. I don't want him to worry about me," Kathi told her parents. "He is a good man, Kathi," her Dad said. "I know, Dad. God has really blessed me," Kathi blushed.

Kathi went to the sunroom and telephoned Jess. "Hello Beautiful, did you make it to your parent's home?" Jess said excitedly. "Yes, I got in about an hour ago. I am sorry I did not call right away, but they wanted to know why I left NASA. It turned into the full story. I am still not sure they believe me. I guess it does sound unbelievable. I am anxious to see you," Kathi said lovingly.

"Me too. I have a couple of things that I must take care of before I leave, but I will be over as soon as possible," he answered. "I think I may just lay down and take a nap then. I am pretty bushed after that drive," she replied. "That sounds like a wonderful idea. I love you, Kath," "Love you too, Jess. See you soon."

Kathi went upstairs to her old bedroom and it hadn't changed since she moved out 15 years ago to go to college. She curled up on her bed, threw her old afghan over her, and was quickly off to sleep.

Kathi began dreaming that an angel came to her in a beautiful garden. "Kathi, Jesus sent me to tell you that many people will not believe you at first. They may mock and ridicule you, but you needn't worry about them. The 300 witnesses will help to spread the message. Wipe the dust off of your feet and continue on. Assemble your team with the astronauts. It is time." The angel disappeared, and Kathi immediately woke up. She couldn't believe that she had been asleep an hour. It seemed like she had just laid down. She lay there listening and did not hear Jess downstairs, so she gently closed her eyes for a few more minutes' rest.

Kathi felt a gentle hand on her shoulder, and it awoke from her nap. "Kathi, Jess is here," her mother said softly. "Oh, thank you, Mom. I didn't mean to sleep so long." "I am sure you needed it after that long drive," her mother assured her. "Please tell him I will be down in a few minutes. I just need to freshen up a bit."

The Appearance of Maye Moon

Within five minutes, Kathi came down the stairs. Jess jumped up and gave her a big hug. "I am so glad to see you Kath," as he hugged her again. "I am so happy to see you too! I've missed you so much," she replied. "You've been busy this morning?" "I sure have. It takes a lot of time to answer emails from the witnesses. We made it over the 200 mark. Seems everyone has questions about the reasons they were chosen to witness Jesus on the Maye Moon Miracle Mission," he said. "I am sure they do. I have to tell you what happened to me this afternoon. I took a nap, and an angel came to me in a dream. He told me that many people would not believe it at first. He also said it was time to assemble my team with the astronauts. I would like to share this with Pastor Scott also," Kathi said.

"Of course, that is a message for sure. I was going to see if you wanted to see our work area and my tiny apartment anyway. Pastor Scott should be around, and he will be very happy to see you. So, do you want to head over there?" Jess asked. "Let me tell Mom I am leaving. I feel like I am a kid again, sleeping in my old room and telling my parents every where I am going. In some ways, it is kinda nice and feels safe."

The two hopped into Jess' car and took a moment to kiss. "I feel like I am sneaking around to kiss," Kathi thought. She was really glad that Jess had some PDA (personal display of affection) boundaries around her parents. The couple headed over to the office first. Jess introduced Kathi to a couple of people who were already working there. Aaron Campbell was the IT guy and website developer. He was very skilled and had been working on the website with remarkable speed.

Kathi was surprised to meet Billy Lewis, who was the author of the Probe article that Kathi had contacted. He had some IT experience but would be writing a lot of the content on the website. Both were also witnesses. Jess showed Kathi an office that he had saved for her. "I haven't spoken to Cora lately, but she is leaving NASA also and moving here to Atlanta. She wants to be a part of this," Kathi explained. "Tell her to come on up. We will put her to work." Pastor Scott just arrived.

"Kathi, it is so good to have you here! We could hardly wait until you arrived," Pastor Scott exclaimed. "I couldn't wait either. I feel so blessed to be a part of this. What are we calling this anyway?" Kathi asked. "Miracle Ministries is all I have come up with so far," Pastor Scott laughed. "Not bad, not bad," Kathi laughed.

"Pastor Scott, I was napping this afternoon, and an angel gave me a message," Kathi said. "There was a time when I wouldn't have believed it, but Jesus made a believer out of me. Let's hear it," he replied. "The angel warned me that people will not believe at first and may mock and ridicule me. He said to wipe the dust off of my feet and continue on. He then told me it was time to assemble my team of astronauts."

"It is good to know that we should proceed with our plan of announcing the 300 witnesses," Pastor Scott nodded. "Yes, I would like to start tomorrow and call each of the astronauts and invite them to assemble here if that is ok?"

"Wonderful! That is a great plan. I hope each of them is still on board," he surmised. "I will find out tomorrow," Kathi said.

"Can I ask another question, Pastor?"

"Sure, Kathi," he replied.

"Would you be able to work my baptism into your service on Sunday? I put it off until I could have you do it. My parents are having some of our extended family in for Thanksgiving, and I would like for them to come,"

Kathi asked. "I would be honored, Kathi. A display of thanks for your salvation. We will do it at the end of the service," he replied. "Thank you, Pastor Scott," Kathi beamed. Jess beamed also. He was so proud of Kathi and was head over heels in love with her.

Chapter 37

K athi got up early and made the telephone calls to the astronauts and was relieved to find they were all onboard and ready to assist. They would all be flying in tomorrow and Kathi would be picking each of them up at the Atlanta airport. It was exciting to get the group together, even though they had all left their families right before Thanksgiving to come. "I will need to tell Mother there will be five more for Thanksgiving. Cora and I will help her out, and it will be fun," Kathy thought.

Cora was moving to Atlanta and had already been working on closing out her apartment. She resigned from NASA, which baffled her superiors. She left Florida late last night and was driving straight through. She was ready for a career change and to be an asset to the ministry. Kathi had made up a list of apartments near the church and would go with her to check them out when they had time. In the meantime, Cora would be staying in the guest room at her parents' home. The five-bedroom home was going to be packed with holiday guests.

Kathi suddenly heard a car pull up in the driveway and went out to greet Cora. "Oh, Cora, it is so good to see you again," Kathi said as she gave her a hug. "You have a beautiful home here. Thank you for having me,"

Cora replied. "Let me show you around, but first, have a seat, and I will get you a cup of coffee. Have you had breakfast?" Kathi asked.

"Coffee sounds perfect. No breakfast for me, though. I munched on junk food to keep wide awake and drank a lot of Energy drinks. May I use your restroom, though?" Cora asked. "Of course, it is just around the corner on the right," Kathi answered as she headed to the kitchen to get them some coffee.

When Kathi returned with the tray of coffee and muffins, Cora had already made her way back to the living room. "Atlanta's roads are crazy in the morning. Do you ever get used to it?" she asked. "Absolutely not. I avoid the interstate at all costs. Fortunately, when you have been here awhile, you will learn how to get to most places without having to get on the interstates. I called the guys last night, and they are flying in tomorrow so we will be picking them up as they arrive. They are staying at the Marriott that is close to the church," Kathi shared. "I could stay there also, Kathi, so I wouldn't be any bother," Cora stated. "Oh no, Sister. I have been looking forward to some girl time. We can start looking at some apartments, condos, or houses after the holidays. Whatever you are interested in," Kathi laughed.

Kathi told Cora that she was getting baptized on Sunday and that several of her family members would be attending.

"Do you think that Pastor Scott would baptize me also?" Cora asked.

"I am sure he would. How cool would that be!" Kathi answered.

"Hey, maybe the guys would want to get baptized also. The five of us starting out our new ministry getting baptized together," Cora said.

"That is a fabulous idea. We will have to ask them, of course but that would be so awesome, following our Savior's example by joining into believer's baptism together. I know Pastor Scott will love being a part of it. You have great ideas already, Cora. Let me show you around the house, and then I will help you take your bags up to your room and let you get settled in. You may want a nap before I drag you around Atlanta and introduce you to Pastor Scott and we see Jess," Kathi laughed.

After a shower and a nap, Cora felt so much better and refreshed. She met Kathi downstairs, and the two of them took off to Atlanta Berea Baptist. Kathi excitedly showed Cora the campus, which housed the various ministries, before heading to the building designated for the Miracle Ministries. They parked and went inside to meet the other workers. "Hey, girls! It is so good to see you," Jess greeted them, "How has your day been? Cora, we are so happy to have you here." "Thank you, Jess. I am happy to be here, too!" Cora answered. Jess made the introductions to the other two guys busy working on the computer. "Tomorrow, we will have a full house and can begin planning our Newsbreak Special for Fox. This is going to make news across the world for Jesus."

The door swung open, and Pastor Scott entered the room. He had a presence and excitement about him that couldn't be explained. "I am pleased to make your acquaintance, Cora. We are happy to have you become a part of the Miracle Ministry. I have watched you during the Miracle Mission, but I just can't believe you are here in person," Pastor Scott smiled. Cora was a little embarrassed but smiled and nodded in affirmation. "I am looking forward to hearing your testimony and all about your career as an astronaut when you have settled in," he continued. "Pastor, Cora was wondering if you would baptize her Sunday also?" Kathi asked.

"I would be happy to. Cora do you affirm you have accepted Jesus as your Savior?" He inquired. "Yes, Pastor, I have,"

she answered quietly.

"We will plan on baptizing you along with Kathi on Sunday, then."

"Is anyone else hungry? I was thinking maybe the four of us could go grab some lunch?" Kathi asked. "That is a great idea. I didn't realize it had gotten so late in the afternoon," Jess answered. "I'm game," Pastor Scott added.

The four of them had a wonderful time fellowshipping and sharing stories. They cut up and laughed like they had been friends their entire lives. It made Cora feel right at home in Atlanta. "I am really going to like it here," she thought, "Pastor Scott is amazing and so handsome."

"Tomorrow, Cora and I will be picking up Bob, Ben, and Larry from the airport. We will be preparing for our interview with Jess. We will plan on being here at 9:00 a.m. the day after tomorrow if that works for you both?" Kathi asked. Both men shook their heads to affirm. "I had some matching polo shirts made for the team. Cora is no longer an employee of NASA and they may not like their shirts being worn in this interview," Kathi explained. "Good thinking, Kathi," Cora said.

As the group walked out to their cars, Kathi asked Jess if he would be by later. "I think I will let you girls have your girl time and try to finish up my project I am working on so I can present it to the group the day after tomorrow. Would that be okay with you?"

He asked.

"That is fine. Can I plan on a group dinner reservation for tomorrow evening?" "Sounds great. Pastor, are you available?" Jess asked.

"Count me in. It is so exciting to see things moving along so beautifully," he said as he glanced over at Cora. They all said their goodbyes and headed on their way.

Kathi and Cora had dinner with her parents at home, played a game of Scrabble with them, and then called it an early evening. Larry's plane was the first to arrive, and they needed to be at the airport around 8:00 a.m. The Atlanta airport is huge, and traffic can be a bear. Larry is supposed to text Kathi when he has found a pickup spot at Departures, then they will take him to the airport to settle in. Bob should arrive around 11:00 a.m. and Ben at 1:20 p.m. The trio will be able to shuttle from the airport to Berea Baptist, so they may not need a rental car.

After reading her Bible and praying, Kathi fell fast asleep. Cora, on the other hand, had some difficulty falling asleep. She kept replaying the conversation at lunch. She found Pastor Scott to be so genuine and easy to talk to. Finally, she could keep her eyes open no longer and drifted off to sleep.

The next morning, Kathi and Cora ate a quick breakfast and headed out to begin their Atlanta airport pick-ups. By 3:00 p.m., everyone was accounted for, and all were delivered to their hotel. Kathi had made reservations at Hal's Steakhouse for 7:00 p.m. so the guys had a chance to rest and relax before meeting everyone.

Everyone arrived on time, and the party began. Introductions were made, and everyone was in a festive mood. Pastor Scott was intrigued by each astronaut's account of meeting Jesus. It was funny because, just like Matthew, Mark, Luke, and John, each astronaut saw and felt something different in their experience. One thing for sure, though, is that each astronaut had a life-changing experience, and each was clear on what Jesus expected them to do. Jesus was giving the Earth a chance to repair itself physically and spiritually. Each of the people seated had a part to play.

"Our first step is to announce to the world that Jesus was on Maye Moon, and he loves us and wants the Earth to be a better place for mankind," Pastor Scott announced. "Jess, how long do you think it will take to be ready to do your interview with our team?" Pastor Scott asked. "I am hoping the day after tomorrow. Tomorrow we will rehearse and work through and shoot the next day. After that, I will go to New York and work with my producers to edit it if needed, and we will be ready for air. I want to make sure we get a perfect time slot with the largest audience and may even work with one of our most popular evening shows. Maybe they will let me take the spot as the commentator and let them have the evening off. I will do my best so that most people will see it. Of course, it will also be posted on social media so people who do not normally tune into Fox can also see it. Fox has international stations, and we will request that it play in all of our markets," "Fantastic Jess. You are the man with the plan!" Pastor Scott exclaimed.

"After our show with Jess, I will offer Winston Warren the next interview. His coverage of the Miracle Mission has earned him a greater following on SNN. I feel confident he will be totally interested," Kathi added. "I think that we should each do a personal testimony individually. We can put it on a video platform and give a more personal account of what happened," Ben added. "Great idea, Ben," they all agreed. "Maybe we could do a tour of some larger arenas and have a very professional presentation. Even take it international," Bob added.

"Absolutely. I love that idea!" Pastor Scott exclaimed.

"Before I forget, I want to invite you fine gentlemen to church Sunday at Berea Baptist. At the end of the service Cora and I are going to get baptized. After church, my parents are hosting a Thanksgiving luncheon at our home. We will have some out of town relatives in for it also. We would be thrilled if you will come," Kathi explained. "I would like to be baptized also Pastor, if it is not too much trouble," Larry asked. "Me too, sir," added Bob. "I would love to be baptized with my fellow travelers, if possible," Ben added. "It would be my honor to baptize each of you," Pastor Scott said as tears fell from his eyes, "A fitting way to begin this new Miracle Ministry."

Chapter 38

A s the group gathered in the Miracle Ministry conference room, Jess led the meeting. "We will have 10 minutes for this interview, so we need to make sure that we can cover our points efficiently and accurately. Who do you think should tell the bulk of the story?" Jess asked. "I think Bob should. He is the Lead Commander. He is a great speaker also," Cora spoke up. "I agree," Ben stated. "I agree, also," Larry confirmed. "Alright, Bob, it is," Jess stated.

"Bob, why don't you find a quiet spot and write a script of what you would like to say? You have 4 ½ minutes to speak," Jess instructed.

"The three of you need to write short, impactful statements of how seeing Jesus made you feel. Tell our audience your interchange with Jesus. Each of you have 1 to 1½ minutes at most," Jess said. "Kathi, you are going to tell the world that 300 witnesses saw Jesus on the ship during the flight to Maye Moon. Ask them to contact us by email if they are one of the witnesses. We will have the address running below on the screen. Can you keep it to one minute?" Jess asked. "I will," she replied.

The group worked diligently on their parts of the interview. When all had finished, they came together and practiced their parts. Jess did a magnificent job of asking probing questions and making sure that it went smoothly. They decided it was time to have some lunch and asked Pastor Scott to come along and watch the interview after lunch. He was quite impressed, and they decided to break for the day and start filming in the morning.

"Do you mind if I run some errands this afternoon? I need to get a few things at the W-Mart and look for a dress for Sunday. I want to look nice for church. You are welcome to come along if you like," Cora said.

"If you don't mind, I think I will spend a little time with Jess. We haven't spent much time together since I arrived," she answered. "No, that is alright. I really hate shopping, so I probably won't be gone that long. If you aren't here, I will begin the new book I brought with me," Cora replied.

Jess and Kathi decided to take a walk in the nearby park. It was a brisk November day, but the sun was shining brightly. "Kathi, I never dreamed my life would be like this a couple of years ago. I was only concerned about my career and advancing up the ladder at Fox. I only associated with a few people that I worked with. I thought I was happy, but I was far from it. I had a relationship with God, but I was neglecting it a lot for work. You have really made a difference in my life." Suddenly, Jess got down on one knee and said, "Kathi, I love you so much and would like to make you my wife." Kathi was shocked, so shocked that she began trembling like a leaf in the wind. Finally, she got her wits about her and cried, "Yes, Jess, I will marry you!"

The two embraced and sealed the deal with a long kiss. Jess pulled out a small velvet box and slowly opened it for Kathi to see the most beautiful diamond ring she had ever seen. He slipped it on her left ring finger, and it fit perfectly. The tears of happiness came down her cheeks. "Jess, you are really full of surprises," she said through the tears. Jess even shed a tear or two himself. "This is one of the happiest days of my life. The Lord has blessed me so much," Kathi sighed. The two continued walking hand in hand through the park.

"Should we let everyone know that we are engaged?" Kathi asked. "I was thinking I could fly my parents in for dinner tomorrow night with your parents. That way, we can break the news to them all at once. I will ask them to come for your baptism on Sunday," Jess said. "That is a great idea! They can come for Thanksgiving dinner also. Mom has hired some help for the dinner and it won't be any trouble having a few others.

Do you want to invite your brothers?" Kathi asked. "Not this time. Let's just make it the six of us," Jess answered. "Agreed,"

Kathi replied. "We have some guests coming in tomorrow morning, but I will get my sister to entertain them at our house, and they can order some pizzas. That will be no problem," Kathi said.

Kathi and Jess hung out the rest of the day and into the evening, just happy to be together. They went to a nearby lake to sit and enjoy the beautiful view when they suddenly saw the full moonrise on the horizon. Just a few minutes later, Maye Moon began appearing in all of her glory and brilliance. "Maye Moon's appearance is kinda where it all started. If Maye Moon had not appeared, we might not have ever crossed paths with one another," Jess surmised. "You are right, Jess. I think it was God's miraculous plan for us to be together," Kathi replied.

When Kathi arrived home the house was dark, but her mother met her in the kitchen as she was getting herself a cup of tea. "Mother, I know tomorrow is going to be a busy day, but I need you and Daddy to have dinner with Jess and me and his parents. They are coming in to attend my baptism on Sunday, and I want you to meet them ahead of time." "Oh, Kathi, the timing is off. I will be a mess," her mother said. "I will help you all day. I am sure Cora would love to help, too. We have extra help coming in. I am going to ask Kate if she can entertain the early guests during the evening when we are gone. I will treat everyone here with pizza and the works. I really need you both to have dinner with them," Kathi pleaded. "Okay, if it is that important. We will make it work. I will telephone the agency and see if I can get additional help for Saturday and Sunday."

"Oh, and by the way, Mother, I have invited Pastor Scott, Bob, Larry, Ben, and Jess' parents for Thanksgiving dinner also. I know how you love a house full of guests," Kathi said with a smile. "Kathi, ehhh, alright. We will manage," her mother sighed. "I love you, Mom, and I won't ever forget this," she said as she kissed her mother on the cheek.

The next morning, the Miracle Ministry group assembled to shoot the interview for Fox News. Jess had brought in a cameraman and was already set up to tape. "We will do it a couple of times so that the Producer has some shots to pick from. We want to get the best takes that we can. Thanks to Kathi for ordering the matching polos. Very nice. Does anyone have any questions before beginning?" Jess asked.

"We will let you know if we think of any Jess," Ben answered.

Throughout the morning, they went through the interviews, and Jess was very pleased with the footage. The men decided to head back to the hotel for some rest. Kathi and Cora decided to stay and help Pastor Scott with some office work for the church. Cora was pleased to get to know Pastor Scott better.

"Cora, where did you grow up at?" Pastor Scott asked.

"I grew up an only child in Biloxi, Mississippi. My mother was an Astrophysicist and taught at Ole' Miss. I spent a lot of time with her in the science lab there. I loved mingling with the college students and exploring the campus. When I was ten years old, my mother began showing signs of Multiple Sclerosis, and the doctors confirmed that she did indeed have it. Unfortunately, it got progressively worse, and she had to retire from the university on disability. She has been homebound and wheelchair-bound now for several years. Some days, she can barely move. My father taught Art at the university and was able to continue teaching for several years and my mother had a caregiver to help out while he was at work. Eventually, he retired and became her full-time caregiver. He is able to paint from home and is getting well known in the art world."

"I also had to do a lot to help out, but I don't regret that. She and I are so much alike that it was like being with my best friend. When I went to college, she insisted that I live on campus and have a real college experience. I wanted to be near home after graduation, but she pushed me to go and explore the world. She never wanted to be a burden to me. She rarely leaves the house because she thinks she has lost her beauty, but in my eyes, she is as beautiful as ever."

The Appearance of Maye Moon

"I worked very hard to enter the space program because I wanted her to be proud of me. I was able to advance to secure a place on the space station for six months. She was very proud, and we 'face timed' every day from the space station. Then Maye Moon appeared. I knew right away that I wanted to be one of the astronauts who explored it first. I immediately started my own training program to be in the best shape possible. It was a dream come true when I was chosen. I didn't realize it would save my life, though. Seeing Jesus there has meant more than anything else. I am blessed that I get to enter the ministry to share the gospel with others."

"Wow! I can't believe all of that spilled out of me. I am a rather shy person, and I have never opened up like that to anyone," Cora said softly. She looked over to Pastor Scott and Kathi and saw tears in their eyes. "I am truly blessed," she repeated.

"We are blessed to have you in the Miracle Ministry. Cora, the church has a little house that has opened up recently. We did have a missionary staying there part-time while he was on deputation. If you would like to stay there, you may. It isn't anything fancy, but it is on the edge of our campus, and you may use it as long as you like," Pastor Scott offered. "I would love to take a look at it. I don't need fancy anyways," Cora said. "Kathi, will you go with us to take a look at it?"

Pastor Scott asked. "Sure, that would be my pleasure," Kathi replied.

The three of them drove over in Kathi's car and saw the perfect little cottage. Small and quaint, and Cora fell in love with it. "Are you sure I can stay here?" She asked. "Cora, it is the least I can do. We don't pay astronaut wages around here. We do have a campus security team and you will be safe there. You are welcome to explore our campus anywhere, anytime. I sometimes eat with the college students in the cafeteria. I will get you and Kathi ID badges that state you are staff and no one will ever bother you. We have a library, but it is probably not what you are used to," he chuckled.

Kathi noticed that there seemed to be a spark between Cora and Pastor Scott. "Wouldn't that be wonderful if they both found their soul mate? Oh, I am really jumping to conclusions," Kathi thought.

"Cora, I am going to head home and help my mother get some things ready for tomorrow when our Thanksgiving guests start rolling in. Do you want to stay here or give me a hand?" Kathi asked.

"I will be happy to give you a hand, Kathi. I so appreciate you putting me up for a few days. I will move into the cottage Monday if that is ok with you?" "Sounds like a plan. I will miss having you around, but we will still see each other every day. This has been fun," she replied.

The Appearance of Maye Moon

The two young women set up the two guest rooms for Kathi's grandparents and Uncle Felix and Aunt Jill. "Maybe I should go ahead and move a few things into the cottage and start staying there so you have an extra guest room," Cora offered.

"I hate to ask you to do that. I want you to be a part of all the festivities," Kathi replied.

"No, I offered. I'll be back over here early in the morning, so I can help where needed," Cora assured her. "Well, if you are sure you don't mind. My sister Kate and her husband were going to be stuck in the basement. She will thank you. I will call Pastor Scott and let him know," Kathi said. Cora packed up the few things she had unpacked at Kathi's home and put them in her car. They did some light cleaning and changed the bed and it looked good as new. Kathi was going to share her room with her five nieces and nephews. It will be a slumber party! Holidays are always special, and Kathi and Jess will share their happy news and make it an extra special Thanksgiving.

Chapter 39

J ess made reservations at Houston's for 7:00 p.m. He picked up his parents and was supposed to meet Kathi and her parents there. He was very nervous about the parents all meeting each other for the first time. Kathi had met his family a couple of times and everything had gone well. He had spent more time with her parents because he worked in Atlanta occasionally, and they had always got together. "It will be fine," he thought. "They have us in common."

Kathi was so nervous she was trembling. Her Dad, Charlie, drove his black Cadillac to the restaurant and complained mildly that he was missing a good football game with Kate's husband. Kim was worried she had forgotten to do something for Sunday.

"Everything will be perfect!" Kathi assured her.

"I bought some donuts, and I am planning to do some breakfast casseroles in the morning. What do you think, Kathi?" Kim asked. "I think that is a wonderful idea. I love your breakfast casserole."

"Your Grandmother will want to help,"

Kim replied. "She can make coffee and pour orange juice. Then she can rest,"

Kathi replied. "Good idea. Good idea," Kim said anxiously, "I am a mess. I hate to meet Jess' folks when I am such a mess." "It will all work out fine," Kathi assured her.

Charlie parked, and they walked in together and found Jess and his parents, Bill and Bev, waiting in the lobby. Jess greeted them and gave Kathi a kiss on the cheek. He looked nervous. The maitre'd showed them to their table and Jess helped the mothers and Kathi be seated. He then made the introductions, and the group started getting to know one another. It was going fine. "I wonder when he is going to tell them?" Kathi thought. "Should I tell them before or after dinner? I should have asked Kathi for her opinion," Jess thought. The waiter brought some appetizers to the table, and Jess decided to wait. "I would like to say a prayer before we eat. If you will join me in bowing your heads," he said and asked a wonderful blessing for their food.

Everyone seemed to enjoy their meal, and the table was cleared. "If Kathi and I could have everyone's attention, we have an announcement to make. I asked Kathi to marry me, and she accepted," Jess said with a huge grin on his face. Kathi looked radiant and so happy. Both sets of parents clapped and looked thrilled at the news. "Have you made any definite plans yet?" Kathi's mother, Kim asked. "No, no, not yet. This just happened yesterday," Kathi replied. "Oh, I have always wanted a daughter," Jess's mother exclaimed. "My little girl," Kathi's Dad, Charlie, said with tears running down his cheek. "He is a good man, Kathi, and I couldn't be happier for you," her Dad added. "Son, you have made me proud," Jess' father added. As the group left the restaurant, they all hugged. "We look forward to seeing you Sunday," Kim called after them. It was a very special evening.

When Kathi got home, she found five munchkins in her bedroom, fast asleep. No slumber party tonight. She grabbed a blanket out of the closet and curled up on the family room couch. She thanked the Lord for helping her find such an amazing man and for the wonderful evening that they had with their parents. She drifted off almost immediately in blissful sleep.

It seemed like she was asleep for only a few minutes when she heard a tapping on the door. Her mother was already up and making preparations for the Thanksgiving dinner. Cora had arrived and was ready to help. Kathi headed to the kitchen to see if her Mother needed her to do anything. Kim had already popped her breakfast casseroles into the oven. She had baked blueberry muffins and had the coffee brewing. The kitchen smelled wonderful! The help for the Thanksgiving dinner was starting to arrive. The caterer will arrive at 11:00 with the food. By then, the breakfast will be cleaned up and the Thanksgiving tables set.

"Your Mother is amazing. She has everything under control," Cora said. "I know she loves the holidays, and she has always made each one special. I think my sister inherited her homemaking genes. Speaking of homemaking, Jess and I got engaged yesterday. We shared the news with our parents last night over dinner," Kathi exclaimed. "Oh, that is wonderful! I am so happy for you. Have you made any wedding plans yet?" Cora exclaimed. "No, not yet. I haven't even got used to the whole fiancé thing yet," Kathi laughed. "So much is happening this weekend. I am thankful you and the guys are also getting baptized with me. It makes it extra special," Kathi said with a smile.

"Mom has this all under control, so I am going to go upstairs and get dressed. Others should start getting up. Grab yourself a cup of coffee and relax. It shouldn't be too long. Jess will be here soon. Church starts at 10:30. We should go kinda early to save three pews for our family and guests," Kathi said as she headed upstairs.

As the church started filling up, Jess, Kathi, Cora, Bob, Ben, and Larry filled up a pew. The rest of the family nearly filled the other three pews. A few of Kathi's cousins and their families also came. Jesse's parents sat amongst Kathi's family and still had smiles on their faces from last night's announcement. Pastor Scott delivered a traditional Easter message from the four gospels, and the choir did an outstanding job on "He Arose" and the "Hallelujah Chorus." The church sang "He Lives" and "The Old Rugged Cross". Traditional hymns just seemed most appropriate this day.

At the end of the service, Pastor Scott invited the church to stay for the baptisms. Kathi and the others had left their seats during the offering to put on the baptismal robes and await Pastor Scott's direction. Kathi was the first to be baptized. Kathi walked down the steps with Pastor Scott's help. As he baptized her, he said, "Based upon your profession of faith in the Lord Jesus Christ, I now baptize you, my sister Kathi Calloway, in the name of the Father, Son, and Holy Ghost. Buried with Him in the likeness of His death, raised in the likeness of His resurrection, to walk in the newness of life." Kathi came up out of the water and heard many around the church say, "Amen." She exited the baptismal with the help of Pastor Scott, and Cora entered. Each of the Miracle team took their turns and returned to the dressing rooms.

"Thank you, Kathi, for sharing this day with us," Cora said. "Thank you, Cora, for sharing this day with me also. I feel so fortunate to have such good friends. The Lord has truly blessed me. We will get dressed and all head home for Thanksgiving dinner," she said with a smile. When they came out, several family members were waiting for them. An added surprise was her friends Tessie and Earl were there.

"Tessie, Earl, I did not know you were here today! It is so good to see you. How have you been?" Kathi exclaimed. "We are wonderful. It was so nice to be able to witness your baptism. We are here for Thanksgiving with our daughter, Jenny. This was just an added bonus!" "Guess what? Jess proposed to me yesterday, and I said yes!" Kathi gushed. Oops, some of her family members overheard the good news, too. "God Bless you, child. I am so happy for you and Jess. I pray you have many blessed years like Earl and I have had." Tessie said. "Jess, you are a very lucky man," Earl added. "Believe me, I know," Jess responded.

"We have to head home for my mother's Thanksgiving dinner, but we would love to get together with you both while you are here in Atlanta. I have a lot of updates to share with you," Kathi said. "That sounds wonderful. Give us a call Monday, and we will set something up," Tessie said. Hugs were exchanged, and they all headed home to Kathi's parents.

"It's about time!" Kathi's uncle Felix exclaimed. The aroma of the delicious food permeated the room. "We're sorry, we're sorry…we ran into some old friends we did not know were here in Atlanta visiting," Kathi explained. "Well, you should have invited them. The more the merrier," Felix laughed. Kathi received several hugs and kisses from the relatives who came for Thanksgiving. Jess found his parents and started to introduce them to Kathi's grandparents and, Cora, Bob, Ben and Larry. There was a lot of family he was not familiar with. Kathi's Dad, Charlie, tapped on a glass with a spoon and said, "Could I have everyone's attention? I have an announcement to make. Kathi and Jess are officially engaged, and I would like to wish the happy couple a lifetime of happiness." The crowd cheered and clapped. "I would also like to introduce Jess's parents, Bill and Bev, and say welcome to our family," Charlie shouted over the noise.

"We are so happy that our daughter was baptized today along with her good friends from NASA. I would like to introduce the astronauts who commanded the Miracle I to Maye Moon, Cora, Bob, Ben, and Larry. We are honored to have you all in our home. Jess, would you like to say the blessing for the food?" Jess obliged, and the group lined up to have a marvelous Thanksgiving meal. Pastor Scott finally arrived and got to the end of the line. Cora just happened to save a place for him to sit.

"How blessed am I getting to sit by Miss Cora," he said as he sat down. The two chatted through dinner like they were old friends. "Maye Moon has certainly brought a lot of people together. Our next step is to host a conference for the 300 witnesses who saw Jesus on the spaceship. Did you sense He was there with you?" "In all honesty, I did not. I guess I had a lot on my mind. I had controls to watch and concerns that everything was going the way it was supposed to go. I guess there was a sense of peace that I hadn't considered," Cora explained. "The peace that passeth all understanding?" Pastor Scott inquired.

"Yes, I guess that it could be described like that. I felt very sure that we would all be alright in my heart," Cora replied.

Kim made her way around the rooms where her guests were seated to make sure that everyone was taken care of. "Can I get you anything?" Echoed several times. Her help was also taking care of her guest's needs. As she approached Cora and Pastor Scott, she said, "I see that you found your way to each other. That is good." "Very good," Pastor Scott replied with a smile. Cora blushed. The two of them did feel an instant connection.

Throughout the dinner, loved ones came by to congratulate Jess and Kathi. Their engagement announcement couldn't have been better than to be with some very special people in their lives. After dinner, Kathi and Jess face-timed with each of his brothers and their families. It would have been nice to have them here also. The men in the house organized a football game in the backyard while the women sat on the sidelines with coffee and cheered. After the game, everyone came in to watch football on television while eating Kim's delicious desserts, including pumpkin pie and pecan pie. Most of the men had fallen asleep before halftime. A few of the guests stayed for leftovers before heading home. It was a fantastic holiday, but tomorrow starts preparation for the Miracle Conference of Witnesses.

Chapter 40

"Good morning, everyone," Pastor Scott greeted. "Let's meet in the conference room in 10 minutes." Everyone brought their coffees and sat about the rectangular table, leaving the end seat for Pastor Scott. "This morning, we are going to plan the conference for the 300 witnesses. First, let's look at a calendar and choose a date. I would like it to be as soon as we can possibly prepare everything, but we have to take into consideration the holidays. We don't want anything to keep the witnesses from coming."

"How about the days following New Year's Eve?" Larry suggested. "A lot of churches have New Year's Eve services, which some may not want to miss," Jess answered. "Good point, especially if they are a pastor of a church," Bob agreed.

"New Year's Eve is on a Sunday this year. How about January 2nd through the 5th?" asked Pastor Scott.

"I think that is perfect," agreed Cora. The others seated at the table shook their heads in agreement.

"Great! That was the easy part. Jess, Can you give us an update on the editing of our interview?" Pastor Scott asked. "Sure, it should be finished in a day or two. Thanksgiving slowed down the process, but I was assured by the editor we would be on it today. I plan on flying to New York in the morning to oversee the process," Jess explained. "You are the man, Jess!" Pastor Scott said with enthusiasm.

"We can have the conference in the church auditorium. Our students will be home on break so our cafeteria can prepare the meals for our attendees. We will need a menu. Who would like to work on lunch and dinner options for 300?"

Pastor Scott asked. Ben and Cora volunteered. "I think that is a good idea to have a male and female perspective," Pastor Scott laughed.

"Next, we need someone to negotiate with a hotel for some good hotel rates with breakfast for the attendees," Pastor Scott requested. "Sounds like a job for me," Bob offered.

"We need someone to work on the technical part of the conference. Can you run a soundboard and camera, Larry?" Pastor Scott asked.

"Absolutely. That is where my expertise lies," Larry replied.

The Appearance of Maye Moon

"Kathi, can you design an invitation and program? I will work with you on the program. We will need to have the group brainstorm what information we need to present to our attendees. The goal is to prepare them to share the news that Jesus wants us to share with the world, the purpose of Maye Moon, and how to make people aware of the need for mankind to clean up our act," Pastor Scott explained. "I think we need to present all the environmental changes that have already taken place since Maye Moon first appeared," Kathi said. "Excellent point, Kathi," Pastor Scott agreed. "I have access to this information by my Press credentials. We keep up to date on this information at Fox," Jess said. "Great, Jess. Find out all the information that you can and list your sources. That will definitely be one of our sessions," Pastor Scott replied. "We should all pray fervently for this conference. I am counting on the Lord to provide us with the gift of tongues."

"Tongues? You mean there will be people speaking gibberish, falling on the floor, and acting all crazy?" Ben asked. "No, No. If you study your Bible, you will find that speaking in tongues actually means that people are able to hear the speaker in their own language. We will have attendees who do not speak English, no doubt. They will be able to hear the speakers in their natural tongue. I believe the Lord will provide us with that gift. I am going to have faith that it will happen," Pastor Scott explained. "I am also having faith that all 300 witnesses will show up to our conference. The Lord wants this to happen."

"Let's meet every morning and every day at noon. We will have lunch here in the conference room, and I will provide it. No peanut butter and jelly sandwiches, I promise. We will surely have other jobs to tackle and hear updates from each of you. We will break for Christmas on December 20th. We will return on December 28th. Larry, if you want to follow me, we will head over to the sanctuary so you can see the equipment we have available," Pastor Scott directed. "Right behind you, boss," Larry replied.

The group disbanded and started working on their assigned areas. Kathi remembered that she had not got back to Tessie and Earl and decided to give them a call. Fortunately, they were available for dinner, so she made a dinner date with them to meet Jess and her at a nearby restaurant. She then returned to her invitation and program designs. Jess was leaving early in the morning and this was the first time that she would not see him for a few days since being engaged. So far, they have not had time to discuss their wedding plans.

Lunchtime came around, and the group met back at the conference room. She had a moment to tell Jess about making dinner plans. "That sounds like fun. Tessie and Earl have become great friends. I wouldn't want to miss them," he responded. "Yes, they were there on our first date," Kathi said. Each member of the team shared their progress, and Kathi was surprised to see how much they accomplished in such a short time. They had a quick lunch and returned to their hard work. Bob worked his charm and was able to get the hotel that the three men were staying at to block 300 rooms at an unbelievable rate with a hot breakfast buffet each day. It paid off being a Miracle Moon astronaut and celebrity. Bob started to plan the speech he would give during the conference. As the Lead Commander of the Mission, he would be the first speaker to discuss the encounter with Jesus on the Maye Moon.

Ben and Cora had an afternoon meeting with the Kitchen Manager to discuss options for the menu. They had jotted down several ideas and would try to accommodate their visitors from other countries and special diets.

Kathi found her hands were tied to a certain extent until others got some of their jobs done. Pastor Scott decided to have her take a large map of the world and place names of the people who had reported that they saw Jesus in the cockpit on the location where they lived. There were still some witnesses who had not been located, but she was sure that Jess' interview would spread the word. Jesus would make sure they were all accounted for.

The group came back together at the end of the day. Kathi had finished the conference invitations that would be sent electronically and by postal. The first invitation was a "Save this date" postcard that reminded her that she would be doing one for her own wedding someday. She was nearly finished with the map Pastor Scott had wanted. It was amazing to see that there were witnesses all over the world. Ben and Cora had confirmed a menu for the conference meals. Larry had been trained to use the church's sound system and technical booth. Bob had the hotel nailed down and a good start on his speech. Everyone was excited about the progress that was made. Since the group had been hand-picked by Jesus, it made sense that they were all go-getters.

"Tomorrow night, the Miracle Mission interview will be aired on Fox. The station has been advertising and building anticipation for it for a couple of days now. I think we will have a large audience. After it is aired, it will be available to view on Fox Nation. I will let you all know audience numbers when I get them," Jess told the group. "I think we should have a viewing party on the big screen in the auditorium. We need to watch it together. I will provide the pizza, popcorn, and soft drinks," Pastor Scott suggested. Everyone was in favor of the party. They had become like one big family since working together each day, and each day began and ended in prayer for each member, the witnesses, and the Miracle Conference, and especially that God's will be done.

Chapter 41

T he next evening, the group convened in a small, intimate area with couches and a movie screen that the church used for smaller group ministries. The room had a kitchenette set up with a popcorn machine. "The pizza will arrive in a few minutes," Pastor Scott said. "I don't know about you, but I am so excited I could shout!" The others laughed at his giddiness and felt exactly the same way. Jess was still in New York at the Fox Studios. He would be a co-host at an after-show discussion of the interview.

"Get your food and come and sit down. It is about to start!" Pastor Scott instructed. "I am starved!" Bob replied. Cora was still a little timid around Pastor Scott and found herself daydreaming about him often. She thought he was interested in her also, but still had not asked her out on an official date.

The show began, and everyone was glued to the big screen. No one said a word. One could only imagine what the public was thinking to hear four prominent astronauts describing this experience on Maye Moon. Satan will be hard at work to dispel their story. Kathi's part of the interview explained that there were 300 witnesses who also saw Jesus in the cockpit—well, it did sound crazy. The group had done what Jesus had asked, and now He would have to give the audience an open mind.

Immediately after the show, Jess and the commentator for that spot, Jay Jackson (J.J. for short), discussed the interview segment.

"Jess, how did you hear about this?" J.J. asked. "I was at NASA during the Maye Moon launch," he replied.

"So do you think they all experienced some mass delusion from being on Maye Moon?" J.J. asked. "No, I know they didn't. They are all personal friends of mine. In fact, I am one of the 300 witnesses. I watched as Jesus rode in the cockpit with the astronauts to Maye Moon," Jess answered. "You are kidding me, man," J.J. said with amazement and disbelief.

"J.J., I know it is hard to believe, but Maye Moon suddenly appearing in the sky was hard to believe also. Here are five highly gifted scientists who are telling you that Jesus appeared on the Maye Moon Mission. They explained why He appeared. All you need is the faith to believe," Jess said with conviction.

"Were you scared when you saw Jesus in the cockpit?" J.J. asked. "At first, I thought someone stole on board, but it became obvious that the astronauts were not able to see Him. He looked like what I imagined Jesus would look like.

Kathi was with me, and she could see Him also. So we discussed it while it was happening and quickly came to the conclusion that it was Jesus. He stood for three days while they traveled through space and did not say a word. I do not think that any man could do that," Jess explained.

"Jess, were you a religious person before the Maye Moon Mission?" J.J. inquired.

"I prefer to say that I am a Christian and saved," Jess answered.

"Is there a difference?" J.J. asked.

"I was saved by faith in believing that Jesus died on the cross to save me from an eternity in hell for my sins. He rose three days later and ascended to heaven and will return again," Jess explained.

"No one can be good enough to earn their way to heaven. It is a gift from God to those who have the faith to believe."

"So is this the Second Coming of Jesus returning to Earth?" J.J. inquired. "No. Jesus appeared in space and on Maye Moon. Jesus is giving the Earth and humans a chance to straighten up. Man has become so sinful. The worst sin is the sin of disbelief. But faith is involved. The 300 witnesses are already believers who are stretched across the world. They will share the message that Jesus has delivered," Jess further explained. "Which is?" J.J. asked intently. "That man has become so evil and selfish. We report about murder, mass shootings, human trafficking, wars, terrorism, and other horrific stories, and people have become hardened and don't even bat an eye. Greed is rampant. Some people never have enough, while others are starving and have nothing. Love is defined as lustful sex. Children are murdered in the womb and sexually and physically abused at an alarming rate. Lying is second nature to most people. I could go on and on," Jess said with such emotion.

"Why would God want to give us a second chance?" J.J. asked seriously. "Because we are His creation…His children. He loves us more than we could possibly understand," Jess concluded.

The group at Berea Baptist sat silent for a minute. Finally, Pastor Scott spoke and said, "Jess was empowered by the Holy Spirit. That was amazing. Let's pray and ask the Holy Spirit to give us the power to speak boldly and His will to be done."

Soon after the program aired, Jess called the group and told them he had the privilege of leading J.J. and three others in the studio to the Lord. The group rejoiced with Jess and was more eager and impassioned to do the work of the Lord than ever. They told Jess they were amazed at the interview and looked forward to seeing him back in Atlanta the next day.

Kathi checked her telephone and had a missed call and voicemail from Winston Warren. He wanted the group on his show as soon as possible and was willing to come to them. Pastor Scott said that the IT guys had several messages from people who claimed to be witnesses. The total was now up to 290. Praise the Lord! The telephone calls kept coming in from CNN, MSNBC, the main networks, 700 Club, and many others who wanted to book them for shows. They were more than happy to come to Atlanta to do the shows with the Miracle Mission group. This is exactly what the Miracle Mission was about! Hallelujah!

The group continued day after day doing interviews and working hard to complete the conference details until December 20th. The witnesses were confirming their attendance to attend the conference in amazing numbers. The Miracle Mission team were all ready for a Christmas break. Bob, Ben and Larry had spent very little time with their families since Miracle Moon had appeared. They each flew home a few weekends and their families came to see them a couple of times, but they were happy to get a little longer family time. Cora was going home to Mississippi to visit her parents. Pastor Scott had duties at the church he needed to tend to. Jess and Kathi were going to spend the holidays with the Wanamaker side of the family since they spent Thanksgiving with hers. Kathi was excited to get to know everyone better and she hoped that she and Jess would get a little time to discuss their wedding plans. She had put off her Christmas shopping and wanted to shop with Jess for his family. Christmas, the celebrated birth of Christ, would be here before you know it.

Chapter 42

P astor Scott woke early to the sound of his telephone ringing. It was Christmas morning, and there was a chill in his bedroom from a light dusting of freshly fallen snow outside.

"Hello, Pastor Scott speaking,"

He said. "Merry Christmas, Pastor Scott! I just wanted to call and wish you a Merry Christmas before your busy morning began," Cora exclaimed. "Oh, Cora, it is so great to hear your voice. It has been so quiet around here, with the Miracle team missing. I hope you are enjoying the time with your family," he replied. "I did, I did. I missed being here and decided to return late last night. My family celebrated Christmas yesterday so I could be here. They are not really into the holidays since my mother got so sick and can't do much," she answered.

"Cora, you can't imagine how happy I am to have you back. Cora, you have a special place in my heart. Would you want to have lunch with me after our church service today?" Pastor Scott asked timidly. "I would love to, Pastor,"

She replied. "I hate to cut our call short, but I must get ready to get to the church. I will see you there," Pastor Scott said. "See you there, Pastor."

As Cora hung up the phone, her heart fluttered, and she smiled to herself. She knew the minute she met Pastor Scott that he was the right man for her. She had waited to see where their friendship would go. She really did not know if he was interested in a relationship or not. She knew he liked and respected her, but she did not know if he had feelings for her like she did him.

Cora put on a solid dark green dress with a Christmas pin she had received from her grandmother. Cora had always been a conservative dresser and preferred not to draw attention to herself. She decided to walk to church that morning even though it was cold and snowy. The church was extra full, surprisingly. Many of the people were those who only came to church on Christmas and Easter. The Children's Choir performed two beautiful songs to start the service off. The congregation sang "Oh Little Town of Bethlehem" and "Hark the Herald Angels Sing." The adult choir performed a couple of beautiful songs next. The music program today was phenomenal. Cora couldn't believe it when the last song was a solo performed by Pastor Scott. She did not even know that he could sing. He sang "Mary Did You Know," and it brought tears to her eyes. She was so moved by it.

Pastor Scott brought a stirring message of the Birth of Christ from Mary's perspective. He had such a way of preaching that was moving and insightful. The service was so wonderful, and there was no place that Cora would rather be on Christmas morning. After the service Pastor Scott shook hands with many, many people. Some even brought him Christmas gifts. Cora sat on the back pew and waited patiently until the church was empty.

"Such an amazing service, Pastor," she said with admiration. "Thank you, Miss Cora. Are you getting hungry?" "I am," she said with a smile. "Well, I wasn't thinking when I said we'd go out for lunch that nothing is open on Christmas Day. Our cafeteria is serving up a Christmas lunch to the aged and homeless. I am sure they will not mind if we crash their party. Plus, after we eat, we can help clean the kitchen up," Pastor Scott laughed. "That sounds like a ball!" Cora smiled.

The two of them walked over to the cafeteria in the softly blowing snow. Cora was glad that she wore her boots. When they arrived, they each grabbed a tray and had a delicious turkey and dressing dinner with all of the fixings. They decided to sit with a small group of homeless men who seemed appreciative of a hot meal. Pastor Scott asked each of them if they knew where they were going to spend eternity. Surprisingly, all but one man shared when they received Christ as their Savior. Before the lost man left, he admitted that he was a sinner and asked the Lord to save him. The church had purchased some gifts for each person who came to the dinner. Cora enjoyed helping to pass the gifts out to the people. Each person also received a "to go" box with another meal, some fruit, and a box of candy.

After the meal ended and everyone left, Cora and Pastor Scott pitched in and did some dishes. They finished their job and decided to have some coffee and sit and talk for a while. "Cora, I think you know that I have become quite fond of you. I feel I have to warn you that I am a fundamentalist when it comes to the Bible. Rather old fashioned. That is probably why I haven't married yet. Although, until Maye Moon I was a bit on the wild side. I was living life dangerously, at least compared to how a Christian should live. Anyway I never met anyone that I thought would be interested in my lifestyle. Even though I have changed, I still feel like most women wouldn't like the life of a Pastor's wife. I want to be totally honest with you. The Bible teaches that the man is the head of the household. I don't take that to mean women are subservient to men or can't make decisions. God holds the man accountable for his household. The man is responsible for final decisions. A Pastor's wife is always under the microscope of the entire congregation. She must set an example for all of the women in the congregation.

Sometimes, she will have to fill in when other women are ill. A pastor is really on call 24-7. You never know when someone might die in the middle of the night or be taken to the hospital with an emergency. People don't expect you to have a private life. You don't take time off being a Christian. God is the head of our home," Pastor Scott explained.

Cora sat there with her mouth slightly open in surprise. "Cora, I would like you to think about these things because I would like to court you," Pastor Scott said seriously.

"What do you mean by courting?" Cora asked.

"Courting is more serious than dating because there is an intent to marry. It is a time when you get to know more about each other before an official engagement. I would like for you to consider whether you think being a Pastor's wife is the life for you. How does that sound?" He asked. "Honestly, this took me a little by surprise. I took an interest in you from the start, but I guess all I was thinking was dating. This sounds more serious and I will definitely think about all that you have said. I know you are a wonderful man. I have never been someone who needed a lot of coddling. My mother wasn't able to show a lot of physical affection due to her illness. I guess I am saying I can be independent when I need to be. How soon do you want to know my answer?" she asked. "You take as much time as you need, Cora," he answered.

"How about I walk you home, Cora? I need to prepare for tonight's candlelight service," Pastor Scott suggested. "That's not necessary. I will see you at church later. Lunch was delicious, and you have given me a lot to think about," Cora answered. They both bundled up and left the cafeteria and went their separate ways.

Cora wasn't sure what she thought about Pastor Scott's proposal. Stunned might be the word to describe it. She had hoped that he would ask her out on a date, but the marriage hadn't really entered her mind. "It was a lot of responsibility being a pastor's wife, but she had gone to Maye Moon, so she knew she could probably handle it. It was like the difference between night and day. Pastor Scott was very handsome and had a great personality. He was easy to talk to, which was important since Cora was shy and introverted. She felt comfortable with her small group of friends, but how would she handle a whole large church that she would have to get to know? The church had made her feel welcome, and there were so many nice people who said hello to her at each service. Was she willing to commit to being in church every service for the rest of her life? Jesus did give His life for her, didn't he? She always feels better, happier after attending church." The thoughts were bouncing around so fast that she was dizzy. "I know I care about him. I could easily call it love if I allowed myself to."

Freshly fallen snow is so beautiful. Cora decided to bundle up and trudge through it back to church for the evening service. The glistening flakes looked like shiny diamonds across the church lawn. Up in the sky was a full moon and a full Maye Moon. She arrived at church and took a seat up near the front. Pastor Scott was busy greeting visitors and members who had not been to church in a while. He had three Associate Pastors with their own duties, but during services, they all shook hands and made attendees feel at home.

It was time for the service to start, and Pastor Scott stood behind the pulpit. He looked over at Cora and gave her a special wink and a smile. She blushed. The song leader went through three Christmas hymns for the last time that year. It was always kinda sad to put the Christmas music away. Tonight, there was a Christmas play that involved some adults and children. It lasted about half of the service, and then Pastor Scott preached a message on the "Greatest Gift of All." Everyone was invited to the fellowship hall for Christmas punch, non-alcoholic eggnog, peppermint hot chocolate, and Christmas cookies. The night was a special ending to Christmas day.

"Please let me walk you home, Cora. I could use the fresh air and company," Pastor Scott asked. "That would be very nice," she answered. "Do you have a lot of special Christmas memories, Cora?" "Well, my father did his best to make Christmas special. My mother would give him a list of gifts for me. Sometimes, he would get it right. Sometimes, he wouldn't. On Christmas, my father would put my mother in the car, and then we would drive around the town looking at Christmas lights. The radio would be turned to Christmas music, and we would sing along with the songs. When we got home, I was allowed to open one present, which would always be pajamas, and then I would have to go to bed so Santa would come." Cora wiped a tear from her eye.

Pastor Scott handed her his handkerchief. "I love that. That sounds like a wonderful Christmas tradition," he said. "It was, but the worse my mother became, she would not want to leave the house," Cora said. "She pulled away from everything and everybody."

They arrived at Cora's cottage, and Pastor Scott said, "Thank you, Cora, for sharing with me. I bought you a small gift." "Oh, you shouldn't have," she said timidly. "Go ahead and open it," he said. She opened the box carefully and found a delicate gold cross necklace inside. "It is beautiful, thank you so much," "You are welcome, Cora. Merry Christmas. Now I must head home. Sweet dreams." "Goodnight, Pastor," she said and watched him walk away in the snow. "Wait, Pastor Scott, I would like to accept your offer to enter into a courtship," Cora called out. Pastor Scott turned and returned to her step. He reached out and put his arms around her and said, "Cora, you have just made me a very happy man."

Chapter 43

T he Miracle Mission group assembled in the conference room, ready to get back to work. "I hope everyone had a very Merry Christmas with your families. It was so quiet around here, but we are only days away from the Miracle Conference, and that will change everything. I would like to let you all know that all 300 witnesses have been accounted for, and all 300 witnesses have confirmed that they will be here for the conference," Pastor Scott announced. "That is a work of God!" Ben said, and the entire group broke out in praise to the Lord. "Our secure website is getting a lot of use, and we have been able to develop an open website so that believers who are not witnesses can know what is going on. I would like to thank Aaron Campbell and Billy Lewis for meeting all of our tech needs for this mission. You guys are great!" Pastor Scott exclaimed. Clapping and cheering broke out again amongst the others.

"I would like each of you to double check your parts in the conference to make sure all details are finished. Finish up your speeches, and if you have slide presentations that you are using, be sure to give them to Aaron or Billy. If anyone has any ideas for some fun activities that will engage the audience, let me know. Some kind of mixer would be good. Aaron and Billy will also be taking pictures during the conference so we will show these at the conclusion of each night."

"I hope that you will all be able to make it tonight to the New Year's Eve service. 8 p.m. to Midnight. We always have a good time. We have a message on Goal setting for the New Year and then we go to the fellowship hall and have finger foods and play games until the New Year rings in. I've been announcing it at church for the past few weeks. The teens and smaller children will be having their own parties here at church also," Pastor Scott explained.

"Our Maye Moon Mission conference goal is to send each person out with the reason Jesus made them a witness to tell the good news to their part of the world. See you at lunch!" Pastor Scott said as he dismissed the team.

Pastor Scott contacted the Music Director and reminded him the choir is to perform at the conference. "How about 'Go Tell it on the Mountain' and 'He's Got the Whole World in His Hands'? Just a couple of ideas. Some solos, too," the Music Director asked. "Great! We will schedule you at the beginning of each night, and you are dismissed when you are finished," Pastor Scott replied. "Two Days until the Conference, and so many things are going on, my head is spinning." Pastor Scott and Cora decided to wait until after the conference to announce their courtship to their friends.

When everyone reassembled for lunch, they all said that they were ready for the conference to begin. "Let's take the rest of the day off. We will be so busy when the conference starts that we can use some rest." Pastor Scott said. They all agreed that was a wonderful idea, and each person headed their own way. Larry waved at the Pastor and mouthed "Naptime" to him. Pastor Scott chuckled.

"Would you like me to walk you home, Cora?" he smiled. "No, that is not necessary. I know you have been busy. I think I may go for a run and clear my head," she said with a smile back at him. "Okay, if you are sure. I am going to go back to my study at the church and pray for tonight's service. I always pray that some lost sinner will find their way here and will get saved," he explained. "I will be there, Pastor," she said.

"If you need me, don't hesitate to call me, Cora. And you can call me Scott when no one is around." They both went their opposite directions.

The New Year's Eve service had a tremendous turnout, and Cora couldn't believe how many people showed up. The different "Anonymous" and homeless groups came and sat together. The Seniors group came and sat together, too. Even a local homeless shelter not affiliated with the church showed up. It was a packed-out house, which was an encouragement to Pastor Scott. Several employees of the church were around to assist with the visitors and attendees. Pastor Scott had an amazing group of church employees who handled a lot of the details so he could focus on the fine details of the Berea Baptist ministry. It took a lot to run a church of this size.

The Maye Moon Mission team sat together towards the front of the sanctuary. They have become like family after spending so much time together over the past few months. So much has happened since the Maye Moon appeared last May. Who would think that their lives could change so much?

The music was wonderful and uplifting, with two soloists performing and a professional gospel Blue Grass group performing a few songs. Pastor Scott started to preach his message on Goal Setting, using examples of Jesus leading his disciples to different towns to present the gospel and perform miracles. His message took a sudden turn to the subject of repentance. He preached how many people are sorry for their sinful actions and asked the Lord to forgive them of their sins. However, true sorrow should include repentance. Jesus forgives, but repentance involves turning away from that sin and not repeating it again and again. He ended his message with a very clear salvation message. Many people were moved by his message and made their way to the altar. Members who were trained to present the salvation gospel went forward to pray with those at the altar. It was a blessing to hear that fourteen people accepted Jesus as their savior.

After the final prayer, the people made their way to the Fellowship Hall for a time of food and festivities. The time passed quickly and it was time for the New Year's ball to drop and the New Year arrived. A new year of hope that God will continue to bless the Earth. The attendees wore their party hats, blew their party horns, and hugged each other in Christian love. Gunshots and fireworks could be heard throughout the city. The group started disbanding to go home and go to bed. It was a wonderful way to start the New Year.

Jess drove Kathi home and gave her a long kiss. Good-good night. They couldn't wait until they were wed and didn't have to say goodbye.

Pastor Scott winked at Cora and walked her home in the chilly night air. "Cora, have you been thinking about setting a date for our marriage? Have you thought about the size of the wedding you would like?" He asked suddenly.

"I have thought about it, but I want to make sure it is something we both want," she calmly answered.

"I was thinking the sooner, the better. How about you?" He stated.

"How soon are you thinking about?" She asked coyly.

"What about a March wedding? I was thinking about the 16th of March. We will never forget the date. We would just think of John 3:16, my favorite verse in the Bible." She giggled and replied, "I guess that is a good idea."

"Then that is settled. We will be married on March 16th. We got one detail out of the way," he said.

They stopped on the porch, and Pastor Scott gave Cora her first kiss. He was careful not to get carried away, but he wanted to show Cora that he did love her. Then he gently said goodnight and turned and started the walk back to the church to get his car.

The next morning, Kathi and Cora positioned themselves at the hotel to greet the witnesses who started arriving. They had made up conference packets to give each person, including name badges and t-shirts. It was so interesting to actually meet each one in person. Almost everyone arrived on New Year's Day. They were invited to have their meals on campus, but many were using the day to sightsee and experience Atlanta. The Atlanta airport can be quite overwhelming, but a shuttle service was prearranged and ran all day long. For some of the witnesses it was the first time to visit and experience such a large modern city. Tomorrow was Day 1 of the conference, and some church volunteers would be there early to check people in.

The Appearance of Maye Moon

Kathi had a hard time sleeping due to the excitement of the Miracle Mission conference. She got up in the middle of the night and went to her computer to read some of the comments being made about the television appearances. She was surprised to find the majority of comments were believers in Jesus' appearance on the moon. Others called the group a bunch of nuts. She and the astronauts made 12 appearances on television and grabbed some pretty large Nielson ratings. The YouTube replays had blown up. She was looking forward to Jess' presentation in the morning because he was sharing a lot of data he had researched about the Earth's environmental recovery. Scientists across the world were baffled by the changes in the air, water, soil, vegetation growth, and many other changes that were taking place.

Finally, after an hour or so, she was very tired and headed back to bed. That morning, her alarm clock went off way too early it seemed, but she had been looking forward to this conference for weeks. She quickly went through her morning routine so that she could get to the church as early as possible. Her only duty was to mingle and listen to people's stories about the Miracle Maye Moon Mission and the sighting of Jesus.

As she arrived at the church, she saw a large group of reporters trying to speak to people as they entered. Pastor Scott had anticipated this and had tight security inside the church building to remove anyone who was not a witness. His security team told the news media they must stand away from the property and not block anyone from entering. The Atlanta P.D. had also arrived to make sure that nothing got out of hand. Security members escorted witnesses to the door and inside the building, where their credentials were verified. "This will definitely hit the news tonight," Kathi thought. Winston Warren was allowed in the conference to report what was happening inside. He was given a private seat on the upper balcony so that he was separated from the witnesses. Pastor Scott will be giving the conference "Welcome" at 10:00 a.m. Day 1 was underway!

Pastor Scott had faith that the gift of tongues would allow everyone in the sanctuary to be able to understand each speaker. He welcomed the group and thanked each one for making the trip to Atlanta for the conference. "This conference will outline the job that Jesus has for each of us who were able to see Jesus in the Miracle spaceship. Jesus wanted to be sure that we would spread the word that the people of Earth must turn from their wicked ways and renew their hearts and minds to love the Lord, thy God, and their fellow man. He has chosen to renew the land, water, and air, but man has free will and must make the choice to change. If not, the tribulation will hasten."

"God loves all people of every race and every nation. Many people have turned away from God, and their spirits have waxed cold. They have turned to a reprobate mind. What has been meant for good, Satan has turned evil. We 300 people have been chosen to help the Lord spread this news to every corner of the Earth. Sure, there will be scoffers, but many will believe. One will become two, and two will become four. A revival will break out across the Earth, and people will decide to destroy the evil that is attacking our world. Believe me, the Lord is speaking through me."

"Let's stop and join hands with the people around you and have 15 minutes of prayer for this conference, that it prepares us for the upcoming Mission," Pastor Scott announced. People all over the large sanctuary began to form prayer groups and fall to their knees. The Holy Spirit could be felt throughout the room. After the prayer session, the choir performed two lively songs for the group. Pastor Scott then introduced Commander Bob, who told his story of meeting Jesus on Maye Moon. After finishing, Bob introduced Ben. Ben told his story and then introduced Cora. Each astronaut's story was similar but told from a different perspective, and each shared their testimony of how it changed their life. Larry, who was left on the spaceship, shared his story and gave a mesmerizing account of Jesus changing his life. This concluded the morning session, and the conference broke for lunch.

A lot of tears had flowed that morning. Jess and Kathi found Tess and Earl and sat with them for lunch. It was so nice to see them again. "This has been the most amazing day," Earl exclaimed. "I am so thankful to be able to do God's work, even though my days are numbered." "Earl, you are just a young man," Kathi replied

"Kathi, my doctors have told me that I have pancreatic cancer. It is stage three," he sighed. "Oh no, Earl, I am so sorry. I didn't know," she softly said back. "Earl, I believe God is going to give you a miracle so you can do his work," Jess said.

"He will use you to demonstrate that many illnesses can be healed by believing in Him." Tessie seemed to light up when Jess said this. Her face had more worry wrinkles than ever before. "Yes, Earl, I stand on his promises. You will be an example to others," she said with hope.

As Kathi and Jess were heading back to the sanctuary, Winston Warren approached them. "Kathi, this conference is absolutely amazing. Thank you so much for arranging for me to cover this. I have found it fascinating. I can't believe I denied the existence of God for so long. My pride has stood in my way of knowing there is a God that could control the things that happen in our lives. Just like meeting you and working with you on the Miracle Mission broadcast. If that hadn't happened, I might not be here today."

"Yes, Warren. We have been so blessed to witness this miracle. I will see you after the afternoon session, and we can talk more."

The Appearance of Maye Moon

The afternoon session began with a "Meet and Greet." Each person was to shake hands with at least five people and tell them what God had done in their lives. Hopefully, by the end of the conference, some new friendships will have been made.

The next session was introduced by Natalie Steubens, who is the United States Ambassador to the United Nations. Jess had met Natalie at Fox and asked her if she would be interested in making the introduction. She graciously agreed. Dr. Moon is a Christian environmental physicist who was employed at UNSD, the United Nations Statistical Division, and was asked to discuss the changes in our air, land, and water quality. Dr. Moon was a lively speaker and was excited to report that across the Earth, the environment had improved by nearly 20%. Additionally, this has affected the weather positively. Many areas of the world that normally had draughts causing many deaths now have adequate water supplies.

Dr. Moon's slide presentation used "easy-to-understand" graphs to illustrate these changes. The slides were available on the group's private website and could be shared and used when the witnesses make presentations in their regions of the world. Day 1 of the conference ended in prayer at 3:00 p.m. Many witnesses stayed for a couple of hours, standing around and talking and getting to know one another.

Kathi and Jess tracked down Warren and were thrilled by his news. "Kathi, I have accepted Jesus as my Lord and Savior. The feeling of Jesus tugging at my heart was too much to resist. I really do not understand why I couldn't see the truth earlier." "I know, Warren, I felt the same. I guess I was just so wrapped up in my career and was brainwashed to believe that Science was everything," Kathi replied.

"Maye Moon appeared, and I couldn't come up with a logical explanation for it, even though I tried," Kathi continued. "I have been a Christian most of my life, Warren, but I was a lukewarm Christian. I did not live like a Christian should live. I was so focused on moving up in my career at Fox. There is a lot of evil going on in the entertainment industry. I just accepted that partaking in it was the way to get ahead. When Maye Moon appeared, it made me question what God was doing. Then I met Kathi, and I fell head over heels in love with her and realized there are a lot more important things in life than my career," Jess shared.

"I knew and respected Kathi and saw what a difference there was in her when she became a Christian. At first, I thought maybe she was in some sort of mental breakdown, he said with a chuckle. But the more I worked with her, I realized she was sincere in her new found faith, and I started questioning my own belief system," Warren said. "Warren, I am thrilled you accepted the Lord as your Savior, and I am sure we will be working a lot more together, Lord willing. We are meeting up with the Miracle team for dinner later. Would you like to join us?" Kathi asked.

"Yes, Warren. We would love it if you joined us. I imagine you would have some great ideas to contribute," Jess added. "I would love to if you think the others wouldn't mind,"

Warren replied. "Then it is set. We will meet you at Paschal's at 7:30," Kathi said.

Chapter 44

D ay 2 of the conference began with prayer groups for the conference. Groups of at least five people were asked to hold hands and form groups across the sanctuary. Again, the Holy Spirit permeated the room, and most people were moved to tears. Praises to the Lord for His Mercy. Soloists from across the world offered to perform, and four were chosen to perform this second morning. Kathi and Jess both said to one another that they had never heard such beautiful singing.

Cora orchestrated a "Meet and Greet" exercise to encourage the witnesses to widen their circle of newfound friends. Each person was instructed to introduce themselves and tell where they were from. Then they were to find a new friend with the same birthday month. This exercise took about 15 minutes, and most people were able to find someone that matched their birthday month. Everyone returned to their seats for Pastor Scott's morning message.

The message this morning was called "Being Chosen by Jesus to Do His Work." Pastor Scott spoke about how the disciples dropped what they were doing and followed Jesus. They trusted the

Lord that their needs would be met. It was difficult for them to leave their families and go with Jesus, but they were compelled to do so and obeyed.

"Why did the disciples drop what they were doing and go forth and spread the gospel? They were looking forward to the coming of the Messiah. Actually, a lot of Jewish people are still looking forward to the coming of the Messiah. They need to know Jesus. Why have we all gathered here at this conference? We all experienced a divine miracle. Just like the Disciples, we look forward to the second coming of Jesus. This is not it. Let me repeat it: this is not it. Jesus appeared to us in space and instructed the astronauts to tell us to share his message that we need to stop the things that are destroying people. The lying, cheating, immorality, perversion, theft, lack of morals, murder, hatred, wars, weapons, and I could go on and on. We have a sinful world because we have chosen to follow Satan. A little white lie here and a little white lie there won't hurt anyone. But it does, yes, it does. There are none righteous, no not one. But couldn't we do better?

Jesus equipped the disciples to do His work. Jesus has instructed our Miracle team to equip you and provide resources to do His work. Our secure website will allow you to message your brothers and sisters here in this room. We hope you will share your successes and failures with one another to make us a stronger group.

Jesus taught his disciples that they were the salt and the light. We must be a light to a dark world. Jesus has given us the task of starting a revival in the world to save the world from destruction. If Jesus had wanted to, He could have made the rapture of the saints take place. We could have come back with Him to reign 1000 years here on Earth. Eventually, it would have led to many, many people being doomed to spend eternity in hell and the destruction of the Earth. But Jesus decided to give us another chance to change. We have always had the opportunity to witness to non-believers and lead others to the saving grace of the Lord. But we were tired. We were busy. We were boating. We had a thousand excuses for not trying. Now, we have a direct commandment to do so.

Jesus taught the disciples how to make disciples of others. Jesus did not want the message of Salvation to end with the disciples. They had to add others to the team. It is like multi-level marketing. You tell five people, and they tell five people, and pretty soon, the number of people who have heard the message is so large that everyone has heard it. With the technology available today, there is no excuse for someone not knowing about Jesus and His saving grace. We must help put a stop to the sin this world offers. Jesus needed the disciples to grow His ministry, and he needs us as much today."

The witnesses were pumped after hearing Pastor Scott's heartfelt message. The group broke for lunch, and there was lively chatter throughout the cafeteria. When everyone convened in the auditorium, the choir began singing "Our God is an Awesome God" and invited the witnesses to sing with them. It was beautiful and brought tears to many eyes. The second song they sang was "Amazing Grace," and "Amens" and "Hallelujahs" were heard throughout the auditorium. The Holy Ghost was moving throughout the crowd.

The last speaker of the day was the Georgia Director of Disease Control and Prevention. He provided the group with some amazing statistics about the decreased numbers of several types of flu and diseases. The most unbelievable was the disappearance of COVID-19 that took place when Maye Moon appeared. It nearly disappeared overnight. The witnesses were not surprised by what the Lord could do. The Lord giveth, and the Lord taketh away. Blessed be the name of the Lord.

At the conclusion of the session, the group was dismissed for the day.

Chapter 45

A light dusting of freshly fallen snow covered the ground, and everything around the church was beautiful and sparkly. Cora felt all warm inside as she walked from her cottage to the church. She and Pastor Scott had not spent much time together the past three days due to his duties at the conference. She understood that there would be times like this because of the nature of his position. She was happy. In fact, she had never been happier. She had come to a point in her life where she doubted she would ever find the right man for her. Her career as an astronaut had left little time for relationships. Jesus had shown her the real purpose of her life, and it was easy to leave that all behind. He had blessed her with a good man and she thanked Him daily.

The sanctuary was full of witnesses, excited for another day. This is the last full day of the conference. Tonight, there would be a pizza party followed by a Praise and Worship service of the best of the old-time hymns. Tomorrow morning will end the conference with a short message from Pastor Scott and a large group breakfast and goodbyes.

Pastor Scott started his message with the question, "Have any of you wondered why Jesus chose you to be a witness?" Hands and amen went up all over the auditorium. He continued with, "I, myself, am a witness, and I have wondered the same thing. I have done some pretty rotten things throughout my life. Before Maye Moon appeared, I was interested in living the fast, extravagant life. Money measured my success. Fancy cars, meetings with bigwigs, and a multi-million-dollar home. But when Maye Moon appeared, the Holy Ghost spoke to my heart and told me I had been living a lie. I had been the preacher of one of the largest churches in America for 12 years and I wasn't saved. I got down on my knees and repented and asked the Lord to save me and change my heart. I vowed to give up my lavish lifestyle and give everything I owned, including myself, to the Lord."

Tears were coming down from Pastor Scott's eyes, and many of the witnesses were also crying. "I want to talk about three men who we would say were not fit to serve God. Maybe you are feeling the same way today. Feeling like you do not deserve God's grace. I understand how it is easy to judge others and feel they do not deserve grace because of the things they have done. If you knew the old me, you would definitely judge me to be unfit.

329

First, let's look at Moses. Moses was a murderer. He fled Egypt so that he would not be put in prison for his crimes. Moses went from living in the King's palace to being a peasant out in the desert. The Lord spoke to Moses and told him that He wanted Moses to go to Pharaoh and tell him to release the children of Israel. Moses said to God, who am I to tell Pharaoh to release the children out of captivity in Egypt? Now, if God asked you personally to do something for him, would you question Him why you should do it? God told Moses, Pharaoh will hearken to your voice. But Moses again said to God, they will not believe me nor hearken to my voice. Sounds like Moses was arguing with God. Then God told Moses, if they do not believe you, I will give you signs to get their attention, and they will believe you."

"Moses then tells the Lord that I am not an eloquent speaker. I am slow of speech and slow in my tongue. The Lord then tells Moses, who made your tongue and mouth. Your brother Aaron is a good speaker, and he will be your spokesman. We might come to the conclusion that Moses really wasn't fit for the job, but he was God's chosen man, and he successfully led the children of Israel out of captivity. Moses had a few good excuses for not wanting to do the job. First, he was a murderer. He did not want to return to Egypt, fearing he would be captured and put in prison. Second, Moses was 80 years old at this point. Some of you might have some grey hair and wrinkles and feel like the younger generation should be doing the heavy lifting. But God chose you, and He had a purpose for choosing you. Third, Moses had a speech impediment and feared he couldn't do the job. Maybe you have some disability that prohibits you from doing much. There must be some purpose God has for you being in this group of 300 witnesses."

"The second man that we might not think was worthy of serving God is Jeremiah. Jeremiah was like Moses in that he did not think he could speak. However, God assured him that He would give him the words to say. Jeremiah also thought he was too young. God told Jeremiah that before he was formed in his mother's belly, he was sanctified and chosen to be a prophet to the nations. It took some convincing. God told Jeremiah that he made him a defenced city, an iron pillar, and brazen walls against the whole land, against the kings of Judah and the princes. They shall fight thee, but they shall not prevail against thee. He went on and became a great servant of the Lord."

"The last man I want to speak about is perhaps the greatest Apostle of the whole Bible. He was a murderer like Moses. He especially liked to persecute the church. I particularly like the verse 1 Corinthians 1:27 But God hath chosen the foolish things of the world to confound the wise, and God hath chosen the weak things of the world to confound the things which are mighty."

"I am sure that many were leery of Paul at first, especially with his history of torturing Christians. Paul went on to have the greatest ministry reported in the Bible. Each of us here in this room needs to put aside our doubts about whether we can be the witnesses that God has called us to be. He has commissioned us to do his work, and he will provide us with the words and tools that we need to do the job. Jess would you please pray for our work as we go forward and for the meal we are about to partake."

Jess prayed more loudly and boldly than ever before after the inspiring message that Pastor Scott presented. The group enjoyed a delicious meal and fellowship amongst the witnesses. When they returned to the afternoon session, an Atlanta weatherman explained the weather changes that have taken place across the world since Maye Moon. Regions that are normally experiencing draughts have received more than enough rain to revive the earth. No reported tornadoes, hurricanes, or earthquakes. The U.S. Weather Service cannot explain what has happened, but the witnesses understand that our God can do anything.

The last presentation of the day was given by Commander Bob. He explained that the World can be changed by putting Jesus back into the places we have asked Him to leave: our schools, our government, the media, our homes, our churches, and especially our hearts. He concluded his message with an altar call for anyone who wished to get anything right with the Lord. Nearly everyone went forward, convicted by how we Christians have allowed God to be removed from our World.

The conference broke for today, but everyone was looking forward to the Pizza Party fellowship and hymn singing that was taking place this evening. Many new friendships have been made during the last three days.

On the last day of the conference, the group was given an additional hour of sleep due to the late hours kept last night. The cafeteria had managed to create a wonderful brunch feast for this last day. No one will go home hungry, for sure. After everyone had finished, the witnesses found seats in the auditorium for the final session. Pastor Scott had Jess, Kathi, and the four astronauts join him onstage and give a final account of what this experience has been like for each of them. Each one gave a heartwarming account and encouraged the witnesses to stay in touch through their secure website. Last to speak was Pastor Scott, who thanked each person for heeding the call to meet. He stressed that Maye Moon's ability to help heal the Earth was not difficult for Jesus. Each night when Maye Moon appears, it serves as a symbol, like the rainbow, of a new promise that God has made to help heal the physical Earth. The hardest challenge is to heal man's hearts, to rid the Earth of the evil and greed that is everywhere you turn. That is our challenge: to challenge others to change. Once again, he asked everyone to form prayer circles and pray that the work of the witnesses changes the world.

Just as Pastor Scott was ready to adjourn the conference, a loud trumpet sound shook the auditorium. A bright, shiny, pure white 10 ft. tall Angel of the Lord appeared, girded in armor so bright and beautiful that the whole sanctuary glowed. He spoke with a voice that sounded like a roll of thunder. "Go forth with goodness and truth and tell the people that God has renewed the Earth. Now, the people must renew their hearts and minds with the Word of the Lord and learn to love one another. That is a commandment of the Lord." The 300 witnesses were awestruck, and most were even afraid. Just as the Angel appeared suddenly, the Angel disappeared. People were paralyzed and afraid to move. One by one, they fell to their knees and began praying. Pastor Scott was stunned and didn't know what to do next. He approached the pulpit, and the only thing that would come out of his mouth was, "Thus saith the Lord."